MODERN CHINESE

现代中文

TEXTBOOK 2A
SIMPLIFIED CHARACTERS

 BetterChinese

MODERN CHINESE 现代中文

Textbook Volume 2A

First Edition

Project Director:	James P. Lin
Editorial Consultant:	Li-Hsiang Yu Shen
Executive Publisher:	Chi-Kuo Shen
Curriculum Advisors:	Norman Masuda and Rebecca Starr
Editorial Team:	Christopher Peacock, Bin Yan, Sue-Ann Ma, Cheuk-Yue Fung, Lillian Klemp, Lauren Chen, Tiantian Gao, and Ying Jin
Illustrations:	Better World Ltd

© 2013 BETTER CHINESE LLC (a Better World LTD company)

Library of Congress Cataloging-in-Publication Data: To be Assigned

ISBN: 978-1-60603-487-3

2 3 4 XLA 20 19 18

For more information about our products, contact us at:

United States

2479 E. Bayshore Road, Suite 110

Palo Alto, CA 94303

Tel: 888-384-0902

Fax: 888-442-7968

Email: usa@betterchinese.com

PHOTO CREDITS

Contents 目录

序言 FOREWORD

It has been a great start for *Modern Chinese*! We are both humbled and excited to hear so many positive things about the program since its inception. As an example of the warm welcome we have received, Professor Hong Jiang at Northwestern University shared with us, "The students can speak freely about their daily lives, only after a few units." That is a great affirmation of our work as we continue to refine and develop *Modern Chinese*.

In this second year program for *Modern Chinese*, we continued our tradition of research, working with both practitioners and linguists. We further refined and developed, through iterative feedback, the program design to ensure engaging, relevant, and effective curricula content.

The characters flourish in this installment with existing and new themes, allowing students to discuss and articulate language experiences that are important to them, such as employment and current events, in more depth. We introduce students to new narration and paragraph formats in addition to existing story dialogues. For practice exercises, we focus on authentic applications of the language so that students can apply them in real scenarios, such as planning a trip and renting an apartment, within a cultural context.

Adding to the cultural context, the curriculum systematically introduces idiomatic expressions to help students understand and authentically communicate with Chinese people. The number of vocabulary words have been increased per lesson but the percentage of new individual Chinese characters has been kept constant, thereby alleviating the challenge of new vocabulary acquisition. Students will explore new grammar points that allow them to achieve proficiency in understanding and presenting ideas, as well as develop fluency when offering their own opinions.

We want to thank everyone who took this journey with us: our Executive Publisher, Chi-Kuo Shen, who curated the Cultural Spotlights; Chief Educator Li-Hsiang Shen, for her editorial overview; Norman Masuda for his insights in creating authentic activities; and Professor Rebecca Starr for her invaluable insights as a linguist and providing a non-native learner's perspective. We would like to express our gratitude to the professors who provided feedback through numerous rounds of reviews: Hong Zeng, Michelle DiBello, Youping Zhang, and Chao Fen Sun of Stanford University; Lilly Cheng of San Diego State University; and Christopher Lupke of Washington State University. We also wish to thank our advisory board professors for their insightful and constructive feedback: Hong Jiang of Northwestern University; Yujie Ge of Santa Clara University; Cynthia Hsien Shen of University of Florida; Li Ma of Florida International University; Xiaojun Wang of Western Michigan University; and Tong Chen of Massachusetts Institute of Technology. Most importantly, Better Chinese would like to recognize the core Modern Chinese team: Project Manager, Angel Yeh, for her creative story-telling abilities and critical eye in overseeing every detail of the Modern Chinese project; Lauren Chen, Cheuk-Yue Fung, Tiantian Gao, Roger Hsieh, Ying Jin, Lillian Klemp, Sue-Ann Ma, Christopher Peacock, and Bin Yan.

Finalizing *Modern Chinese* was a dream come true, but it is not the end. We look forward to further refining the program continuously with feedback from you, as students or as teachers. I want to thank you for giving us the courage to make *Modern Chinese* and for helping us make learning Chinese more approachable and relevant.

James P. Lin
Project Director
July 2013

MODERN CHINESE VOLUME 2 现代中文
Scope and Sequence

Units	Communication Goals	Structure Notes	Language Notes & Cultural Spotlights
天 **UNIT 1** **Weather**	• Describe temperature and humidity. • Compare seasons and weather conditions in different places. • Write about several travel experiences to different places. • Talk about highlights of vacation experiences. • Use common idiomatic expressions to talk about weather. • Use a weather forecast to plan activities.	1. Use 才 to emphasize a small number or amount. 2. Use 左右 after a number to make an estimate. 3. Use 说不定 to express possibility or uncertainty. 4. Use 各 to mean each or different. 5. Use 比较 to strengthen an adjective. 6. Use 听说 to mean "I've heard that." 7. Use A 比 B with an adjective and a quantity to specify an amount in comparison. 8. Use 多了 to express much more. 9. Use 原来 to express "as it turns out."	• Idiomatic Expression: 风和日丽 • Learn about the conventions of writing addresses in Chinese. • Learn about regional, climate-influenced celebrations. • Idiomatic Expression: 四季如春 • Understand a Chinese weather forecast. • Learn adjectives to describe weather. • Learn about the summer in Kunming (昆明) and Lijiang (丽江).
学 **UNIT 2** **Academics**	• Discuss college majors and electives. • Talk about class reports, discussions, and studying abroad. • Explain the procedure for how to apply for a scholarship to a classmate. • Describe one's language proficiency. • Inquire about popular college clubs and organizations. • Describe people's appearance and personality traits. • Talk about meaningful activities and goals toward self improvement.	1. Use 只要 A 就 B (了) to indicate A is the only condition necessary for B to occur. 2. Use 为了 to explain the purpose of doing something. 3. Use 不过 to say "but" to indicate a contrast to the previous statement. 4. Use 变得 / 变成 to describe transformation in state or from one thing to another. 5. Use 等等 to indicate "and so on" at the end of a list. 6. Use 当······的时候 to formally indicate when something happened. 7. Use 由于 to indicate a reason or cause. 8. Use 与 to join two nouns in formal writing.	• Idiomatic Expression: 三人行，必有我师 • Learn how 了 can be used and when it is omitted. • Learn about Chinese students studying overseas. • Idiomatic Expression: 一见如故 • Learn about different ways to describe appearance and personality. • Learn about the differences between Chinese and Western views on education and success. • Learn about Dr. Sun Yat-sen (孙中山), the founder of modern China, and how his experience abroad influenced him.

Units	Communication Goals	Structure Notes	Language Notes & Cultural Spotlights
住 **UNIT 3** **Housing**	• Talk about elements of living in rental housing. • Talk about living with a roommate. • Describe a roommate's habits. • Discuss common housekeeping chores. • Describe steps involved in locating housing, including looking for housing and contract signing. • Recognize common criteria for selecting housing. • Express satisfaction and contentment in a situation.	1. Use 再说 *to bring up additional points.* 2. Use 确实 *to say "indeed" or "really."* 3. Use 一点(儿) 都没/不 *to emphasize "not at all."* 4. Use 恐怕 *to express doubt over an unfortunate situation.* 5. Use 之内/外/前/后 *to indicate that things are within or outside of scope.* 6. Use 可惜 *to express pity at an unfortunate situation.* 7. Use 包括……(在内) *to list included items or examples within a category.* 8. Use 对……(不)满意 *to express satisfaction or dissatisfaction with something.*	• Idiomatic Expression: 一应俱全 • Learn about alternative ways that the Chinese may address each other. • Learn about terminology that describe different types of people and occupations. • Learn about a few of China's unique dwellings. • Idiomatic Expressions: 安家落户 • Understand apartment rental advertisements. • Learn about Beijing's unique city planning design and influence.
买 **UNIT 4** **Shopping**	• Describe the basic elements of shopping online. • Use common terms related to sales promotions and warranty periods accurately. • Discuss sales offers and state reasons for purchasing decisions. • Express apologies and frustrations. • Talk about household items. • Demonstrate understanding of terms related to a store's return policy.	1. Use A 不如 B *to indicate A is not as good as B.* 2. Use 并且 *to mean "also" to connect words or clauses in formal contexts.* 3. Use 既 A 又 B *as a formal way to exprss "both A and B."* 4. Use 最……不过了 *to emphasize superlatives.* 5. Use 得了/不了 *to express ability or inability to complete certain actions.* 6. Use 像…这/那样的… *to describe categories using comparisons.* 7. Use 其实 *to say "actually."* 8. Use 不管…都/还… *to express that something does not matter.*	• Idiomatic Expression: 一分钱一分货 • Understand sales promotions. • Learn about independent boutique culture in major Chinese cities. • Idiomatic Expression: 货比三家 • Learn about a store's return policy. • Discover some of China's time-honored brands.
娱 **UNIT 5** **Hobbies**	• Talk about a recent athletic event. • Express opinions about athletes, sports stars, and their teams. • Discuss the results of a sporting event. • Talk about a musical competition. • Discuss musical performances that include traditional Chinese instruments.	1. Use 另外 *to talk about additional items.* 2. Use (只)不过……而已 *to minimize the significance of something.* 3. Use 与其……(倒)不如 *to indicate a preferred alternative.* 4. Use 依……看 *to formally express someone's opinion.* 5. Use 来自 *to indicate a place of origin.*	• Idiomatic Expressions: 反败为胜 • Learn about terminology specific to sports. • Learn about popular sports and their impact in Chinese-speaking countries. • Learn about traditional Chinese board games and their place in daily life. • Idiomatic Expressions: 多才多艺

Units	Communication Goals	Structure Notes	Language Notes & Cultural Spotlights
	• Express inspirations and aspirations for giving a musical performance. • Express gratitude for encouragement received.	6. Use 收到 to express obtaining physical objects and 受到 for receiving abstract concepts. 7. Use 令 to express making someone feel a certain way. 8. Use (在)……上 to introduce topics.	• Learn about verbs related to playing instruments. • Learn about traditional instruments and the fusion of music from around the world.
食 **UNIT 6** **Cuisine**	• Identify commonly-used Chinese cooking ingredients. • Follow a recipe to make a Chinese dish. • Use idiomatic expressions to describe the appearance and flavor of food. • Talk about necessary ingredients for making a dish. • Discuss freshness and expiration dates of food. • Use idiomatic expressions to make compliments about food. • Talk about the authenticity of dishes.	1. Use 以为 to express mistaken belief. 2. Use 将 to indicate an action performed on a specific object in formal contexts. 3. Use 无论…都… to express "no matter what" something is always the case. 4. Use 实在 to mean "really" and "honestly." 5. Use 于是 to say "hence" or "thus." 6. Use 几乎 to say "nearly." 7. Use 果然 to indicate that something happened as expected. 8. Use 难得 to describe rare situations and opportunities.	• Idiomatic Expression: 津津有味 • Learn to interpret Chinese recipes. • Learn phrases and expressions based on food and eating. • Learn about common ingredients in Chinese cooking. • Discover the historical origins of a popular Chinese dish. • Idiomatic Expression: 五花八门 • Learn how to write an e-mail in Chinese. • Discover street food in Chinese-speaking countries. • Learn about the teahouse culture in Chengdu (成都).
祸 **UNIT 7** **Emergencies**	• Report a traffic accident to the police. • Talk about traffic violations. • Talk about injuries and going to hospitals. • Recognize common traffic and driving terms. • Talk about common natural disasters. • Talk about accidents. • Discuss a disaster report about casualties and damages. • Discuss preparations for a natural diaster.	1. Use 完全 to say "completely." 2. Use 并 to emphasize a negative contrast. 3. Use 因此 to say "therefore." 4. Use 再也(不/没) to emphatically state "never ever again." 5. Use 关于 to say "with regard to" a topic. 6. Use 此外 to introduce additional points. 7. Use 以 to indicate the purpose of an action. 8. Use (从)……以来 to indicate "ever since" a certain time in the past.	• Idiomatic Expression: 丢三落四 • Learn how to use verbs with their directional complements. • Learn about major natural disasters in China and their impact. • Idiomatic Expression: 飞来横祸 • Learn about weather warning signals used on TV. • Learn about commonly used terms in newspapers. • Learn about oracle bones (甲骨) and seisometers (测震仪), two methods for predicting natural disasters. • 大禹治水: Learn about how Da Yu introduced flood control.

Units	Communication Goals	Structure Notes	Language Notes & Cultural Spotlights
行 **UNIT 8** **Travel**	• Talk about the steps involved in checking in at the airport. • Talk about encountering problems at the airport. • Talk about making changes in one's reservations. • Explain the various ways to keep a record of one's travels. • Talk about local dishes while traveling. • Discuss one's impressions regarding a trip.	1. Use 将(要/会) to describe future events in formal contexts. 2. Use 却 to indicate a reversal or contrast. 3. Use 除非…(否则/要不然)… to make "unless" statements. 4. Use 刚才 to talk about events or situations that have just occurred. 5. Use 不是 A 而是 B to emphasize a contrast between A and B. 6. Use 实际上 to explain how things really are. 7. Use 趁(着) to take advantage of a situation. 8. Use 只有…才… to describe necessary conditions for a condition to occur.	• Idiomatic Expression: 一波三折 • Learn to navigate one's way around the airport. • Read about Zheng He (郑和) and Chinese sea explorations • Learn about Marco Polo's Journey to China. • Idiomatic Expressions: 人山人海 and 百闻不如一见 • Learn about various options for train and bus travel in China. • Learn about the real Buddhist monk from *Journey to the West* (西游记) and his travels .
艺 **UNIT 9** **The Arts**	• Talk about elements related to a stage performance. • Explain how one prepares for a show. • Give opinions about a performance. • Describe the different kinds of traditional folk art. • Talk about traditional Chinese pastimes. • Discuss one's ability in performing arts and traditional games.	1. Use 尤其 to mean "especially" or "particularly." 2. Use 在……方面 to talk about a particular aspect of a situation. 3. Use 不如 to suggest a better alternative. 4. Use 替 to indicate doing something for or in place of someone else. 5. Use 可 to emphasize states or events. 6. Use 多 to intensify attributes 7. Use 任何 to mean "any." 8. Use 以…为… to describe using something as something else.	• Idiomatic Expressions: 出神入化 • Learn how to interpret an advertisement for a performance. • 中国结: Discover the folk art of Chinese knotting. • Idiomatic Expression: 琴棋书画 • Learn how to book a show ticket. • 唐诗: Learn about well-known Tang Dynasty poets and their poetry. • 敦煌艺术: Learn about Dunhuang and its significance in art and history in China.
@ **UNIT 10** **Technology**	• Explain signing up for classes online. • Talk about aspects of science and technology in daily life. • Discuss inventions and advances in technology. • Talk about green energy and its impact. • Discuss technology used in the car. • Share criteria for making an evaluation.	1. Use 根据 to mean "according to" or "based on." 2. Use 通过 to say "by means" or "through." 3. Use 以及 to join words or phrases in formal contexts. 4. Use 相当 to intensify attributes. 5. Use 甚至 to say "even (to the extent that)." 6. Use 便 as a formal way to say "then." 7. Use 往往 to mean "often" or "usually."	• Idiomatic Expression: 大开眼界 • Learn how to register for and log in to online accounts. • 互联网世界: Learn about the Internet technologies in China and how they compare to those in the US. • Idiomatic Expressions: 日新月异 • Learn about the terminology for different parts of a car.

Units	Communication Goals	Structure Notes	Language Notes & Cultural Spotlights
		8. Use 而 to mean "but" or "rather." 9. Use 不仅……还 to mean "not only . . . but also . . ." 10. Use 得起 to indicate ability to do something.	• Understand traffic warning signs and other precautionary signs. • 现代科技专家: Learn about major contributions of famous Chinese people to modern science and technology.
商 **UNIT 11** **Business**	• Talk about the procedure for opening a bank account. • Explain the steps in filling out an application at a bank. • Discuss services associated with a bank savings account. • Talk about investing in the stock market. • Explain best practices in financial management. • Discuss real estate investments.	1. Use 反正 to mean "anyway" or "in any case." 2. Use 毕竟 to say "after all" or "actually." 3. Use 免得 to say "so as not to" or "in case." 4. Use 一旦…(就)…to express that something will happen as soon as something else occurs. 5. Use 从而 to mean "thus" or "thereby." 6. Use 凡是…都… to indicate that something applies to everything in a certain category. 7. Use 即使 to say "even if." 8. Use 例如 to introduce an example.	• Idiomatic Expression: 精打细算 挥金如土 • Learn how to open a bank account in China. • 中国经济发展: Learn how major economic milestones altered Chinese history. • 中国货币演变: Learn about the development and evolution of Chinese currency. • Idiomatic Expression: 积少成多 • Understand terminology used for reporting statistics. • 恭喜发财!祝你好运!: Read about things that symbolize money and good fortune.
健 **UNIT 12** **Health**	• Point out some common minor ailments. • Talk about how to maintain a healthy lifestyle. • Discuss eating habits and physical exercise. • Talk about one's sleep and exercise routines. • Describe healthy eating habits. • Discuss the effects of a healthy lifestyle.	1. Use 总是 to describe something that always happens. 2. Use 一切 to mean "everything" or "all." 3. Use 要么…要么… to say "either . . . or . . ." 4. Use 何况 to mean "let alone" or "moreover." 5. Use 于 as a formal preposition meaning "to," "for," "in," or "at." 6. Use 尽量 to mean "as much as possible." 7. Use 居然 to indicate that some event was unexpected. 8. Use 要不是 to mean "if it were not for."	• Idiomatic Expression: 早睡早起 • Learn about visiting a doctor in China. • 奇妙气功: Learn about the traditional Chinese exercise Qigong. • Idiomatic Expression: 精神焕发 • Learn about the food guide pyramid. • 治病强身 — 中草药: Learn about Chinese herbal remedies.
史 **UNIT 13** **History**	• Describe a famous architectural structure. • Talk about a person's place in history. • Explain the impacts of an action, both good and bad.	1. Use 然而 to mean "however" or "but." 2. Use 结果 to mean "as result of" or "as consequence." 3. Use 既然…就… to mean "since . . . then . . ." 4. Use 至于 to introduce a topic.	• Idiomatic Expression: 顺其自然 古今中外 • Learn how to ask and express opinions on a topic. • 中华瓷器: Learn about the significance of Chinese porcelain.

Units	Communication Goals	Structure Notes	Language Notes & Cultural Spotlights
	• Discuss opportunities with others. • Talk about a couple of influential philosophers in Chinese history. • Describe basic teachings of Confucius. • Describe basic teachings of Laozi.	5. Use 使 to mean "make" or "cause." 6. Use 简直 to mean "simply" or "just." 7. Use 互相 to mean "mutually" or "each other."	• 瓷器与中国: Learn about how the word "China" became the name of the nation. • Idiomatic Expression: 上善若水，勿施于人 己所不欲 • Learn about phrases to express politeness. • 外来侵略 民族意识: Learn how wars with foreign powers in the past influenced China's view on foreign relations.
绿 **UNIT 14** **The Environment**	• Describe various ways to reduce waste, reuse materials, and recycle. • Discuss protecting the environment. • Talk about secondhand markets as a means to reuse goods. • Explain ways to improve environmental awareness • Talk about renewable resources. • Discuss causes of and ways to reduce pollution.	1. Use 根本 to mean "at all" or "simply." 2. Use 难免 to mean "unavoidable." 3. Use 把…视为… to express viewing something in a particular way. 4. Use 况且 to mean "moreover" or "besides". 5. Use 向 to mean "to" or "torward" in formal contexts. 6. Use 对于 to introduce a topic or issue. 7. Use 则 as a formal way to express "then." 8. Use 就算…也… to say "even if…still…"	• Idiomatic Expression: 物尽其用 • Learn about China's geography and related environmental issues. • 天津生态城: Explore how the development of Tianjin's Eco-City will be a model of sustainable development. • Idiomatic Expression: 前人种树，后人乘凉 • Learn about recycling in China • 环境保护: Learn about China's efforts and progress in conservation and developing green technologies.
社 **UNIT 15** **Society**	• Discuss various fund-raising activities. • Talk about making donations. • Explain one's idea for improving everyone's future lives. • Talk about doing volunteer work. • Discuss a teaching experience. • Describe living conditions. • Share one's feelings and opinions about volunteer work.	1. Use 如何 to express "how" in formal contexts. 2. Use 本来 to mean "originally." 3. Use 哪怕…也… to indicate "even if…still…" 4. Use 假如 to introduce a possible or hypothetical situation. 5. Use 个 to describe certain manners of performing actions. 6. Use 作为 to mean "as" or "being." 7. Use 固然 to say "to be sure" or "admittedly."	• Idiomatic Expression: 齐心协力 • Learn about charitable activities and organizations. • 茶馆 — 南北饮茶文化: Explore the differences of the tea-drinking culture in Northern and Southern China. • Idiomatic Expressions: 助人为乐 • Understand charity and environmental protection slogans. • 微薄文化: Learn about microblogging and its influences.

Units	Communication Goals	Structure Notes	Language Notes & Cultural Spotlights
梦 **UNIT 16** **Dreams**	• Discuss ideals and goals. • Talk about plans for the future and various career options. • Describe the development in relationships. • Talk about achievements. • Express uncertainty toward a future career path. • Discuss steps toward achieving one's dreams.	1. *Use* 到底 *to create emphatic questions.* 2. *Use* 更别说 *to mean "not to mention."* 3. *Use* 没有…就没有… *to express that something would be impossible without something else.* 4. *Use* 千万 *to emphasize warnings.* 5. *Use* 多亏 *to mean "thanks to."* 6. *Use* 终于 *to say "finally."* 7. *Use* 这么说来 *to introduce a conclusion.* 8. *Use* 及时 *to mean "in time" or "promptly."*	• Idiomatic Expression: 雄心大志 • Learn how to write a resume. • Learn about common interview questions and ways to respond. • 禅的人生态度: Learn about the Zen way of life. • Learn how to express congratulations and good wishes. • Idiomatic Expression: 美梦成真 • 但愿人长久 千里共婵娟: Understand friendships in Chinese culture — expectations and behavior.

Classroom Expressions

Chinese	Pinyin	English
上课。	Shàng kè.	Let's begin class.
下课。	Xià kè.	Class dismissed.
很好!	Hěn hǎo!	Very good!
请举手。	Qǐng jǔ shǒu.	Please raise your hand.
跟我念。	Gēn wǒ niàn.	Read aloud after me.
你来念。	Nǐ lái niàn.	Now you read it.
你懂吗?	Nǐ dǒng ma?	Do you understand?
我懂/我不懂。	Wǒ dǒng/wǒ bùdǒng.	I understand/I don't understand.
对不对?	Duì búduì?	Is this correct?
对/不对	Duì/búduì	Right/Correct/Wrong/Incorrect
请大声一点。	Qǐng dà shēng yì diǎn.	A little louder please.
请看___。	Qǐng kàn ___.	Please look at ___.
请看黑/白板。	Qǐng kàn hēi/báibǎn.	Please look at the black/whiteboard.
请翻到第___页。	Qǐng fāndào dì ___ yè.	Please turn to page ___.
请看第___段。	Qǐng kàn dì ___ duàn.	Please look at paragraph ___.
请看第___行。	Qǐng kàn dì ___ háng.	Please look at the ___ line.
我没听清楚。	Wǒ méi tīng qīngchu.	I didn't hear it clearly.
可不可以再说一遍?	Kě bu kěyǐ zài shuō yí biàn?	Could you say it one more time?
可不可以说慢一点?	Kě bu kěyǐ shuō màn yì diǎn?	Could you speak more slowly?
我有一个问题。	Wǒ yǒu yí ge wèntí.	I have a question.
___是什么意思?	___ shì shénme yìsi?	What does ___ mean?
请问___中文怎么说?	Qǐngwèn ___ Zhōngwén zěnme shuō?	Excuse me, how do you say ___ in Chinese?
今天的功课/作业是___。	Jīntiān de gōngkè/zuòyè shì___.	The homework/assignment is ___.
功课/作业要在___交。	Dōngkè/zuòyè yào zài ___ jiāo.	The homework/assignment is due ___.
___有考试/测验。	___ yǒu kǎoshì/cèyàn.	There will be an exam/test on ___.

Lesson Organization

Modern Chinese is organized by units, each representing a particular theme. In each unit, there are two lessons presenting different scenarios. The organization of each lesson is as follows:

Sections	Subsections	Description
Communication Goals		Communicative skills that will be emphasized in the lesson for the student.
Lesson Story		Lesson dialogue or narrative type text in illustrated format with simplified Chinese characters and pinyin for new vocabulary.
Lesson Text		Lesson dialogue or narrative type text in simplified Chinese characters.
Language Tips		Brief explanations on usage of specific words and phrases in the Lesson Text.
Vocabulary	Lesson Vocabulary	Newly introduced core new words with with simplified Chinese characters, traditional Chinese characters (if different), pinyin, part of speech, and definition.
	Required Vocabulary	Fundamental words and phrases that are not in the Lesson Text but are required. They are part of the core vocabulary and are used in the Structure Notes and Practice sections.
Idiomatic Expressions		Explanations of expressions, sayings, and *chengyu* (Chinese idioms) that are found in the Lesson Text.
Language Notes		Language and culture notes pertaining to the lesson theme and vocabulary.
Structure Notes		Grammar explanations, examples, and practices.
Practice	Notes	Highlighted new vocabulary words that are used in the Practices for the purpose of understanding and completing the exercises. Students are not required to learn these words. They can be used for extended learning.
Practice	Speaking	Individual, partner, and group speaking exercises through conversations and presentations.
	Writing	Stroke order is displayed for characters that students are required to be able to write for the lesson. These are the most frequently-used characters. Exercises that involve writing Chinese characters are provided.
	Research	Group projects that require students to do research in order to complete an exercise.
	Online Chat	Typing Chinese characters in authentic digital contexts. A prompt is provided for students to create their own written conversations in the form of an online chat with a classmate.
	Reading	Reading comprehension sections contain vocabulary from the Lesson Vocabulary and Required Vocabulary sections.
Cultural Spotlight		Cultural information relevant to the lesson theme.
Text in Pinyin and English		Lesson Text in pinyin and English.
What Can You Do		Summary of interpretive, interpersonal, and presentational communication skills achieved by the student.
Unit Review		Found at the end of the second lesson for each unit, this is a summary of all vocabulary and structure notes learned in the unit. To assess comprehension of the material from the two lessons, a short list of role-play suggestions are provided for extended communicative practice.

Abbreviations of Grammatical Terms

adj	Adjective
adv	Adverb
av	Auxiliary Verb
cj	Conjunction
ie	Idiomatic Expression
interj	Interjection
mw	Measure Word
n	Noun
nu	Number
on	Onomatopoeia
p	Particle
pr	Pronoun
prep	Preposition
qph	Question Phrase
qw	Question Word
rc	Resultative Complement
rv	Resultative Verb
v	Verb
dc	Directional Complement
vo	Verb-Object Compound

Icons

 Speaking Practice

 Writing Practice

 Reading Practice

 Practice that requires using a computer or mobile device.

Character Profiles

孙玛丽
Sūn Mǎlì

An American student from Boston

Spent a summer interning in Beijing and is now studying at a university there

Friendly, lively, and independent and loves learning new things

In her junior year

李中平
Lǐ Zhōngpíng

An American student from Texas

Majoring in mathematics but has broad interests, including Chinese culture

Cheerful, studious, and determined

In his junior year

陈大东
Chén Dàdōng

A Canadian student from Montreal

Very interested in studying Chinese history and literature

Responsible and hard-working

In his sophomore year

Xiang'an's roommate

王小美
Wáng Xiǎoměi

An American student who was born in Beijing and raised in California

Artistic and a little shy

Loves humanities and the arts, especially music

In her sophomore year

张安娜
Zhāng Ānnà

A Russian student and dancer from Moscow

Loves dancing and shopping but is also frugal

Seems aloof but has a sensitive side

In her junior year

黄祥安
Huáng Xiáng'ān

A South African student from Johannesburg

Loves soccer and photography and is interested in blogging

Easygoing and kind-hearted

In his sophomore year

Dadong's roommate

Character Profiles

周信
Zhōu Xìn

A Chinese student that lives in Beijing

Majoring in business and helps to look after Mali when she arrived in Beijing during the summer in her junior year

Very confident and ambitious

In his senior year

Xiaomei's cousin

杨冰冰
Yáng Bīngbīng

A Brazilian recent college graduate

University coordinator of the "Green Earth" Club

Outgoing, with a sunny outlook on life

天

Weather

第一单元
UNIT 1

Communication Goals

Lesson 1: 天气 **Weather**
- Describe temperature and humidity.
- Compare seasons and weather conditions in different places.
- Write about several travel experiences to different places.

Lesson 2: 旅游和气候 **Travel and Climate**
- Talk about highlights of vacation experiences.
- Use common idiomatic expressions to talk about the weather.
- Use a weather forecast to plan activities.

天气
Weather

中平刚旅游回来，收到了朋友们寄来的明信片：
（lǚ yóu 旅游）（míng xìn piàn 明信片）

qīn ài de
亲爱的中平：

　　暑假过得好吗？北京的夏天就跟小美的
zhōu xìn　　　　　　　qì wēn yì bān　huá shì
表哥周信说的一样热，气温一般在华氏八十
dù　　　　　　　　liáng kuai　　　　　mí shàng
多度，但是下雨以后会凉快一点儿。我迷上
jì xù liú
了中国的文化，打算继续留在北京念书。天

气没那么热的时候，希望你能来北京玩！

　　　　　　　　　玛丽

　　　　　　　　　八月九日

中平，你好！

　　我们已经到伦敦了。伦敦的夏天很凉快，平均气温才七十度左右，可是常常下雨，难怪人们出门都带着雨伞。小美很喜欢这样的天气，常常自已出去逛街。对了，说不定过几天我们会去巴黎和别的地方旅游。希望我们能游遍欧洲的各个大城市！

大东

八月十六日

嗨，中平！

　　你玩得怎么样？南非现在是冬季，但是天气很好，比较暖和。安娜有一个舞蹈团的面试，已经回俄罗斯了。等我下星期回去再跟你聊吧！

祥安

八月二十日

LESSON TEXT 1.1

Weather 天气

The end of summer is almost here and Zhongping has just returned from his trip. He goes through his mail and reads postcards from his friends Mali, Dadong, and Xiang'an.

中平刚旅游回来，收到了朋友们寄来的明信片：

亲爱的中平：

暑假过得好吗？北京的夏天就跟小美的表哥周信说的一样热，气温一般在华氏八十多度，但是下雨以后会凉快一点儿。我迷上了中国的文化，打算继续留在北京念书。天气没那么热的时候，希望你能来北京玩！

玛丽

八月九日

中平，你好！

我们已经到伦敦了。伦敦的夏天很凉快，平均气温才七十度左右，可是常常下雨，难怪人们出门都带着雨伞。小美很喜欢这样的天气，常常自己出去逛街。对了，说不定过几天我们会去巴黎和别的地方旅游。希望我们能游遍欧洲的各个大城市！

大东

八月十六日

嗨，中平！

　　你玩得怎么样？南非现在是冬季，但是天气很好，比较暖和。安娜有一个舞蹈团的面试，已经回俄罗斯了。等我下星期回去再跟你聊吧！

祥安

八月二十日

Language Tips

| 对了 (duìle) | In the Lesson Text, Dadong uses 对了 to mention that he and Xiaomei might be going to Paris and some other places. This expression literally means "correct," but when used as an exclamation, it can also mean "by the way" or "that's right." |

Examples:

| 对了，你明天去哪里？ | 对了，就是这样做。 |
| By the way, where are you going tomorrow? | That's right, that's how you do it. |

| 游 (yóu) | In Dadong's postcard, Dadong uses 游遍 to express his wish of traveling to various cities in Europe. The original meaning of 游 is to swim; the traditional character is 遊, and its radical 辶 means walking. In the simplified version, 游 also means to travel or visit, such as 游遍, 游园, 游玩, etc. |

Example: 他一个人游遍了欧洲。
He traveled through Europe alone.

LESSON VOCABULARY 1.1

	SIMPLIFIED	TRADITIONAL	PINYIN	WORD CATEGORY	DEFINITION
1.	旅游	旅遊	lǚyóu	*v, n*	to tour; tourism
	游	遊	yóu	*v*	to travel
2.	明信片		míngxìnpiàn	*n*	postcard
3.	亲爱的	親愛的	qīn'àide	*adj, n*	dear; darling
4.	气温	氣温	qìwēn	*n*	temperature
5.	一般		yìbān	*adv*	generally; ordinary
6.	华氏	華氏	huáshì	*n*	Fahrenheit (°F), °F = °C × 1.8 + 32
7.	度		dù	*n, mw*	degree; (used as a unit of measurement of temperature)
8.	凉快	涼快	liángkuai	*adj*	pleasantly cool
9.	迷上		míshàng	*rv*	be fascinated by
	迷		mí	*v*	to become enchanted with
10.	继续	繼續	jìxù	*v*	to continue
11.	留		liú	*v*	to stay in a place, to remain
12.	平均		píngjūn	*adj, adv*	average; on average
13.	左右		zuǒyòu	*adv*	about, approximately
14.	出门	出門	chūmén	*vo*	to be away from home; to go on a journey
15.	雨伞	雨傘	yǔsǎn	*n*	umbrella
16.	对了	對了	duìle	*interj*	by the way; that's right
17.	说不定	説不定	shuōbudìng	*adv*	maybe, perhaps
18.	遍		biàn	*adv, mw*	all over; (used for repetitive times and occurrences)
19.	各		gè	*adj*	each, every
20.	冬季		dōngjì	*n*	winter
21.	暖和		nuǎnhuo	*adj*	warm
22.	舞蹈团	舞蹈團	wǔdǎotuán	*n*	dance troupe

LESSON VOCABULARY 1.1 (continued)

SIMPLIFIED	TRADITIONAL	PINYIN	WORD CATEGORY	DEFINITION
舞蹈		wǔdǎo	*n*	dance
团	團	tuán	*n*	troupe, group
23. 面试	面試	miànshì	*n, v*	audition, interview; to have an interview or audition

PROPER NOUN

24. 周信		Zhōu Xìn	*n*	Zhou Xin
25. 伦敦	倫敦	Lúndūn	*n*	London
26. 巴黎		Bālí	*n*	Paris

REQUIRED VOCABULARY 1.1

27. 季节	季節	jìjié	*n*	season
28. 零下		língxià	*n*	below zero
29. 摄氏	攝氏	shèshì	*n*	Celsius (°C), °C = (°F - 32) / 1.8

Idiomatic Expression

fēng hé rì lì
风和日丽

风和日丽 means "the breeze is gentle and the sun is bright."

This expression appears in the novel *Painful History* (《痛史》: *Tòng Shǐ*), written during the Qing Dynasty (1644 – 1912 AD). In the novel, imperial officials take advantage of a beautiful day to sweep tombs and honor their ancestors. This was the phrase used to describe that day. Today, it is often used to describe warm and sunny weather, especially in the springtime.

Example:
今天风和日丽，我们出去走走吧！
Today is warm and sunny; let's go for a walk!

How to Write an Address in Chinese

Writing an address in Chinese is different from writing one in the United States. For addresses written in English, the order progresses from the most specific to the most general information. For instance, if you write a letter from the United States to China, the format might look like this:

Zhongping Li
100 University Road
Palo Alto, CA 94301
U.S.A.

Ms. Mali Sun
Wenhua Bei Road, Building 6, Apt. 219
Chang'an District, Xi'an, Shaanxi Province 200001
People's Republic of China

In Chinese, an address is written so that the largest units — the country and province — come first, before narrowing down to the recipient. For instance, if you send a letter in China, the pattern of the address should be:

Zip Code (邮编: yóubiān)
China (中国) + Province (省: shěng) + City (市: shì)
District (区: qū) + Street (街: jiē) / Road (路: lù) + Building (楼: lóu) + Apartment (室: shì)
Recipient (收件人: shōujiànrén)

2 0 0 0 0 1

陕西省西安市
长安区文化北路6号楼219室

孙玛丽小姐 收

北京市朝阳区建国路2号　周信
100000

The zip code consists of six digits and is always located on the top left corner. It is also recommended that you include the title of the person that you are addressing. For instance, if you are writing to your teacher, you would address the letter to Teacher Li (李老师). You can also write the word receive (收: shōu) after the name of the recipient. In contrast to the American format, the sender's name and address (寄件人名址: jìjiànrén míng zhǐ) are written on the bottom right corner, while the recipient's details appear on the top left corner of the envelope. The four cities that are province-level municipalities — Shanghai, Beijing, Tianjin, and Chongqin — are not part of any province and the province part of the address is ommitted.

STRUCTURE NOTE 1.1

Use 才 to emphasize a small number or amount

才 *has been used previously to express "not until," indicating that an event was later than expected.* 才 *can also be used similarly to* 只, *"only," meaning that the amount or level of something is small.*

Subject + 才 + Phrase

From the Lesson Text: 平均气温才七十度左右。
Píngjūn qìwēn cái 70 (qīshí) dù zuǒyòu.
The average temperature is only about 70 degrees.

Other examples: 妹妹今年才三岁。
Mèimei jīnnián cái sān suì.
My little sister is only three years old.

我每年才回家一次。
Wǒ měinián cái huíjiā yí cì.
I only go home once a year.

Practice: Change the following sentences to questions using 才.

Example: 我昨天晚上十点吃饭。
→ 你昨天晚上十点才吃饭吗？

1. 那条红色的裤子五十元。
   _____

2. 这个学期她选了一门课。
   _____

3. 表弟每天做十五分钟的功课。
   _____

STRUCTURE NOTE 1.2

Use 左右 after a number to make an estimate

左右 *(zuǒyòu) means "left and right" but can also be used to express "approximately" — the actual number can be a bit more or less than the estimate. Unlike other estimation expressions such as* 差不多 *or* 大概, 左右 *is placed after the estimate, not before.*

Number + Measure Word (+ Noun) + 左右

From the Lesson Text: 平均气温才七十度左右。
Píngjūn qìwēn cái 70 (qīshí) dù zuǒyòu.
The average temperature is only about 70 degrees.

Other examples:	我们公司有一百个人左右。	每一课的生词有二十个左右。
	Wǒmen gōngsī yǒu yìbǎi ge rén zuǒyòu.	Měi yí kè de shēngcí yǒu èrshí ge zuǒyòu.
	Our company has approximately 100 people.	Every lesson has about 20 vocabulary words.

Practice: Answer the following questions using the word in the brackets and 左右.

Example: 今天的气温多少度？（九十度）
→ 今天的气温九十度左右。

1.   你们买了多少本书？（二十本）
_____

2.   你们吃饭吃了多长时间？（一个小时）
_____

3.   中平参加了几次游泳比赛？（四次）
_____

STRUCTURE NOTE 1.3
Use 说不定 *to express possibility or uncertainty*

说不定 *(shuōbudìng) literally means "can't say for certain." This phrase is used either at the beginning of a sentence or following the subject to indicate "maybe" or "possibly." To add further emphasis,* 说不定 *can be used in conjunction with other expressions of uncertainty, such as* 可能.

> 说不定 + Sentence

> Subject + 说不定 + Verb Phrase

From the Lesson Text:	说不定过几天我们会去巴黎和别的地方旅游。
	Shuōbudìng guò jǐ tiān wǒmen huì qù Bālí hé biéde dìfang lǚyóu.
	We might travel to Paris and some other places in a few days.

Other examples:	如果下个星期有空，说不定我们可以去旅游。	我们说不定明年能一起去公司实习。
	Rúguǒ xià ge xīngqī yǒu kòng, shuōbudìng wǒmen kěyǐ qù lǚyóu.	Wǒmen shuōbudìng míngnián néng yìqǐ qù gōngsī shíxí.
	If we have time next week, perhaps we could take a trip.	Next year, we might be able to intern at a company together.

Practice: Insert 说不定 to the sentences below to express uncertainty.

Example: 这个暑假我会去中国旅游。
→ 说不定这个暑假我会去中国旅游。

1. 毕业以后我会在舞蹈团工作。

   _____

2. 今天会下雨，你出门的时候还是带着雨伞吧！

   _____

3. 最近他晚上常常睡不着，他的生活太紧张了。

   _____

STRUCTURE NOTE 1.4
Use 各 *to mean each or different*

各 *(gè) is a pronoun meaning "each" or "different." It can be used before a noun or a measure word to indicate different individual items in a specific category, such as an organization, group, or country. For example:* 各国 *means different countries, while* 各家 *means each family.*

各 + Noun (limited to a specific group)

各 + Measure Word

From the Lesson Text: 希望我们能游遍欧洲的各个大城市！
Xīwàng wǒmen néng yóubiàn Ōuzhōu de gège dà chéngshì!
Hopefully, we can travel through Europe's various major cities!

Other examples:

各人有各人的想法。
Gè rén yǒu gè rén de xiǎngfǎ.
Everyone has his/her own way of thinking.

我想学习各种语言。
Wǒ xiǎng xuéxí gè zhǒng yǔyán.
I want to learn all kinds of languages.

Practice: Choose the correct word from the word bank to fill in the blanks.

各地　　各位　　各家　　各国

1. 他参观过欧洲_____的博物馆。
2. 菜很快就能做好，请_____先等一下。
3. 每年元宵节，_____餐厅都有用花灯装饰的传统。

STRUCTURE NOTE 1.5
Use 比较 *to strengthen an adjective*

In previous lessons, expressions like 好一点, *"a little better," have been used to express the relative degree of adjectives.* 比较, *meaning "relatively" or "comparatively," is used to indicate that something is relatively or quite the case.* 比较 *cannot be used within direct comparison sentences, as in A* 比 *B* 比较 *Adjective, since the* 比 *already expresses the comparative meaning in those cases.*

Subject + 比较 + Adjective

From the Lesson Text:
南非现在是冬季，但是天气很好，比较暖和。
Nánfēi xiànzài shì dōngjì, dànshì tiānqì hěn hǎo, bǐjiao nuǎnhuo.
It's currently wintertime in South Africa, but the weather is really nice and relatively warm.

Other examples:
这家书店的书比较便宜。
Zhè jiā shūdiàn de shū bǐjiao piányi.
The books in this bookstore are quite cheap.

开车上学比较方便。
Kāichē shàngxué bǐjiao fāngbiàn.
Driving to school is relatively convenient.

Practice: Answer the following questions using the word in the brackets and 比较.

Example: 明天的天气怎么样？（暖和）
→ 明天的天气比较暖和。

1. 你觉得语法课怎么样？（难）

   _____

2. 晚上的天气怎么样？（凉快）

   _____

3. 你觉得这场京剧表演怎么样？（有意思）

   _____

练习 1.1：课文理解

Paired Activity: Discuss the following questions based on the Lesson Text. Be prepared to share your thoughts with the class.

> 1. 玛丽觉得北京的天气怎么样？
>
> 2. 如果你要去英国旅游，你会选哪个季节去？你会带什么东西？
>
> 3. 除了南非以外，哪些国家八月的时候也是冬天？你喜欢这样的气候吗？

练习 1.2（上）：中国城市天气预报

Paired Activity: Working with a partner, plan a trip to China. Pick three cities in China that you would like to visit and discuss what the temperatures will be like at the time of your travel. Use the key words and weather forecast below when composing your descriptions.

> 早上　晚上　气温　热　冷　下雨　晴天　阴天　下雪

Example: 今天上海阴天，有点冷；早上气温华氏四十五度，晚上气温华氏三十九度。

中国城市天气预报

哈尔滨 -2 / -20
北京 17 / 28
上海 39 / 45
广州 53 / 66
昆明 41 / 62

Notes:
哈尔滨 (Hā'ěrbīn): *n.* Harbin
上海 (Shànghǎi): *n.* Shanghai
广州 (Guǎngzhōu): *n.* Guangzhou

Paired Activity: Let us suppose that you and your partner decide to visit Beijing. While researching with your friend, you come across a graph sharing Beijing's average temperatures throughout the year. Taking into account your own personal weather preferences, decide when would be the best time for you and your friend to go to Beijing. Describe the temperature at that time using the key words provided below.

春天　夏天　冬天　热　暖和　凉快　冷　才　比较　左右

Example: 我想秋天的时候去北京旅游。北京十月的平均最高气温才六十六度左右，不冷也不热，很舒服！

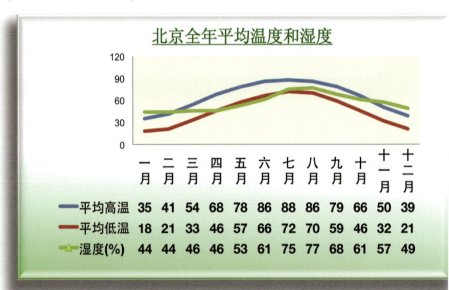

北京全年平均温度和湿度

Notes:
高 (gāo): *adj.* high
低 (dī): *adj.* low
湿度 (shīdù): *n.* humidity

	一月	二月	三月	四月	五月	六月	七月	八月	九月	十月	十一月	十二月
平均高温	35	41	54	68	78	86	88	86	79	66	50	39
平均低温	18	21	33	46	57	66	72	70	59	46	32	21
湿度(%)	44	44	46	46	53	61	75	77	68	61	57	49

练习 1.4（下）：你喜欢哪个城市？

Group Activity: Compare Beijing's climate to the climate in the two other cities that you plan to visit. Identify the two cities, research the expected climate at the time you are going, then compare the temperature and humidity of the three cities.

温度　高　低　天气　舒服　闷热　凉快　冷

Example: 在这三个城市里，我最喜欢北京，因为北京的温度和湿度不高也不低。我比较喜欢这样的天气。

季节：_____	城市1：_____	城市2：_____	北京
平均高温			
平均低温			
湿度			

	Radical	Stroke Order
旅	方 fāng square	丶 亠 方 方 方 方 旅 旅 旅
游	氵(水) shuǐ water	丶 冫 氵 汸 汸 汸 汸 游 游
温	氵(水) shuǐ water	丶 冫 氵 氵 沪 沪 汩 沮 温 温 温
般	舟 zhōu boat	丿 亻 𠂤 舟 舟 舟 舟 舮 船 般
华	十 shí ten	丿 亻 亻 化 化 华
氏	氏 shì clan	丿 𠂢 𠃊 氏
凉	冫(冰) bīng ice	丶 冫 冫 广 广 浐 浐 浐 凉 凉
迷	辶 chuò walk	丶 丷 丷 半 半 米 米 迷 迷
留	田 tián field	丿 𠃌 𠂎 𠃌 卯 卯 留 留 留
平	一 yī one	一 二 二 平 平
均	土 tǔ earth	一 十 土 圴 均 均 均
雨	雨 yǔ rain	一 一 冂 币 雨 雨 雨
遍	辶 chuò walk	丶 冫 㝵 户 户 肩 肩 扁 扁 遍 遍
各	夂 zhǐ walk slowly	丿 夂 夂 冬 各 各
季	禾 hé grain	一 二 千 千 禾 禾 季 季

练习 1.6: 线上聊天

Online chat: You are going to travel to a new city with your friend. Discuss where and when you want to go. Include details such as what the weather and season will be at that time, and what you need to do to prepare for the weather.

练习 1.7: 阅读理解

这个暑假大东和小美一起去欧洲旅游。他们先去了英国。大东迷上了英国的博物馆，一有空就和小美去参观博物馆。虽然英国常常下雨，出门一定要带着雨伞，但是小美很喜欢英国的下雨天。他们去的第二个地方是巴黎。巴黎是一个又古老又现代的城市。巴黎的天气风和日丽，他们逛了不同的景点，认识了很多新朋友。然后他们还去了别的几个大城市。这次旅游非常有意思，让大东和小美都不想回家了。

Read the passage and answer the following questions.
1. What does Xiaomei think about the weather in England? Why?
2. Why do Dadong and Xiaomei not want to go home?
3. If you were to go to Europe, where would you go to and why?

练习 1.8: 阅读理解

旅游网9月20日：

你了解巴黎吗？巴黎是法国的首都，不但有古老的历史，还是法国教育和文化的中心。如果你想要了解法国的历史和文化，你可以去参观巴黎的大学和博物馆。在巴黎旅游，你一定要去尝一下世界有名的法国菜，或者在路边喝杯咖啡。巴黎是一个很大的城市，逛街的时候最好带着地图，小心不要迷路。

Read the travel website and answer the following questions.
1. What kind of city is Paris?
2. What should you bring with you while shopping in Paris? Why?
3. How would you introduce your city to foreign visitors and why?

Notes:
法国 (Fǎguó): *n.* France
首都 (shǒudū): *n.* capital
尝 (cháng): *v.* to taste
世界 (shìjiè): *n.* world

Seasonal Chinese Festivals

There are a number of Chinese festivals and fairs related to the different seasons. Two popular locally-centered celebrations are the Flower Fair (花市: Huāshì) in Guangzhou, Guangdong Province, and the Harbin International Ice and Snow Sculpture Festival (哈尔滨国际冰雪节: Hā'ěrbīn Guójì Bīngxuě Jié) in Harbin, Heilongjiang Province.

Flower Fair

The Flower Fair is held annually from the 28th to the 30th of the twelfth lunar month in Guangzhou. With plenty of rainfall, Guangzhou generally enjoys warm and humid weather year-round. This provides ideal conditions for cultivating flowers, giving the city its nickname, "Flower City."

The origin of the Flower Fair goes back 500 years to the time of the Ming Dynasty (1368 AD – 1644 AD). Local flower growers from one village would bring their flowers to sell in another, and this became the first Flower Fair.

Today, the Flower Fair is spread across Guangzhou's eight major flower markets. Several days before the official start of the fair, vendors begin setting up flower stands and many people go buy flowers (mostly peach blossoms and narcissi) to decorate their homes. The streets are decorated with fresh flowers, Chinese bonsai, pachira plants (also known as "money" trees), and kumquat trees that symbolize prosperity and good luck. Crowds also enjoy traditional Chinese performances, face painters, calligraphers, and more.

Harbin International Ice and Snow Sculpture Festival

Situated in Northeastern China, Harbin is known as the "Ice City." As its nickname implies, Harbin has some of the longest and coldest winters in China, and snow and ice are part of everyday life in the city, as well as its most well-known festival.

The Harbin International Ice and Snow Sculpture Festival began in 1963 as a continuation of a much longer local tradition and is considered by many to be one of China's top tourist attractions. On January 5, the festival officially begins when the temperature is typically below zero degree Fahrenheit (-17 °C). The festival continues for more than a month and attracts hundreds of thousands of international tourists to the area.

As far back as the Qing Dynasty, locals have used ice lanterns during the winter to provide secure and practical lighting. Ice lanterns are traditionally made by filling a bucket with water, partially freezing the water, and then boring a hole at the top and pouring out the remaining unfrozen water to provide a space for a candle. The resulting lantern is windproof and cheap to produce. As a result, ice lanterns became enormously popular around Harbin and developed into a staple at winter festivals.

Today, the term "ice lantern" encompasses a much larger range of ice-based sculptures with light sources. Many ice lanterns now integrate materials such as plastics, multicolored LEDs, and music with the traditional snow and ice sculpture. The festival hosts a number of sculpting competitions and record-breaking structures, with the scale of the work and the technological sophistication of the structures reaching new heights each year.

Pinyin

Zhōngpíng gāng lǚyóu huílai, shōudào le péngyoumen jìlái de míngxìnpiàn:

Qīn'ài de Zhōngpíng:

Shǔjià guò de hǎo ma? Běijīng de xiàtiān jiù gēn Xiǎoměi de biǎogē Zhōu Xìn shuō de yíyàng rè, qìwēn yìbān zài huáshì bāshí duō dù, dànshì xiàyǔ yǐhòu huì liángkuai yìdiǎnr. Wǒ míshangle Zhōngguó de wénhuà, dǎsuàn jìxù liú zài Běijīng niànshū. Tiānqi méi nàme rè de shíhou, xīwàng nǐ néng lái Běijīng wán!

Mǎlì

Bā (8) yuè jiǔ (9) rì

Zhōngpíng, nǐ hǎo!

Wǒmen yǐjīng dào Lúndūn le. Lúndūn de xiàtiān hěn liángkuai, píngjūn qìwēn cái qīshí dù zuǒyòu, kěshì chángcháng xiàyǔ, nánguài rénmen chūmén dōu dàizhe yǔsǎn. Xiǎoměi hěn xǐhuan zhèyàng de tiānqì, chángcháng zìjǐ chūqù guàngjiē. Duìle, shuōbudìng guò jǐtiān wǒmen huì qù Bālí hé biéde dìfang lǚyóu. Xīwàng wǒmen néng yóu biàn Ōuzhōu de gège dà chéngshì!

Dàdōng

Bā (8) yuè shíliù (16) rì

English

Zhongping has just returned from his travels. He has received postcards sent by his friends.

Dear Zhongping,

How was your summer break? Summers in Beijing sure are hot, as Xiaomei's cousin, Zhou Xin, said they would be. The temperature is generally in the 80s but cools down a bit after it rains. I have become fascinated by the Chinese culture and plan to continue my studies in Beijing. When the weather is not so hot, I hope you can come visit me here in Beijing!

Mali

August 9

Hello Zhongping!

We have already arrived in London. It's very cool in London in the summer. The average temperature is only about 70 degrees, but it often rains. It's no wonder the locals all carry umbrellas with them. Xiaomei really likes this type of weather and frequently wanders around on her own. Oh, by the way, we might travel to Paris and some other places in a few days. Hopefully, we can travel through Europe's various major cities.

Dadong

August 16

Hēi, Zhōngpíng!

Nǐ wánde zěnmeyàng? Nánfēi xiànzài shì dōngjì, dànshì tiānqì hěn hǎo, bǐjiao nuǎnhuo. Ānnà yǒu yí ge wǔdǎotuán de miànshì, yǐjīng huí Éluósī le. Děng wǒ xiàxīngqī huíqù zài gēn nǐ liáo ba!

Xiáng'ān

Bā (8) yuè èrshí (20) rì

Hey Zhongping!

How was your trip? It's currently wintertime in South Africa, but the weather is really nice and relatively warm. Anna had an interview with a dance troupe, so she already went back to Russia. Let's talk more after I return next week!

Xiang'an

August 20

What Can You Do?

INTERPRETIVE
- I can recognize the four seasons and their descriptions in a narrative.
- I can identify weather conditions based on specific descriptions.

INTERPERSONAL
- I can discuss a vacation experience with others.
- I can exchange information about weather conditions using weather-related vocabulary and corresponding temperatures.

PRESENTATIONAL
- I can present a weather forecast from outside sources.
- I can talk about weather conditions during a trip.

旅游和气候
Travel and Climate

hǎo jiǔ bú jiàn
好久不见。暑假实习还好吗？

jié shù
好极了！实习结束以后，我去了中国各地旅游。

yún nán
这是我从云南给你带回来的茶叶。

yún nán
谢谢！你去了云南的哪些地方旅游？

kūn míng
我到了昆明，那
fēng jǐng
里的风景很漂亮，
shān
有山有水。

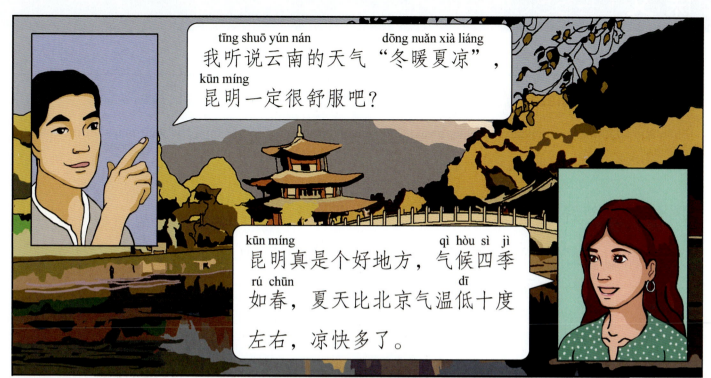

我听说云南的天气"冬暖夏凉"，昆明一定很舒服吧？

昆明真是个好地方，气候四季如春，夏天比北京气温低十度左右，凉快多了。

是"驴友"，不是"女友"。"驴友"就是一起旅游的朋友。

真羡慕你，北京这几天特别闷热。下次去旅游一定要叫上我，我要当你的"驴友"！

什么？你要当我的女友？

原来是这个意思啊！对了，这个周末我打算去爬山，你想和我一起去吗？

星期六

29c°/17c°

下午

3mm

好，让我看看天气预报……预报说周六早上是晴天，可是下午会刮风，还可能下雨。白天最高温度二十九度，晚上会下降到十七度。我们要不要改天再去？或者去别的地方？

没关系，我们带着帽子和雨衣，早一点儿出发就行了。

LESSON TEXT 1.2

Travel and Climate 旅游和气候

Zhou Xin and Mali meet up after summer break. They talk about Mali's trip to China and their plans for the coming weekend.

周信： 好久不见。暑假实习还好吗？

孙玛丽： 好极了！实习结束以后，我去了中国各地旅游。这是我从云南给你带回来的茶叶。

周信： 谢谢！你去了云南的哪些地方旅游？

孙玛丽： 我到了昆明，那里的风景很漂亮，有山有水。

周信： 我听说云南的天气"冬暖夏凉"，昆明一定很舒服吧？

孙玛丽： 昆明真是个好地方，气候四季如春，夏天比北京气温低十度左右，凉快多了。

周信： 真羡慕你，北京这几天特别闷热。下次去旅游一定要叫上我，我要当你的"驴友"！

孙玛丽： 什么？你要当我的女友？

周信： 是"驴友"，不是"女友"。"驴友"就是一起旅游的朋友。

孙玛丽： 原来是这个意思啊！对了，这个周末我打算去爬山，你想和我一起去吗？

周信： 好，让我看看天气预报……预报说周六早上是晴天，可是下午会刮风，还可能下雨。白天最高温度二十九度，晚上会下降到十七度。我们要不要改天再去？或者去别的地方？

孙玛丽： 没关系，我们带着帽子和雨衣，早一点儿出发就行了。

Language Tips

気温 (qìwēn)

温度 (wēndù)

In the Lesson Text, 气温 and 温度 are used, and both refer to temperature. However, 气温 means air temperature (e.g., The temperature today is 70 degrees), while 温度 simply means temperature. 温度 is used more broadly and can describe the temperature of a variety of things.

Examples:

夏天平均气温八十度左右。
The average temperature in summer is about 80 degrees.

人发烧的时候身体温度会上升。
When human beings have a fever, the body's temperature rises.

驴友 (lǘyǒu)

In the Lesson Text, Zhou Xin explained to Mali that he said 驴友 rather than the similar-sounding 女友. 驴友 literally means "donkey friend." It refers to people who like outdoor activities and like to travel on their own — essentially backpackers, who carry all their daily necessities in a backpack while traveling — and it is a term that such people use to refer to each other. The word "donkey" is used because donkeys can carry heavy loads on their backs and are able to bear hardships, a quality that these backpackers are proud to share.

Example:

我和我的驴友朋友们要去游遍欧洲。
My group of traveling mates and I are going to explore Europe.

字 词 VOCABULARY

LESSON VOCABULARY 1.2

	SIMPLIFIED	TRADITIONAL	PINYIN	WORD CATEGORY	DEFINITION
1.	好久不见	好久不見	hǎojiǔ bújiàn	*ie*	long time no see
	久		jiǔ	*adj*	longtime
2.	结束	結束	jiéshù	*v*	to end, to finish
3.	风景	風景	fēngjǐng	*n*	scenery
4.	山		shān	*n*	hill; mountain
5.	听说	聽說	tīngshuō	*v*	to be told; to hear of
6.	冬暖夏凉	冬暖夏涼	dōngnuǎn xiàliáng	*ie*	warm in the winters and cool in the summers
7.	气候	氣候	qìhòu	*n*	climate
8.	四季如春		sìjì rúchūn	*ie*	like spring all year-round
	季		jì	*n*	season
	如		rú	*adj*	to be like
9.	低		dī	*adj*	low
10.	闷热	悶熱	mēnrè	*adj*	humid, muggy
11.	叫上		jiàoshang	*rv*	to ask someone to go with
12.	驴友	驢友	lǘyǒu	*n*	traveling mates
13.	原来	原來	yuánlái	*adv, adj*	all along, turns out; original
14.	爬山		páshān	*vo*	to hike; to climb a mountain
	爬		pá	*v*	to climb; to crawl
15.	天气预报	天氣預報	tiānqì yùbào	*n*	weather forecast
	预报	預報	yùbào	*n*	forecast; to forecast
16.	晴天		qíngtiān	*n*	sunny day
17.	刮风	颳風	guāfēng	*vo*	to be windy
	刮	颳	guā	*v*	to blow
	风	風	fēng	*n*	wind
18.	白天		báitiān	*n*	daytime
19.	高		gāo	*adj*	high

LESSON VOCABULARY 1.2 (continued)

SIMPLIFIED	TRADITIONAL	PINYIN	WORD CATEGORY	DEFINITION
20. 温度		wēndù	*n*	temperature
21. 下降到		xiàjiàngdào	*v*	to drop to; to fall to
22. 改天		gǎitiān	*n*	another day, some other day
23. 雨衣		yǔyī	*n*	raincoat
24. 出发	出發	chūfā	*v*	to depart, to set out

PROPER NOUN

25. 云南	雲南	Yúnnán	*n*	Yunnan (province)
26. 昆明		Kūnmíng	*n*	Kunming (city)

REQUIRED VOCABULARY 1.2

27. 上升		shàngshēng	*v*	to rise, to go up
28. 干燥	乾燥	gānzào	*adj*	dry, arid
29. 潮湿	潮濕	cháoshī	*adj*	humid; damp

 ONLINE RESOURCES
Visit *http://college.betterchinese.com* for a map and list of China's major cities.

Idiomatic Expression

sì jì rú chūn
四季如春

四季如春 means "four seasons like spring." Often associated with the city of Kunming and its "eternal spring-like weather," this phrase is broadly used to describe a place with a mild climate where it feels like spring throughout the year.

Example:
这里的气候四季如春。
The climate here feels like spring all year-round.

Weather Forecast

Unlike the United States, which uses the imperial system of measurement, China uses the metric system. Temperatures in the United States are measured in Fahrenheit (°F), while temperatures in China are given in Celsius (°C). Here is a weather forecast, along with its associated vocabulary:

Terms	Pinyin	Meaning
相对湿度	xiāngduì shīdù	relative humidity
风向	fēngxiàng	wind direction
风力	fēnglì	wind strength
级	jí	level
微风	wēifēng	gentle breeze
强风	qiángfēng	strong wind
晴	qíng	fine, clear
多云	duōyún	cloudy

In addition to the terms found above, the list below provides other terms that are commonly used to describe different kinds of weather phenomena (天气现象: tiānqì xiànxiàng):

Weather	Pinyin	Meaning	Weather	Pinyin	Meaning
阴	yīn	overcast	阵雪	zhènxuě	snow shower
阵雨	zhènyǔ	shower	小雪	xiǎoxuě	light snow
雷阵雨	léizhènyǔ	thunderstorm	中雪	zhōngxuě	moderate snow
小雨	xiǎoyǔ	drizzle	大雪	dàxuě	heavy snow
中雨	zhōngyǔ	moderate rain	暴雪	bàofēngxuě	snowstorm
大雨	dàyǔ	downpour	雾	wù	foggy
暴雨	bàoyǔ	rainstorm	沙尘暴	shāchénbào	sandstorm

Adjectives to Describe Weather

These are terms frequently used in everyday conversations:

冰冻	寒冷	凉爽	温暖	炎热	酷热
bīngdòng	hánlěng	liángshuǎng	wēnnuǎn	yánrè	kùrè
freezing	cold	cool	warm	hot	scorching

STRUCTURE NOTE 1.6

Use 听说 *to mean "I've heard that"*

The phrase 听说 *(tīngshuō) literally means "heard said." It is used in two common ways: first, to report some information about the subject that someone, usually the speaker, has heard. In this pattern, the subject is often omitted before* 听说. *Second, the verb phrase* 听说过 *expresses that the subject has heard of something before.*

> (Subject +) 听说 + Sentence

> Subject + 听说过 + Noun Phrase

From the Lesson Text:
我听说云南的天气 "冬暖夏凉"。
Wǒ tīngshuō Yúnnán de tiānqì "dōngnuǎn xiàliáng".
I hear Yunnan's winters are warm and summers are cool.

Other examples:
听说你明年去中国旅游。
Tīngshuō nǐ míngnián qù Zhōngguó lǚyóu.
I hear that you are traveling to China next year.

我没有听说过这个人。
Wǒ méiyǒu tīngshuō guo zhè ge rén.
I've never heard of this person before.

Practice: Change the following sentences by using 听说.

Example: 他去过很多国家。
→ 听说他去过很多国家。

1. 中平今年选修了中国文学课。

   _____

2. 明天会下大雨。

   _____

3. 他篮球打得很好。

   _____

4. 昆明的气候四季如春。

   _____

5. 你知道申请奖学金的事吗？

   _____

STRUCTURE NOTE 1.7
Use A 比 B with an adjective and an amount to specify an amount in comparison

We have learned how to use 比 *to compare two things in Modern Chinese Textbook Vol. 1B, Unit 9, Lesson 1, Structure Note 9.3. However, if you want to specify the amount in the comparison, then the number word and the measure word should be placed after the adjective.*

> A 比 B + Adjective + Number Word + Measure Word

From the Lesson Text:　　（昆明的）夏天比北京气温低十度左右。
(Kūnmíng de) Xiàtiān bǐ Běijīng qìwēn dī shí dù zuǒyòu.
Summer temperatures in Kunming are lower than Beijing by about 10 degrees.

Other examples:　　这本书比那本贵十块钱。　　她比我大两岁。
Zhè běn shū bǐ nà běn guì shí kuài qián.　　Tā bǐ wǒ dà liǎng suì.
This book is ten dollars more expensive　　She is two years older than me.
than that one.

Practice: Create complete sentences using 比 and the information provided below.

Example:　教授五十一岁/教授的太太四十九岁
→ 教授比他的太太大两岁。

1.　这杯咖啡十五元/那杯花茶十八元

　　_____

2.　我选了三门课/她选了七门课

　　_____

3.　我的公司有十个实习生/他的公司有五个实习生

　　_____

4.　这个城市的人口有五十万/那个城市的人口有一百万

　　_____

5.　今天北京的最高温度是二十五度/波士顿的最高温度
　　是二十二度

　　_____

STRUCTURE NOTE 1.8
Use 多了 *to express much more*

The previous Structure Note described a comparative adjective followed by a quantity to indicate a specific amount of difference, as in 我比他大两岁, *"I am two years older than he is." To describe greater degrees of difference, phrase such as* 多了 *and* 得多 *are added following the adjectives to mean "by a lot." This is similar to Modern Chinese Textbook Vol. 1B, Unit 9, Lesson 1, Structure Note 9.5, where* 一点 *is added after the adjective to indicate a small degree of difference.*

> A + 比 + B + Adjective + 得多 / 多了

From the Lesson Text:

（昆明的）夏天比北京气温低十度左右，凉快多了。

(Kūnmíng de) Xiàtiān bǐ Běijīng qìwēn dī shí dù zuǒyòu, liángkuai duō le.
Summer temperatures in Kunming are lower than Beijing by about 10 degrees, so it's much cooler.

Other Examples:

这个城市比十年前美多了。
Zhè ge chéngshì bǐ shí nián qián měi duō le.
This city is much more beautiful than ten years ago.

在我们学校，学习日语的学生比学习汉语的少多了。
Zài wǒmen xuéxiào, xuéxí Rìyǔ de xuésheng bǐ xuéxí Hànyǔ de shǎo duōle.
In our school, there are far fewer students studying Japanese than Chinese.

Practice: Create complete sentences using the following word pairs with 比……多了.

Example: 他的中文 / 我的 / 好 → 他的中文比我的好多了。

1. 北京的夏天 / 云南的 / 热

   _____

2. 这里的气候 / 那里的 / 舒服

   _____

3. 这个学期的文学考试 / 上个学期的 / 难

   _____

4. 教授写的书法 / 我的 / 漂亮

   _____

5. 出国旅游 / 在家看电视 / 有意思

   _____

STRUCTURE NOTE 1.9
Use 原来 *to express "as it turns out"*

原来 *has several different uses. In its most literal sense, it means "original" or "originally," as in,* 这家商店原来是我爷爷开的, *"this shop was originally opened by my grandfather."* 原来 *can also be used to indicate that the speaker has discovered the way things are in the present, or the way that something has turned out; often contrary to expectations. In this use, it is similar to "as it turns out" or "all along." When* 原来 *is used in this way, it generally precedes the rest of the sentence.*

> 原来 + Sentence

From the Lesson Text:

原来是这个意思啊！
Yuánlái shì zhè ge yìsi a!
So that's what it means!

Other Examples:

原来学习中文的语法是一件很有意思的事。
Yuánlái xuéxí Zhōngwén de yǔfǎ shì yí jiàn hěn yǒuyìsi de shì.
It turns out learning Chinese grammar is a very interesting thing.

他每次生病的时候都不想去医院，原来是因为他怕打针。
Tā měi cì shēngbìng de shíhou dōu bù xiǎng qù yīyuàn, yuánlái shì yīnwèi tā pà dǎzhēn.
Whenever he was sick, he hasn't wanted to go to the hospital. As it turns out, it is because he's afraid of injections.

Practice: Change the following sentences into Chinese by applying the 原来 and using the information provided below.

Example: I thought you were in the library, but you were here all along.
→ 我以为你在图书馆，原来你一直在这儿。

1. As it turns out, he also likes to eat Chinese food.

   _____

2. It turns out you live on campus, too.

   _____

3. It turns out that I don't have a Chinese exam today.

   _____

4. As it turns out, he is from Boston, too.

   _____

练习 1.9: 课文理解

Paired Activity: Discuss the following questions based on the Lesson Text. Be prepared to share your thoughts with the class.

1. 玛丽暑假过得怎么样？她去了哪里旅游？

2. 玛丽为什么喜欢昆明？

3. 如果有机会，你想去中国哪个地方旅游？为什么？

练习 1.10: 北京旅行

Individual Activity: You and your classmate are visiting Beijing for five days. Based on the forecast, create an itinerary covering Beijing's famous tourist spots. Use the word bank below to describe what activities you will do on each day and why.

晴天　阴天　多云　小雨　大雨　雷阵雨　舒服　温暖　凉爽　微冷

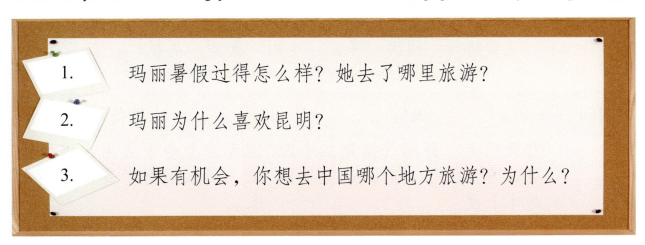

天气预报

5日 星期五	6日 星期六	7日 星期日	8日 星期一	9日 星期二
28°C 18°C	26°C 17°C	24°C 15°C	27°C 19°C	30°C 20°C

旅游景点	什么时候去？为什么？
Example: 长城	星期五白天天气晴朗，去爬长城的时候最好选这种天气。
故宫	
颐和园 (Yíhéyuán: Summer Palace)	
奥林匹克公园 (Àolínpǐkè gōngyuán: Olympic Park)	
秀水街 (Xiùshuǐjiē: Silk Market)	

练习 **1.11:** 旅游计划

Paired Activity: Working with a partner, review and choose three days from the itinerary you just created. What will you need to prepare before you go out? Fill out the chart and then create a dialogue in which you discuss your preparations for the weather.

晴天　阴天　多云　小雨　大雨　刮风

时间	天气	准备
Example: 星期日	白天阴天，最高气温是二十四度。晚上会下大雨，最低气温是十五度。	因为晚上会下大雨，温度比较低，所以最好带着雨伞和大衣。

练习 **1.12:** 和季节有关的节日

Group Activity: Working in groups, research a seasonal event held in one of China's cities. Write a short report using the words provided and be prepared to present it to the class.

才　左右　比较　比……低/高　听说……

Example: 听说哈尔滨的国际冰雪节非常有名。每年一月，很多游客去哈尔滨看漂亮的冰灯。我很喜欢这样的节日！虽然我非常怕冷，但我也希望能有机会去哈尔滨看那么美的冰灯。

	Radical	Stroke Order
度	广 yǎn shelter	丶 亠 广 广 庐 庐 度 度 度
久	一 yī one	丿 夂 久
山	山 shān mountain	丨 屮 山
冬	夂 zhǐ walk slowly	丿 夂 冬 冬 冬
暖	日 rì sun	丨 冂 冂 日 日 日 日 日 晒 晒 暖 暖 暖
束	木 mù wood	一 一 一 一 束 束 束
低	亻(人) rén person	丿 亻 亻 仁 低 低 低
闷	门 mén door	丶 丶 门 门 闷 闷 闷
原	厂 hǎn cliff	一 厂 厂 尸 原 原 原 原 原 原
预	页 yè page	乛 マ 了 予 予 预 预 预 预
爬	爪 zhǎo claw	丿 厂 爪 爪 爪 爪 爬
晴	日 rì sun	丨 冂 冂 日 日 日 晴 晴 晴 晴 晴 晴
降	阝 fù hill	了 阝 阝 阝 阵 降 降 降
云	厶 sī self	一 二 云 云
南	十 shí ten	一 十 十 内 南 南 南 南

Online chat: Working with a classmate, discuss where you would ideally like to spend a winter vacation. Provide details about how the weather and temperature factor into your decision.

练习 1.15: 阅读理解

玛丽打算实习结束以后去旅行。旅行前，她做了很多准备。首先，她在网络上看了很多中国旅游介绍。介绍说云南的昆明有山有水，很漂亮，而且气候四季如春，非常舒服。然后玛丽问了她的中国朋友，朋友们告诉她昆明有很多有名的旅游景点。玛丽打算去昆明看看。

Read the passage and answer the following questions.
1. What is the weather in Kunming like?
2. Why does Mali want to visit Kunming?
3. How have the weather and temperature influenced your travel plans in the past?

练习 1.16: 阅读理解

朋友们，晚上好！今天是八月五日，星期日，天气晴转多云。让我为您介绍明、后两天的城市天气情况。

八月六日，多云转雨，白天最高气温三十度。晚上气温会下降到十八度，部分地方有小雨。

八月七日，小雨转大雨，最高气温二十六度，白天有大风，全市大部分地方有大雨，晚上风力减小，最低气温十五度。

Read the radio transcript of the weather forecast and answer the following questions.
1. What is the weather like on August 5?
2. Compare the differences between the weather forecasts on August 6 – 7.
3. Using August 6 – 7 as examples, write a weather forecast for August 8.

Notes:
转 (zhuǎn): *v.* to change
多云 (duōyún): *adj.* cloudy
部分 (bùfen): *n.* part of, portion
风力 (fēnglì): *n.* wind strength
减小 (jiǎnxiǎo): *v.* to decrease

Summer in Kunming and Lijiang

Located in the southern province of Yunnan, the cities of Kunming and Lijiang (丽江: Lìjiāng) are two of the best places to experience summer in China. Unlike many other places in China, which have hot and humid summers punctuated by sudden thunderstorms, summer in mountaneous Yunnan is mild and temperate.

Kunming

The capital of Yunnan Province, Kunming is known as "the City of Eternal Spring." Surrounded by mountains, Kunming has a mild climate all year-round (四季如春, see Idiomatic Expression, page 25). In particular, the summers are long with temperatures ranging from 63 – 75 °F (17 – 24 °C). Each year, millions of tourists visit Kunming to enjoy the eternal spring.

Two picturesque sites to visit in Kunming are the Stone Forest Scenic Area (石林: Shílín) and Jiuxiang Scenic Area (九乡: Jiǔxiāng). The Stone Forest began as a shallow sea about 270 million years ago, where deposits of sandstone covered by limestone accumulated. Over time, the ocean subsided, exposing the deposits to erosion from air and water. This eventually created the Stone Forest we see today, with stones sculpted by the natural elements into all shapes and sizes. Aside from hiking through the majestic landscape, meeting the Sani people that live in this forest home, is another experience that should not be missed. One of the best times to go is on the 24th day of the sixth lunar month during the annual Yi Torch Festival to enjoy activities such as wrestling matches, bullfighting, pole-climbing, singing, and dancing.

The Jiuxiang Scenic Area is another natural wonder that transports visitors to an underground world of caves. Formed some 600 million years ago, the entire system consists of over 100 caves covering 77 square miles (200 square kilometers). Many of these caves are so enormous that some have their own gorges, waterfalls, ponds, and even a village! Aside from touring the region by foot, you can also take a boat ride along the cave river. At the end of a tour through the underground system, a cable car transports people back up, allowing tourists to enjoy majestic views of the surrounding mountains.

Lijiang

The small city of Lijiang is located in the northwestern part of Yunnan Province, where the Qinghai-Tibet Plateau and Yunnan-Guizhou Plateau meet. Close to the equator and at a high elevation, this region enjoys clear weather most of the year, along with plenty of rainfall.

With average temperatures ranging between 50 – 79 °F (10 – 26 °C), the summer is a good time to visit the Old Town of Lijiang (丽江古镇: Lijiāng Gǔzhèn), constructed during the late Song Dynasty (960 – 1279 AD). When it was built, water was brought in from the Yushui River to form rivers small and large that crisscrossed the entire town. Walking around the town, one can see many waterways and bridges, while experiencing charming cobblestone streets and viewing houses with beautiful architecture representing different ethnic groups. With plenty of restaurants, shops, and cultural destinations, such as the Wufeng Pavilion and the Lijiang Museum of Dongba Culture, there is always something to do in this cozy town.

Another scenic destination not too far away is the Old Town of Shuhe (東河古镇: Shùhé Gǔzhèn). A small, peaceful village tucked away in a forest, the Old Town of Shuhe is a well-preserved location along the Ancient Tea Horse Road, which served as a trade route across Yunnan. It is also a great place to buy fur and leather goods — a local specialty — within the central square marketplace. Off the beaten path of more well-traveled spots, Shuhe brings visitors a glimpse of a time gone by.

Pinyin	**English**
Zhōu Xìn: Hǎojiǔbújiàn. Shǔjià shíxí hái hǎo ma?	Long time no see! How was your summer internship?
Sūn Mǎlì: Hǎo jí le! Shíxí jiéshù yǐhòu, wǒ qùle Zhōngguó gè dì lǚyóu. Zhè shì wǒ cóng Yúnnán gěi nǐ dài huílai de cháyè.	It was terrific! After the internship, I traveled to various parts of China. Here is some tea that I brought back for you from Yunnan.
Zhōu Xìn: Xièxie! Nǐ qùle Yúnnán de nǎ xiē dìfang lǚyóu?	Thank you! Where did you visit in Yunnan?
Sūn Mǎlì: Wǒ dàole Kūnmíng, nàlǐ de fēngjǐng hěn piàoliang, yǒushān yǒushuǐ.	I went to Kunming. It's really beautiful there, with scenic mountains and rivers and lakes.
Zhōu Xìn: Wǒ tīngshuō Yúnnán de tiānqì "dōngnuǎn xiàliáng", Kūnmíng yídìng hěn shūfu ba?	I hear Yunnan's winters are warm and summers are cool. Kunming must have been very comfortable, right?
Sūn Mǎlì: Kūnmíng zhēn shì ge hǎo dìfang, qìhòu sìjì rúchūn, xiàtiān bǐ Běijīng qìwēn dī shí dù zuǒyòu, liángkuai duō le.	Kunming really is a great place. It feels like spring all year-round. Summer temperatures in Kunming are lower than Beijing by about 10 degrees, so it's much cooler.
Zhōu Xìn: Zhēn xiànmu nǐ, Běijīng zhè jǐtiān tèbié mēnrè. Xiàcì qù lǚyóu yídìng yào jiàoshang wǒ, wǒ yào dāng nǐ de "lǚyǒu".	I'm so envious! It's been particularly hot and muggy in Beijing these past few days. Next time you go traveling, you must ask me to join you so I can be your "lǚyǒu" (travelling friend).
Sūn Mǎlì: Shénme? Nǐ yào dāng wǒde nǚyǒu?	What? You want to be my girlfriend?
Zhōu Xìn: Shì "lǚyǒu", bú shì "nǚyǒu". "Lǚyǒu" jiù shì yìqǐ lǚyóu de péngyou.	I said "traveling friend," not "girlfriend." "Lǚyǒu" means friends who travel together.
Sūn Mǎlì: Yuánlái shì zhège yìsi a! Duìle, zhège zhōumò wǒ dǎsuan qù páshān, nǐ xiǎng hé wǒ yìqǐ qù ma?	So that's what it means! Oh, by the way, I plan to go hiking this weekend. Do you want to go with me?

Zhōu Xìn:	Hǎo, ràng wǒ kànkan tiānqì yùbào…… Yùbào shuō zhōuliù zǎoshang shì qíngtiān, kěshì xiàwǔ huì guāfēng, hái kěnéng xiàyǔ. Báitiān zuì gāo wēndù èrshíjiǔ dù, wǎnshang huì xiàjiàng dào shíqī dù. Wǒmen yàobuyào gǎitiān zàiqù? Huòzhě qù biéde dìfang?	Sure, let me check the weather forecast . . . According to the forecast, it will be sunny on Saturday morning, but it will be windy and it might rain in the afternoon. The highest daytime temperature will be 29 degrees, with evening temperatures dropping to about 17 degrees. Should we go some another day? Or go somewhere else?
Sūn Mǎlì:	Méi guānxi, wǒmen dàizhe màozi hé yǔyī, zǎo yìdiǎnr chūfā jiù xíng le.	It's okay. As long as we take hats and raincoats, and go a bit earlier, it'll be fine.

What Can You Do?

INTERPRETIVE
- I can interpret a weather forecast and prepare accordingly.
- I can recognize the difference between what one has actually experienced and opinions about those experiences.

INTERPERSONAL
- I can exchange details about a trip.
- I can discuss preferences for places and weather.

PRESENTATIONAL
- I can present information about a place and its climate.
- I can propose a plan for an activity based on the weather.

ACT IT OUT

Working in groups, compose an original two-minute skit that utilizes the vocabulary and structures introduced in Unit 1. Each of you should assume a role and have a roughly equal number of lines in the skit. Be prepared to perform your skit in class. You can either come up with your own story or choose from one of the following situations:

A) You and your friends are going to visit Beijing during the summer break. Discuss with your friends what the weather will be like there and what you will need to prepare for the trip.

B) Your friend returned from a trip to Europe and brought various souvenirs for you and your friends. Discuss what he/she brought for each person.

C) Discuss what the weather will be like this weekend and what activities you and your friends plan to do.

CHECK WHAT YOU CAN DO

RECOGNIZE

Adjectives
- ☐ 凉快
- ☐ 各
- ☐ 暖和
- ☐ 低
- ☐ 闷热
- ☐ 高
- ☐ 干燥
- ☐ 潮湿
- ☐ 平均
- ☐ 亲爱的

Adverbs
- ☐ 一般
- ☐ 左右
- ☐ 说不定
- ☐ 原来
- ☐ 遍

Idiomatic Expressions
- ☐ 好久不见
- ☐ 冬暖夏凉
- ☐ 四季如春

Interjection
- ☐ 对了

Name
- ☐ 周信

Nouns
- ☐ 明信片
- ☐ 气温
- ☐ 华氏
- ☐ 雨伞
- ☐ 冬季
- ☐ 舞蹈团
- ☐ 季节

- ☐ 零下
- ☐ 摄氏
- ☐ 巴黎
- ☐ 伦敦
- ☐ 风景
- ☐ 山
- ☐ 气候
- ☐ 驴友
- ☐ 天气预报
- ☐ 晴天
- ☐ 白天
- ☐ 温度
- ☐ 改天
- ☐ 雨衣
- ☐ 云南
- ☐ 昆明
- ☐ 度
- ☐ 面试

Resultative Verb
- ☐ 迷上

Verbs
- ☐ 继续
- ☐ 留
- ☐ 听说
- ☐ 叫上
- ☐ 刮风
- ☐ 下降到
- ☐ 出发
- ☐ 上升
- ☐ 旅游

Verb-Object Compounds
- ☐ 出门
- ☐ 爬山

WRITE

- ☐ 旅
- ☐ 游
- ☐ 温
- ☐ 般
- ☐ 华
- ☐ 氏
- ☐ 凉
- ☐ 迷
- ☐ 留
- ☐ 平
- ☐ 均
- ☐ 雨
- ☐ 遍
- ☐ 各
- ☐ 季

- ☐ 度
- ☐ 久
- ☐ 山
- ☐ 冬
- ☐ 暖
- ☐ 束
- ☐ 低
- ☐ 闷
- ☐ 原
- ☐ 预
- ☐ 爬
- ☐ 晴
- ☐ 降
- ☐ 云
- ☐ 南

USE

- ☐ Use 才 to emphasize a small number or amount.
- ☐ Use 左右 after a number to make an estimate.
- ☐ Use 说不定 to express possibility or uncertainty.
- ☐ Use 各 to mean each or different.
- ☐ Use 比较 to strengthen an adjective.
- ☐ Use 听说 to mean "I've heard that."
- ☐ Use A 比 B with an adjective and an amount to specify an amount in comparison.
- ☐ Use 多了 to express much more.
- ☐ Use 原来 to mean "as it turns out."

Academics

第二单元
UNIT 2

Communication Goals

Lesson 1: 申请留学 **Applying to Study Abroad**
- Discuss college majors and electives.
- Talk about class reports, discussions, and studying abroad.
- Explain the procedure for how to apply for a scholarship to a classmate.
- Describe one's language proficiency.

Lesson 2: 加入社团 **Joining a Student Club**
- Inquire about popular college clubs and organizations.
- Describe people's appearance and personality traits.
- Talk about meaningful activities and goals towards self improvement.

申请留学
Applying to Study Abroad

中平，你选修^{xuǎn xiū}的中国文化课怎么样？

这门课很有意思，我们用中文讨论^{tǎo lùn}和写报告^{bào gào}。你呢？这个学期选了什么课？

暑假的时候我迷上了中国历史小说^{xiǎo shuō}，所以这个学期我主^{zhǔ}修^{xiū}中国历史课和中国文学课，教授要我们读很多历史书和中文小说^{xiǎo shuō}。

我觉得学习知识不见^{zhī shi bú jiàn}得^{dé}只在书本^{shū běn}上，特别是学习中国文化或历史，最好的办法^{bàn fǎ}就是去中国走一趟^{tàng}，学习一段^{duàn}时间。

去中国学习听起来挺有意思的！你想去中国哪个地方呢？

我只是想顺便去看看玛丽……我查了一下怎么申请留学，只要准备必需的资料就可以了，我们还能申请奖学金。

中平当然想去北京！这样他就可以去看玛丽了，对吧？

没想到这么简单。到中国留学能更好地了解和学习中国历史，而且我一直很想去参观故宫和爬长城。

那我也要去中国留学，这样我就能吃到地道的饺子和北京烤鸭啦！

哈哈，你去中国是为了吃啊？不过我也很喜欢吃中国菜。这真是个好主意。如果你们都去中国留学，那么我也去吧！

太好了！那以后我们都能变成中国通了。我要把这个好消息告诉玛丽！

LESSON TEXT 2.1

Applying to Study Abroad 申请留学

The new school year has just begun. Dadong, Zhongping, and their friends run into each other at the school cafeteria.

陈大东： 中平，你选修的中国文化课怎么样？

李中平： 这门课很有意思，我们用中文讨论和写报告。你呢？这个学期选了什么课？

陈大东： 暑假的时候我迷上了中国历史小说，所以这个学期我主修中国历史课和中国文学课，教授要我们读很多历史书和中文小说。

李中平： 我觉得学习知识不见得只在书本上，特别是学习中国文化或历史，最好的办法就是去中国走一趟，学习一段时间。

王小美： 去中国学习听起来挺有意思的！你想去中国哪个地方呢？

黄祥安： 中平当然想去北京！这样他就可以去看玛丽了，对吧？

李中平： 我只是想顺便去看看玛丽……我查了一下怎么申请留学，只要准备必需的资料就可以了，我们还能申请奖学金。

陈大东： 没想到这么简单。到中国留学能更好地了解和学习中国历史，而且我一直都很想去参观故宫和爬长城。

黄祥安： 那我也要去中国留学，这样我就能吃到地道的饺子和北京烤鸭啦！

王小美： 哈哈，你去中国是为了吃啊？不过我也很喜欢吃中国菜。这真是个好主意。如果你们都去中国留学，那么我也去吧！

李中平： 太好了！那以后我们都能变成中国通了。我要把这个好消息告诉玛丽！

Language Tips

不见得 (bújiàndé)	In the Lesson Text, Zhongping uses 不见得 to say that books are not the only way to acquire knowledge. It is a more casual way of saying "not necessarily," 不一定.

Example:

中国菜不见得难做。
Chinese food is not necessarily difficult to make.

地道 (dìdao)	In the Lesson Text, Xiang'an uses 地道 to say the dumplings and Peking Duck in China are authentic. 地道 and 道地 both mean authentic. However, 地道 is primarily used in Northern China, while 道地 is often used in Southern China.
道地 (dàodì)	

Example:

这个餐厅的中国菜很地道。
This restaurant's Chinese food is very authentic.

中国通 (Zhōngguó tōng)	In the Lesson Text, Zhongping says he hopes he and his friends can become 中国通 after they study in China. The word 通 literally means "to go through." However, 通 can also mean an expert in a certain area, as in 中国通.

Example:

在中国住了十年，她变成了一个中国通。
After living in China for ten years, she became a on an expert of China.

字 词 VOCABULARY

LESSON VOCABULARY 2.1

	SIMPLIFIED	TRADITIONAL	PINYIN	WORD CATEGORY	DEFINITION
1.	选修	選修	xuǎnxiū	v	to take as an elective course
2.	讨论	討論	tǎolùn	v, n	to discuss; discussion
3.	报告	報告	bàogào	n, v	report; to report
4.	小说	小説	xiǎoshuō	n	novel, fiction
5.	主修		zhǔxiū	v	to major in
6.	知识	知識	zhīshi	n	knowledge
7.	不见得	不見得	bújiàndé	adv	not necessarily
8.	书本	書本	shūběn	n	books
9.	办法	辦法	bànfǎ	n	method; means
10.	趟		tàng	mw	(used to indicate a trip or trips made)
11.	段		duàn	mw	a section; a part
12.	挺		tǐng	adv	very, rather, quite
13.	顺便	順便	shùnbiàn	adv	in passing; in addition to what one's doing
14.	查		chá	v	to check; to investigate
15.	申请	申請	shēnqǐng	v	to apply
16.	留学	留學	liúxué	v	to study abroad
17.	必需		bìxū	adj	necessary; indispensable
18.	资料	資料	zīliào	n	data, material, information
19.	奖学金	獎學金	jiǎngxuéjīn	n	scholarship
20.	地道		dìdao	adj	real, authentic
21.	为了	爲了	wèile	prep	for the purpose of; for the sake of
22.	不过	不過	búguò	cj	but; however
23.	主意		zhǔyi	n	idea
24.	变成	變成	biànchéng	rv	to become, to turn into
25.	中国通	中國通	Zhōngguótōng	n	an expert of China, an old China hand

SIMPLIFIED	TRADITIONAL	PINYIN	WORD CATEGORY	DEFINITION
通		tōng	n	expert
26. 消息		xiāoxi	n	news

REQUIRED VOCABULARY 2.1

SIMPLIFIED	TRADITIONAL	PINYIN	WORD CATEGORY	DEFINITION
27. 辅修		fǔxiū	v, n	to minor in; minor
28. 学分	學分	xuéfēn	n	course credit
29. 成绩	成績	chéngjì	n	result; grades
30. 填表格		tián biǎogé	vo	to fill out the form
填		tián	v	to fill out
表格		biǎogé	n	form

Idiomatic Expression

sān rén xíng   bì yǒu wǒ shī
三人行，必有我师

三人行，必有我师 literally means "out of three people walking together, there must be one that is my teacher."

This expression appears in *The Analects* (《论语》: *Lún Yǔ*), a collection of Confucius' sayings and ideas. He believed that one could always learn something new from among any three people. A phrase directly following the expression, 择其善者而从之, 其不善者而改之 (zé qí shàn zhě ér cōng zhī, qí bú shàn zhě ér gǎi zhī), adds that you can learn to attain good qualities and avoid bad qualities. This expression is often used to express a modest attitude or to encourage people to learn from others.

Example:
我们应该有"三人行，必有我师"的态度，多跟别人学习。
We should have the attitude that "out of three people walking together, there must be one that I can learn from" — we should learn more from others.

Using and Omitting 了 Appropriately

Deciding when to use 了, especially in a narrative situation, can be very challenging. Native speakers themselves do not completely agree on where 了 should be used in a particular passage. There are, however, certain places where they agree that 了 cannot be used, and where it must be used.

Keep in mind that 了 does not need to be used simply to mark past events. 了 indicates a change of state, and should be used to emphasize that a situation has completed or started.

Refresher: common usages of 了

When describing an event involving specific amounts or lengths of time:		
我打了一个小时的篮球。	Wǒ dǎle yí ge xiǎoshí de lánqiú.	I played an hour's worth of basketball.

When describing a change from a normal state (see *Modern Chinese* Textbook Vol. 1A, Unit 3, Lesson 2, Structure Note 3.10):		
我生病了。	Wǒ shēngbìng le.	I'm sick.

When using a verb that has a built-in endpoint that indicates something that has taken place or an action that has been completed (see *Modern Chinese* Textbook Vol. 1A, Unit 5, Lesson 2, Structure Note 5.11 Unit 6, Lesson 2, Structure Note 6.11):		
窗户打破了。	Chuānghu dǎ pò le.	The window is broken.

When NOT to use 了:

When describing habitual activities:		
我以前常常喝 ~~了~~ 咖啡。	Wǒ yǐqián chángcháng hē~~le~~ kāfēi.	I often drank coffee before.

When reporting what someone said or thought using verbs including 说, 问, 告诉, and 知道:		
他说 ~~了~~ 他没有笔。	Tā shuō~~le~~ tā méiyǒu bǐ.	He said he didn't have a pen.

When describing states or feelings using verbs such as 喜欢, 觉得, and 想:		
以前他不喜欢 ~~了~~ 吃辣。	Yǐqián tā bù xǐhuan~~le~~ chī là	He previously didn't like to eat spicy foods.

When using a verb that must be followed by a clause:		
我以前觉得 ~~了~~ 这个餐厅的菜很好吃。	Wǒ yǐqián juéde~~le~~ zhège cāntīng de cài hěn hǎo chī.	I used to think that the food at this restaurant tasted good.

After the verb that is not the main one a speaker wants to emphasize within a series of verbs in a related sequence of events. The main verb emphasized is usually the final verb.		
我去 ~~了~~ 超市买了东西。	Wǒ qù~~le~~ chāoshì mǎile dōngxi.	I went to the supermarket to go shopping.

STRUCTURE NOTE 2.1

Use 只要 A 就 B (了) to indicate A is the only condition necessary for B to occur

只要 A, 就 B (了) *expresses the meaning "As long as A happens, B will happen." If there is a subject in the B clause, it precedes* 就.

> 只要 + Condition, (+Subject) + 就 + Result (+ 了)

From the Lesson Text:

只要准备必需的资料就可以了。
Zhǐyào zhǔnbèi bìxū de zīliào jiù kěyǐle.
As long as you prepare the necessary materials, you will be fine.

Other examples:

只要好好上课，考试就没有问题。
Zhǐyào hǎohao shàngkè, kǎoshì jiù méiyǒu wèntí.
As long as you attend your classes as expected, the exam won't be a problem.

只要明天不下雨，我们就去爬山吧！
Zhǐyào míngtiān bú xiàyǔ, wǒmen jiù qù páshān ba!
As long as it won't rain tomorrow, let's go hiking!

Practice: Create complete sentences using 只要…就… pattern and information provided.

Example: 我们 / 买好飞机票 / 能去北京
→ 只要我们买好飞机票，就能去北京。

1. 你们 / 上课好好听课 / 功课都会做

   _____

2. 你 / 多练习 / 能把汉字写得更好

   _____

3. 不下雨的话 / 我们 / 出去散步

   _____

4. 你们 / 申请 / 有机会去实习了

   _____

5. 我 / 有奖学金 / 能去留学了

   _____

STRUCTURE NOTE 2.2
Use 为了 *to explain the purpose of doing something*

为了 *(wèile) means "for," "for the purpose of," or "in order to," and is used to introduce the reason for taking some action. The reason clause must come before the action, not after. The subject of the sentence generally goes in the second clause but can also be placed at the beginning of the sentence, before* 为了*. Normally, the reason, marked by* 为了*, always precedes the action. To emphasize the reason, however, the alternate pattern "action +* 是为了 *+ reason" may be used.*

> Action + 是为了 + Reason

> Subject + 为了 + Reason + Action

> 为了 + Reason, + Subject + Action

From the Lesson Text:

你去中国是为了吃啊？
Nǐ qù Zhōngguó shì wèile chī a?
You just want to go to China for the food?

Other examples:

他为了照顾妹妹，每天一下课就回家。
Tā wèile zhàogù mèimei, měitiān yí xiàkè jiù huíjiā.
In order to take care of his sister, he returns home as soon as he gets out of class every day.

为了学习中文，我常常听录音。
Wèile xuéxí Zhōngwén, wǒ chángchang tīng lùyīn.
In order to learn Chinese, I often listen to recordings.

Practice: Match the following sentences on the basis of the information given.

1. 为了上课不迟到，　　　　我买了最早的火车票。
2. 为了能回家过春节，　　　　小美申请去中国留学。
3. 为了给爷爷买生日礼物，　　　他每天都去练习游泳。
4. 为了学习中文，　　　　她每天早上6点半起床。
5. 为了参加学校的运动会，　　　哥哥暑假去咖啡店打工了。

STRUCTURE NOTE 2.3
Use 不过 to say "but" to indicate a contrast to the previous statement

不过 *(búguò) literally means "not exceeding," and can be used to indicate "only." In this lesson,* 不过 *expresses the meaning "but," and is a more colloquial version of similar phrases* 但是 *and* 可是*.*

不过 + Sentence

From the Lesson Text:

你去中国是为了吃啊？不过我也很喜欢中国菜。
Nǐ qù Zhōngguó shì wéile chī a? Búguò wǒ yě hěn xǐhuan Zhōngguó cài.
You just want to go to China for the food? But, I also really like Chinese food.

Other Examples:

这个城市的环境很好，不过房租非常贵。
Zhè ge chéngshì de huánjìng hěn hǎo, búguò fángzū fēicháng guì.
This city's environment is very good, but rent is extremely high.

虽然很多人都说住城市很方便，不过我还是比较喜欢乡下的生活。
Suīrán hěnduō rén dōu shuō zhù chéngshì hěn fāngbiàn, búguò wǒ háishì bǐjiao xǐhuan xiāngxia de shēnghuó.
Although a lot of people say that living in the city is convenient, I still prefer living in the country.

Practice: Create complete sentences using 不过.

Example:
我想在学校附近租一个公寓，不过……
→ 我想在学校附近租一个公寓，不过那里的公寓比较难找。

1. 我听说那家中国饭馆的菜很好吃，……

   _____

2. 她今天想把她的室友介绍给我，……

   _____

3. 安娜想买那个手机，……

   _____

4. 中平想刷卡买那条项链，……

   _____

5. 他这个暑假打算去旅游，……

   _____

STRUCTURE NOTE 2.4
Use 变得 / 变成 *to describe transformation in state or from one thing to another*

变成 *(biànchéng) and* 变得 *are used in different sentence patterns to express that something has changed.* 变成 *means "to turn into," and is only used before nouns, while* 变得 *means "to turn" or "to get" and is only used before adjectives.*

Subject + 变成 + Noun Phrase

Subject + 变得 + Adjective Phrase

From the Lesson Text:
那以后我们都能变成中国通了。
Nà yǐhòu wǒmen dōu néng biànchéng Zhōngguótōng le.
Then, afterwards we can all become experts of China.

Other Examples:

这条胡同以前一点也不出名，现在变成了旅游景点。
Zhè tiáo hútong yǐqián yī diǎn yě bù chūmíng, xiànzài biànchéngle lǚyóu jǐngdiǎn
This hutong wasn't famous at all before, and now it becomes a scenic spot.

冬天来了，天气变得越来越冷了。
Dōngtiān lái, tiānqì biànde yuèláiyuè lěng le.
Winter has arrived, the weather has gotten colder and colder.

Practice: Choose the correct phrase to fill in the blanks.

变成　　变得

Example: 弟弟想要**变成**一只小狗。

1. 我希望＿＿＿＿一条鱼，在水里快乐地游来游去。

2. 她穿了一件新裙子，她想要＿＿＿＿更可爱。

3. 看了哥哥的比赛，弟弟＿＿＿＿越来越喜欢打球了。

练习 2.1: 课文理解

Paired Activity: Discuss the following questions based on the Lesson Text. Be prepared to share your thoughts with the class.

1. 大东为什么打算主修中国历史课和中国文学课？

2. 中平觉得学习中国文化或者历史最好的办法是什么？

3. 你知道怎么申请去中国留学吗？

练习 2.2: 你会选哪一所大学？

Paired Activity: Below are some of China's most well-known universities. Assign the characters to the university that best matches his or her major, interests, and relationships. Refer to the character profiles on page xii as needed.

北京大学
优势学科: 文学、数学

清华大学
优势学科: 工商管理、理工

中央音乐学院
优势学科: 音乐学、音乐表演

南京大学
优势学科: 历史学

Characters	University	Why?
	清华大学	因为我对工商管理很有兴趣。毕业后我想要做跟商务有关的工作。

Universities:

北京大学 (Běijīng Dàxué): Peking University

南京大学 (Nánjīng Dàxué): Nanjing University

清华大学 (Qīnghuá Dàxué): Tsinghua University

中央音乐学院 (Zhōngyāng Yīnyuè Xuéyuàn): Central Conservatory of Music

Notes:

优势学科 (yōushì xuékē): *n.* dominant program

工商管理 (gōngshāng guǎnlǐ): *n.* business management

理工 (lǐgōng): *n.* science and engineering

ONLINE RESOURCES

Visit *http://college.betterchinese.com* for a list of academic major and minor programs in Chinese.

练习 **2.3**（上）：你会选哪门课？

Paired Activity: You and a classmate are planning to study at a Chinese university, and you will be required to take four classes. Below is a list of majors and courses available at the university. Based on your own major and interests, discuss what courses you would like to take and why. Compare your preferences with your partner.

主修课	选修课			
汉语言	现代汉语1	现代汉语2	现代汉语3	古代汉语
中国历史	古代历史	近现代历史	博物馆学	中西历史
中国文化	传统文化	电影学	茶文化	现代艺术
中国文学	电影文学	现代文学	古代文学	古代哲学

Notes:

现代艺术 (xiàndài yìshù): *n.* modern art

中国古代哲学 (Zhōngguó gǔdài zhéxué): *n.* ancient Chinese philosophy

练习 **2.4**（中）：申请留学

Individual Activity: You have decided to study in China next semester. The application requires a short passage explaining why you would like to study abroad. Use the questions and space below to write your passage.

1. 你想申请去哪个大学留学？为什么？
2. 你对哪门课有兴趣？为什么？
3. 你到了中国以后，除了念书以外还有什么计划？

练习 **2.5**（下）：海外留学项目

Group Activity: Working in small groups, research a Chinese study-abroad program (海外留学项目: hǎiwài liúxué xiàngmù) that you would be interested in attending. Discuss why this program appeals to your group.

Example: 因为可以申请奖学金，而且学费也不贵，所以我们想去北京大学留学一个学期。北京的秋天很舒服，我们还可以去游故宫、爬长城……

	Radical	Stroke Order
讨	讠(言) yán speech	丶 讠 讠 讨 讨
论	讠(言) yán speech	丶 讠 讠 论 论 论
报	扌(手) shǒu hand	一 十 扌 扌 护 报 报
主	王 wáng king	丶 二 二 主 主
修	亻(人) rén person	丿 亻 亻 仃 仈 修 修 修
趟	走 zǒu walk	一 十 土 丰 丰 走 走 走 赵 赵 趟 趟 趟 趟
段	殳 shū to strike	丶 丆 丆 丆 乍 乍 郎 段 段
挺	扌(手) shǒu hand	一 十 扌 扌 扌 扦 挺 挺
查	木 mù wood	一 十 才 木 木 杏 杏 杏 查
必	丶 diǎn dot	丿 心 心 必 必
资	贝 bèi shell	丶 冫 冫 次 次 次 咨 资 资
料	米 mǐ rice	丶 丷 丷 半 半 米 米 米 料 料
申	丨 shù line	丨 口 口 日 申
奖	大 dà big	丶 冫 丬 丬 丬 奖 奖 奖
通	辶 chuò walk	乛 乛 冖 丆 甬 甬 甬 甬 诵 通

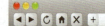

练习 2.7:线上聊天

Online chat: Working with a classmate, discuss the current Chinese language course you are both enrolled in. Share your opinions about the course and what you hope to achieve.

练习 2.8:阅读理解

> 这个学期中平选修了中国文化课。他的教授常常说"三人行必有我师",希望学生们能多跟别人学习。他也让同学们看一些和中国文化有关的电影,然后让每个人用中文写报告。中平第一次写的报告有很多语法问题,但是教授说中平的中文不错。教授还告诉中平如果他想了解更多的中国文化,就应该去中国留学,而且他还可以申请奖学金。

Read the passage and answer the following questions.
1. What kind of activities does the professor do with the students during class?
2. What does the professor suggest that Zhongping do?
3. What kind of activities does your instructor do with the students in your class?

练习 2.9:阅读理解

美国大学生的中国留学热持续

2012年8月12日

　　今年九月,美国女孩丽娜会在北京大学开始留学生活。丽娜还成功申请到了这个大学的奖学金。丽娜说她一直对中文和中国文化很感兴趣,想游遍中国,变成一个中国通。据报告,越来越多的美国大学生跟丽娜一样,希望有机会去中国留学。在2012年,有13,910个美国学生在中国学习;但在1995年,留学中国的美国学生只有1,400人。中国一所大学的教授表示,从现在中文学习的情况看,美国大学生的中国留学热还会持续。

Notes:
持续 (chíxù): *v.* to continue
(根)据 (jù): *prep.* according to
所 (suǒ): *mw.* measure word for buildings and institutions

Read the article and answer the following questions.
1. Why did Lina go to study abroad in China?
2. Why does the professor believe the interest in learning Chinese will continue?
3. Do you agree that the interest in learning Chinese will continue and why or why not?

Chinese Studying Abroad

The first part of the 20th century saw many Chinese students begin to go abroad, a marked difference from the traditional educational system which was centered around the imperial examinations. With the encouragement from the government, the majority of students went abroad to places such as Japan, United States, United Kingdom, and France. These students proved to have a significant influence on the development of modern China. Three prominent examples of influential thinkers whose careers were influenced by their experience abroad are the writer Lu Xun (鲁迅: Lǔ Xùn), the philosopher and educator Hu Shi (胡适: Hú Shì), and the rocket scientist Qian Xuesen (钱学森: Qián Xuésēn).

Lu Xun was one of the most influential writers of the 20th century. Originally, he wanted to become a doctor. He received a government scholarship to study at Sendai Medical Academy in Japan, where he was the academy's first foreign student. While at Sendai, Lu decided that it was more important "to cure China's spiritual ills rather than its physical ailments," and left school to pursue a career in writing. After returning to China, he began to write critically about social issues and became a leading figure in Chinese intellectual and political life.

Hu Shi arrived at Cornell University in 1910 to study agriculture. After changing majors to philosophy and literature, Hu continued his studies at Columbia University where he studied philosophy with one of the leading scholars of the time, the educator and philosopher John Dewey. When he returned to China, he was involved in important cultural and political movements, becoming a prominent intellectual in China. Hu eventually served as China's ambassador to the United States and the chancellor of Beijing University. Hu's most important contribution to literacy in China was in promoting the reform of written Chinese. He advocated replacing classical Chinese with vernacular Chinese, making it far easier for the average person to read literature and newspapers.

Scientist Qian Xuesen was a landmark figure in the missile and space programs in the United States and in China. He first studied mechanical engineering at MIT in 1936, and then went on to graduate studies at the California Institute of Technology (Caltech). There, Qian pursued an interest in space rockets and became a cofounder of the Jet Propulsion Laboratory (JPL). After his return to China in 1955, he led the development of Chinese missile and space programs for several decades. Revered as "the Father of Chinese Rocketry," Qian would see his work used to develop and send China's first man into space.

Today, China sends more students abroad than any other country in the world. Between 1978 and 2003, over 700,000 Chinese students studied in over 100 countries, and the number of students studying abroad is still rising. Growing up with the knowledge that many prominent Chinese scholars and politicians have studied abroad, students look to foreign education as a means of achieving success.

Pinyin

Chén Dàdōng: Zhōngpíng, nǐ xuǎnxiū de Zhōngguó wénhuà kè zěnmeyàng?

Lǐ Zhōngpíng: Zhè mén kè hěn yǒuyìsi, wǒmen yòng Zhōngwén tǎolùn hé xiě bàogào. Nǐ ne? Zhège xuéqī xuǎnle shénme kè?

Chén Dàdōng: Shǔjià de shíhou wǒ míshangle Zhōngguó lìshǐ xiǎoshuō, suǒyǐ zhège xuéqī wǒ zhǔxiū Zhōngguó lìshǐ kè hé Zhōngguó wénxué kè, jiàoshòu yào wǒmen dú hěn duō lìshǐ shū hé Zhōngwén xiǎoshuō.

Lǐ Zhōngpíng: Wǒ juéde xuéxí zhīshi bújiànde zhǐ zài shūběn shang, tèbié shì xuéxí Zhōngguó wénhuà huò lìshǐ, zuì hǎo de bànfǎ jiù shì qù Zhōngguó zǒu yí tàng, xuéxí yí duàn shíjiān.

Wáng Xiǎoměi: Qù Zhōngguó xuéxí tīng qǐlai tǐng yǒuyìsi de! Nǐ xiǎng qù Zhōngguó nǎge dìfang ne?

Huáng Xiáng' ān: Zhōngpíng dāngrán xiǎng qù Běijīng! Zhèyang tā jiù kěyǐ qù kàn Mǎlì le, duì ba?

Lǐ Zhōngpíng: Wǒ zhǐshì xiǎng shùnbiàn qù kànkan Mǎlì… Wǒ chá le yíxià zěnme shēnqǐng liúxué, zhǐyào zhǔnbèi bìxū de zīliào jiù kěyǐ le, wǒmen hái néng shēnqǐng jiǎngxuéjīn.

English

Zhongping, how's your elective course on Chinese culture going?

It's very interesting. We use Chinese to have discussions and write reports. How about you? What classes did you select for this school term?

I became fascinated with Chinese historical novels this summer, so I'm taking Chinese history and Chinese literature this semester as my major electives. The professor wants us to read a lot of history books and Chinese novels.

I think learning and knowledge don't necessarily come only from books, especially when you're studying Chinese culture or history. The best way to learn is to take a trip to China and study there for a while.

Going to study in China sounds quite interesting! Where in China do you want to go?
Of course Zhongping wants to go to Beijing! This way, he can go see Mali, right?

I wouldn't mind seeing Mali in passing . . . I did a bit of research on how to apply to study abroad. As long as you prepare the necessary materials, you will be fine. We can also apply for scholarships.

Chén Dàdōng:	Méixiǎngdào zhème jiǎndān. Dào Zhōngguó liúxué néng gèng hǎo de liǎojiě hé xuéxí Zhōngguó lìshǐ, érqiě wǒ yìzhí dōu hěn xiǎng qù cānguān Gùgōng hé pá Chángchéng.	I never thought it'd be that simple. Going to study abroad in China can allow us to better understand and learn about Chinese history. Furthermore, I've always wanted to visit the Imperial Palace and climb the Great Wall.
Huáng Xiáng'ān:	Nà wǒ yě yào qù Zhōngguó liúxué, zhèyàng wǒ jiù néng chīdào dìdao de jiǎozi hé Běijīng kǎoyā la!	Then I also want to go study abroad in China! This way I can eat authentic dumplings and Peking duck.
Wáng Xiǎoměi:	Hāha, nǐ qù Zhōngguó shì wèile chī a? Búguò wǒ yě hěn xǐhuan chī Zhōngguó cài. Zhè zhēn shì ge hǎo zhǔyi. Rúguǒ nǐmen dōu qù Zhōngguó liúxué, nàme wǒ yě qù ba!	Haha, you just want to go to China for the food? But, I also really like Chinese food, so this is a good idea. If everyone is going to study abroad in China, then I will go too!
Lǐ Zhōngpíng:	Tài hǎo le! Nà wǒmen yǐhòu dōu néng biànchéng Zhōngguótōng le. Wǒ yào bǎ zhège hǎo xiāoxi gàosu Mǎlì.	Great! Then, afterwards we can all become experts of China. I will tell Mali the good news!

What Can You Do?

INTERPRETIVE
- I can state reasons to study abroad based on others' experiences.
- I can list activities to do while studying abroad.

INTERPERSONAL
- I can debate reasons for enrolling in a specific class.
- I can discuss objectives for studying abroad.

PRESENTATIONAL
- I can describe activities occurring in my classes.
- I can provide information on applying for a study abroad program.

加入社团
Joining a Student Club

新学期开始了，我很高兴能留在北京念书。今天下午我参加了大学社团的招募^{shè}^{zhāo mù}活动。这里的社团多得不得^{shè}了，有武术社、吉他社、文^{shè}^{shè}学社等等。^{shè}

当我正在烦恼不知道^{dāng}^{fán nǎo}要加入哪一个社团的时候，^{jiā rù}^{shè}碰见了周信。他给我介绍^{pèng jian}了杨冰冰，她是"绿色地^{yáng bīng bīng}^{dì}球社"的负责人。^{qiú shè}^{fù zé}

由于社团准备在北京发展一个环境保护项目，所以在招募大学生志愿者。我与冰冰一见如故！冰冰是巴西人，个子挺高的，超过一米七。她的性格很开朗，难怪周信说冰冰很受大家欢迎。

冰冰常常有机会在中国各地参加和举办很多的环保活动。我觉得她的工作很有意思！我决定加入这个社团，做一名志愿者，希望和大家一起努力。

LESSON TEXT 2.2

Joining a Student Club 加入社团

In her diary, Mali writes about attending the university's club day. While there, she runs into Zhou Xin and he introduces Mali to his friend, Yang Bingbing.

玛丽的日记：

　　新学期开始了，我很高兴能留在北京念书。今天下午我参加了大学社团的招募活动。这里的社团多得不得了，有武术社、吉他社、文学社等等。

———————

　　当我正在烦恼不知道要加入哪一个社团的时候，碰见了周信。他给我介绍了杨冰冰，她是"绿色地球社"的负责人。由于社团准备在北京发展一个环境保护项目，所以在招募大学生志愿者。我与冰冰一见如故！冰冰是巴西人，个子挺高的，超过一米七。她的性格很开朗，难怪周信说冰冰很受大家欢迎。

　　冰冰常常有机会在中国各地参加和举办很多的环保活动。我觉得她的工作很有意思！我决定加入这个社团，做一名志愿者，希望和大家一起努力。

Language Tip

碰见 (pèngjiàn)

In Mali's diary, Mali uses 碰见 to say that she ran into Zhou Xin at the university club recruitment event. 碰 literally means "to bump and touch." However, it can also mean "to meet or run into someone" or "to meet unexpectedly," as in 碰见.

Example:

今天我逛街的时候碰见了老师。
We ran into our teacher today when we were shopping.

字词 VOCABULARY

LESSON VOCABULARY 2.2

	SIMPLIFIED	TRADITIONAL	PINYIN	WORD CATEGORY	DEFINITION
1.	日记	日記	rìjì	*n*	diary
2.	社		shè	*n*	organization; agency
3.	招募		zhāomù	*v*	to recruit
4.	当	當	dāng	*cj*	when
5.	烦恼	煩惱	fánnǎo	*adj, n*	worried; worry, trouble
6.	加入		jiārù	*v*	to join; to add
	入		rù	*v*	to join; to enter
7.	碰见	碰見	pèngjiàn	*rv*	to meet unexpectedly, to run into
	碰		pèng	*v*	to bump into; to hit
8.	地球		dìqiú	*n*	earth
9.	负责	負責	fùzé	*v, adj*	to be in charge of; conscientious
10.	由于	由於	yóuyú	*cj*	because, due to
11.	发展	發展	fāzhǎn	*v, n*	to develop; development
12.	保护	保護	bǎohù	*n, v*	protection; to protect
13.	项目	項目	xiàngmù	*n*	project; item
14.	志愿者	志願者	zhìyuànzhě	*n*	volunteer
	志愿	志願	zhìyuàn	*v, n*	to volunteer; aspiration, wish
	者		zhě	*n*	person (who does something), one who (is) . . .
15.	与	與	yǔ	*cj*	and
16.	一见如故	一見如故	yíjiàn rúgù	*ie*	friends at first sight
17.	个子	個子	gèzi	*n*	height
18.	超过	超過	chāoguò	*rv*	to exceed
19.	米		mǐ	*n*	meter
20.	性格		xìnggé	*n*	character
21.	开朗	開朗	kāilǎng	*adj*	optimistic

LESSON VOCABULARY 2.2 (continued)

SIMPLIFIED	TRADITIONAL	PINYIN	WORD CATEGORY	DEFINITION
22. 受欢迎	受歡迎	shòu huānyíng	adj	be popular
受		shòu	v	to receive; to bear
23. 举办	舉辦	jǔbàn	v	to hold
24. 决定	決定	juédìng	v, n	to decide; decision
25. 名		míng	mw	(used for people or ranking)

PROPOER NOUNS

26. 巴西		Bāxī	n	Brazil
27. 杨冰冰	楊冰冰	Yáng Bīngbīng	n	Yang Bingbing

REQUIRED VOCABULARY 2.2

28. 成员	成員	chéngyuán	n	member
29. 爱好	愛好	àihào	n	hobby, interest
30. 邀请	邀請	yāoqǐng	v, n	invite; invitation

ONLINE RESOURCES

Visit *http://college.betterchinese.com* for a list of different positions within a club.

Idiomatic Expression

> yí jiàn rú gù
> 一见如故

一见如故 means "friends at first sight."

This expression appears in *Zuo Zhuan* (《左传》: *Zuǒ Zhuàn*). In the book, Fang Xuanling, a government counselor, and Li Shimin, an emperor of the Tang Dynasty (618 – 907 AD), become close friends upon their first meeting. It is often used to describe a situation where there is a meeting of kindred spirits and how fast friendships form.

Example:
她们的性格不同，但是一见如故，很快变成好朋友。
They have different personalities, but they felt like they were friends at first sight. They immediately became good friends.

Adjectives to Describe Appearance

The following terms are commonly used to describe appearance:

Chinese	Pinyin	Meaning
身高：	shēngāo	height
高	gāo	tall
矮	ǎi	short
头发长度：	tóufa chángdù	hair length
长	cháng	long
适中	shìzhōng	moderate
短	duǎn	short
体重：	tǐzhòng	weight
重	zhòng	heavy
正常	zhèngcháng	normal
轻	qīng	light, not heavy

Chinese	Pinyin	Meaning
身材：	shēncái	figure
瘦	shòu	thin, skinny
胖	pàng	fat
娇小	jiāoxiǎo	petite
匀称	yúnchèn	well-proportioned
魁梧	kuíwú	tall and sturdy
苗条	miáotiao	slender, slim
外表：	wàibiǎo	external appearance
美	měi	beautiful
漂亮	piàoliang	pretty, beautiful
帅	shuài	handsome

Adjectives to Describe Personality

The following terms are commonly used to describe personality:

Chinese	Pinyin	Meaning	Chinese	Pinyin	Meaning
活泼	huópo	lively	安静	ānjìng	quiet
热情	rèqíng	enthusiastic, warmhearted	害羞	hàixiū	shy
开朗	kāilǎng	optimistic, cheerful	悲观	bēiguān	pessimistic
乐天	lètiān	cheerful, happy-go-lucky, optimistic			
善良	shànliáng	kindhearted, kind	刻薄	kèbó	unkind
友善	yǒushàn	friendly			
勇敢	yǒnggǎn	brave	胆小	dǎnxiǎo	timid, cowardly
幽默	yōumò	humorous	严肃	yánsù	serious
有耐心	yǒu nàixīn	patient	急躁	jízào	impatient
勤劳	qínláo	hard-working, industrious, diligent	懒	lǎn	lazy
认真	rènzhēn	serious; conscientious; diligent	马虎	mǎhu	careless; casual; sloppy

ONLINE RESOURCES

Visit *http://college.betterchinese.com* for more vocabulary about appearance and personality.

STRUCTURE NOTE 2.5
Use 等等 *to indicate "and so on" at the end of a list*

等, *meaning "to wait," can be reduplicated as* 等等 *to express "and so on" or "et cetera" at the end of a list. Unlike the English expressions,* 等等 *is generally not preceded by a comma.*

> Item A ＋ 、 ＋ Item B … ＋ 等等

From the Lesson Text:

这里的社团多得不得了，有武术社、吉他社、文学社等等。

Zhèlǐ de shètuán duō de bùdéliǎo, yǒu wǔshù shè, jítā shè, wénxué shè děngděng.

There is an amazing number of clubs here; there's a Martial Arts Club, Guitar Club, Literature Club, etc.

Other examples:

商店的衬衫有很多颜色：红色、黄色、绿色等等。

Shāngdiàn de chènshān yǒu hěnduō yánsè: hóngsè, huángsè, lǜsè děngděng.

The shirts in the store come in many colors: red, yellow, green, etc.

他会打乒乓球、羽毛球、网球等等。

Tā huì dǎ pīngpāngqiú, yǔmáoqiú, wǎngqiú děngděng.

He can play ping pong, badminton, tennis, etc.

Practice: Express the following sentences in Chinese by applying 等等 and using the information provided below.

Example:　This hat comes in many colors: black, red, white, blue, etc.

　→ 这个帽子有很多颜色：黑色、红色、白色、蓝色等等。

1.　I received many gifts at my birthday party, such as a book, a hat, a movie ticket, etc.

　　_____

2.　He has been to China, Russia, America, Canada, Britain, etc.

　　_____

3.　His family has many pets: dogs, cats, fish, etc.

　　_____

4.　The university has many clubs: Kung Fu Club, Guitar Club, Literature Club, etc.

　　_____

5.　This semester I am taking history, mathematics, literature, etc.

　　_____

STRUCTURE NOTE 2.6
Use 当……的时候 *to formally indicate when something happened*

Previously, the pattern (在) + *Phrase* + 的时候 *has been used to indicate that an event took place at a particular time. A more formal way of indicating a time is to use the pattern* 当 (dāng) + *Phrase* (+ 的时候). *In more formal situations,* 的时候 *can be replaced with* 时. *In this pattern,* 当 *serves as a preposition similar to* 在.

当 + Phrase (+ 的时候 / 时) , + Sentence

From the Lesson Text:
当我正在烦恼要参加哪一个社团的时候，碰见了周信。
Dāng wǒ zhèngzài fánnǎo yào cānjiā nǎ yí ge shètuán de shíhou, pèngjiànle Zhōuxìn.
Just as I was puzzling over which club to join, I ran into Zhou Xin.

Other examples:
当他从外国回来的时候，女朋友已经找了别人。
Dāng tā cóng wàiguó huílai de shíhou, nǚpéngyou yǐjīng zhǎole biérén.
When he returned from abroad, his girlfriend had already found someone else.

当我正要出去时，外面就开始下雨了。
Dāng wǒ zhèngyào chūqu shí, wàimian jiù kāishǐ xiàyǔ le.
As I was about to go out, it started to rain outside.

Practice: Create complete sentences using 当……的时候 and the information provided.

Example: 做功课，弹钢琴
→ 当我正在做功课的时候，听到有人弹钢琴。

1.   跳舞，拍照片
_____

2.   打网球，弹吉他
_____

3.   约会，下雪
_____

4.   散步，放烟火
_____

5.   看电影，朋友给我打电话
_____

STRUCTURE NOTE 2.7
Use 由于 *to indicate a reason or cause*

由于 *(yóuyú) meaning "due to (the fact that)," is a more formal way of saying* 因为, *"because." In contrast to* 因为, 由于 *is most often used when identifying the cause that led to a particular result.* 由于 *generally starts the sentence, but it can also follow the subject. The outcome clause can optionally be introduced with* 所以, *"therefore," or other similar expressions.*

> 由于 + Reason, (+ 所以) + Outcome

> Subject + 由于 + Verb Phrase, (+ 所以) + Outcome

From the Lesson Text:

由于社团准备在北京发展一个环境保护项目，所以她在招募大学生志愿者。

Yóuyú shètuán zhǔnbèi zài Běijīng fāzhǎn yí ge huánjìng bǎohù xiàngmù, suǒyǐ tā zài zhāomù dàxuéshēng zhìyuànzhě.

The club is preparing to develop an environmental protection project in Beijing, so she is recruiting university student volunteers.

Other Examples:

由于我没时间学习，这次考得不好。

Yóuyú wǒ méi shíjiān xuéxí, zhè cì kǎo de bù hǎo.

Because I didn't have time to study, I did poorly on the test this time.

他由于生病了，不能来学校。

Tā yóuyú shēngbìngle, bùnéng lái xuéxiào.

Due to illness, he can't come to school.

Practice: Match the following sentences on the basis of the information given.

1. 由于他想参加运动会，　　　　　　所以周末要在家复习功课。
2. 由于她家有四个孩子，　　　　　　所以每天早上都跑步。
3. 由于爸爸工作很忙，　　　　　　　所以晚上去咖啡店打工。
4. 由于我们要准备考试，　　　　　　所以每天很晚才回家。
5. 由于我想买新的电脑，　　　　　　所以她和姐姐共用一个房间。

STRUCTURE NOTE 2.8
Use 与 to join two nouns in formal writing

There are many different ways to express "and," depending on the types of things being connected and the level of formality. In formal writing, 和 is often replaced by 与 (yǔ). Like 和, 与 is most often used to join two nouns (people, objects, ideas, etc.) rather than adjectives, verbs, or full clauses.

Noun Phrase + 与 + Noun Phrase

From the Lesson Text:

我与冰冰一见如故！
Wǒ yǔ Bīngbīng yíjiàn rúgù!
I hit it off with Bingbing right away!

Other Examples:

春节与中秋节是中国重要的传统节日。
Chūnjié yǔ Zhōngqiūjié shì Zhōngguó zhòngyào de chuántǒng jiérì.
The Spring Festival and the Mid-Autumn Festival are important traditional festivals in China.

北京的春季与秋季是我最喜欢的季节。
Běijīng de chūnjì yǔ qiūjì shì wǒ zuì xǐhuan de jìjié.
The spring and summer in Beijing are my favorite seasons.

Practice: Reorganize the words and create a sentence with 与.

Example:
武术 / 书法 / 中国传统文化
→ 武术与书法是中国传统文化。

1. 他 / 学习 / 打算 / 中国文化 / 中国历史

   _____

2. 晚辈 / 尊敬 / 老人 / 照顾 / 要

   _____

3. 端午节 / 吃粽子 / 划龙舟 / 重要活动

   _____

4. 巴黎 / 伦敦 / 欧洲 / 古老而美丽的城市

   _____

5. 很重视 / 中国人 / 孔子的思想 / 礼节

   _____

练习 2.10: 课文理解

Paired Activity: Discuss the following questions based on the Lesson Text. Be prepared to share your thoughts with the class.

> 1. 冰冰是一个什么样的人？
>
> 2. 冰冰在"绿色地球社"负责的工作是什么？
>
> 3. 你参加过社团吗？社团有什么样的活动？如果没有，你会对怎么样的社团有兴趣？

练习 2.11: 你想参加哪个社团？

Paired Activity: You and your partner are at a university club fair. Think about your current schedule and interests, and discuss what club(s) you would like to join.

社团活动资料

社团	人数	活动时间	活动简介
现代艺术社	25人	周一 下午 7:00-9:30	欣赏中国与欧洲的现代艺术作品
茶学社	20人	周二、四 下午 6:00-7:00	认识东方与西方的茶文化 学习各种泡茶的方法
文学社	30人	周三、五 下午 5:30-6:30	学习写作方法 欣赏文学作品
学生书画社	35人	周六 上午 9:00-12:00	学习书画知识 参加书画作品展
汉语社	50人	周六 下午 3:30-5:30	学习汉语与中国文化 欣赏中国电影、音乐

Notes:

人数 (rénshù): *n.* number of people
简介 (jiǎnjiè): *n.* brief introduction
欣赏 (xīnshǎng): *v.* to appreciate

写作 (xiězuò): *v.* to write
作品展 (zuòpǐn zhǎn): *n.* exhibition
艺术 (yìshù): *n.* art

ONLINE RESOURCES

Visit *http://college.betterchinese.com* for additional names of different types of clubs.

练习 2.12 (上)：参加社团调查

Individual Activity: The student council (学生会: xuéshēnghuì) asks you to collect opinions regarding a Chinese club on campus. Create a short survey (调查: diàochá), then ask three other classmates for their answers.

Questions	Answers
Example: 你对与中国文化有关的社团有兴趣吗？	

练习 2.13 (中)：比较不同大学的社团

Group Activity: Taking into account the survey answers in Practice Exercise 2.12 above, work together to create a club related to the Chinese language or culture that is not yet available at your school. Describe the club's focus and what kinds of events will be held.

练习 2.14 (下)：社团活动海报

Group Activity: Using the poster below as an example, create a poster (海报: hǎibào) for an upcoming event that the Chinese club will hold.

Example:

现代艺术社

你想欣赏中国画吗？你想参观中国各地的艺术吗？二月一日来参加现代艺术社举办的山水画活动吧！

活动时间：二月一日 下午2:00–5:00
活动地点：艺术大楼

社团名字：

活动简介：

活动时间：

活动地点：

Notes:
地点 (dìdiǎn): *n.* location

	Radical	Stroke Order
社	礻(示) shì show	丶 ㇀ 礻 礻 礻 社 社
欢	又 yòu again	乛 又 ㇇ 欢 欢 欢
招	扌(手) shǒu hand	一 扌 扌 扣 扣 招 招 招
入	入 rù enter	丿 入
负	刀 dāo knife	丿 ㇈ 夕 负 负 负
责	贝 bèi shell	一 二 丰 主 青 青 责 责
由	㇑ shù line	丨 冂 日 由 由
于	一 yī one	一 二 于
护	扌(手) shǒu hand	一 扌 扌 扩 护 护
目	目 mù eye	丨 冂 月 月 目
与	一 yī one	一 与 与
性	忄(心) xīn heart	丶 忄 忄 忄 忄 忄 性 性
格	木 mù wood	一 十 才 木 术 权 柊 格 格 格
举	丶 diǎn dot	丶 丷 丷 丷 兴 兴 兴 举
杨	木 mù wood	一 十 才 木 杓 杨 杨

Online chat: Working with a classmate, discuss a school event/activity you recently attended. Describe someone you met at the event and what you had in common.

练习 2.17: 阅读理解

　　大学社团招募活动以后，玛丽交了一个新朋友，她叫杨冰冰，是"绿色地球社"的负责人。为了让大家都了解和参加环境保护，冰冰常常在中国各地举办活动。冰冰不但漂亮而且性格非常开朗。玛丽觉得冰冰的性格和自己的很像，她和冰冰一见如故。玛丽很高兴能认识一个这么棒的朋友。

Read the passage and answer the following questions.
1. What additional details are provided about Bingbing in this passage?
2. Provide three reasons why Mali likes her new friend.
3. Describe a new friend you met recently and talk about why you like this person.

练习 2.18: 阅读理解

武术社团招募

　　新的校园生活马上就要开始了，你想学习中国武术吗？想有更健康的身体吗？想认识更多的朋友吗？快加入我们的社团吧！
　　有兴趣的同学请在9月5日到10日去活动中心报名。武术社欢迎你！

武术社
9月3日

Notes:
报名 (bàomíng): *vo.* to sign up

Read the notice and answer the following questions.
1. What are the benefits of joining the Wushu club?
2. Where, when, and how do you sign up for the club?
3. Describe a club or organization you have joined. How did you hear about and join the club or organization?

Chinese vs. Western Views on Education and Success

There is a strong tradition of valuing education in Chinese culture. This comes largely from Confucian ideals that pervade the Chinese educational system.

Confucius believed that everyone could be educated, even perfected. Consequently, Chinese people tend to de-emphasize innate ability, stressing that effort and work ethic can make up for any inborn disadvantage. Struggle is traditionally seen as an important part of success in education and in life. Chinese students who work extremely hard often do so because they believe it will ensure them success. This view on the importance of hard work is different from the Western educational system, which generally encourages people to find their talents and natural abilities.

For many Chinese families, their children's educational success is also the way towards financial stability. This belief dates back to the imperial era, when scholars of all classes would take the grueling imperial exam to become administrative officials. This merit-based system would enable a poor but clever scholar to succeed and thus raise his family out of poverty.

Even today, a similar attitude towards education prevails. Rich or poor, many Chinese families focus their resources on helping their child succeed educationally from a very young age. Financial security begins with the all-important university entrance exam. Students, who pass the exam and enter a prestigious university, hope their education will lead to a high-paying job, thereby ensuring their family's financial stability.

Sun Yat-sen Abroad

The father of the Chinese Republic, Dr. Sun Yat-sen, (孙中山: Sūn Zhōngshān), was a famous revolutionary who played a critical role in Chinese politics during the late 19th and early 20th century. He spent much of his life abroad, beginning at the age of 12, when he moved to Hawaii to attend boarding school and learn English. Sun also studied medicine in Hong Kong (then a British colony), where he became increasingly frustrated with the Qing Dynasty (1644 - 1912 AD) government.

Sun's experience overseas helped him form his strategy for bringing about change in China. In Hong Kong, he quit his medical practice and became a revolutionary, dedicated to overthrowing the Qing Dynasty and modernizing China. Sun would spend much of his life in exile for his political activities, but even abroad, he was able to connect with local Chinese students and leaders in other countries. He also spent an enormous amount of time and effort attracting foreign support and aid for political revolution and economic development.

Although he was not in China at the time, Sun would come to play an important part in the 1911 Revolution that led to the demise of the Qing Dynasty, ending two thousand years of imperial rule. After the emperor abdicated, Sun was elected the first provisional president of the new republic upon his return to China in December 1911. Before his death in 1925, Sun worked to keep the new country unified in the face of political chaos. Sun is credited as a driving force in the birth of modern China.

Pinyin

Xīn xuéqī kāishǐ le, wǒ hěn gāoxìng néng liú zài Běijīng niànshū. Jīntiān xiàwǔ wǒ cānjiāle dàxué shètuán de zhāomù huódòng. Zhèlǐ de shètuán duō de bùdeliǎo, yǒu wǔshù shè, jítā shè, wénxué shè děngděng.

Dāng wǒ zhèngzài fánnǎo bù zhīdào yào jiārù nǎ yí ge shètuán de shíhou, pèngjiànle Zhōu Xìn. Tā gěi wǒ jièshàole Yáng Bīngbīng, tā shì "Lǜsè Dìqiú Shè" de fùzérén. Yóuyú shètuán zhǔnbèi zài Běijīng fāzhǎn yí ge huánjìng bǎohù xiàngmù, suǒyǐ zài zhāomù dàxuéshēng zhìyuànzhě. Wǒ yǔ Bīngbīng yíjiàn rúgù! Bīngbīng shì Bāxī rén, gèzi tǐng gāo de, chāoguò yì mǐ qī. Tā de xìnggé hěn kāilǎng, nánguài Zhōu Xìn shuō Bīngbīng hěn shòu dàjiā huānyíng.

Bīngbīng chángcháng yǒu jīhuì zài Zhōngguó gèdì cānjiā hé jǔbàn hěn duō de huánbǎo huódòng. Wǒ jué de tā de gōngzuò hěn yǒuyìsi! Wǒ juédìng jiārù zhège shètuán, zuò yì míng zhìyuànzhě, hé dàjiā yìqǐ nǔlì.

English

The new school term has begun. I am so happy to be able to stay in Beijing for my studies. This afternoon, I attended the University's club recruitment event. There is an amazing number of clubs here; there's a Martial Arts Club, Guitar Club, Literature Club, etc.

Just as I was having trouble not knowing which club to join, I bumped into Zhou Xin. He introduced me to Yang Bingbing, who is the representative for the "Green Earth Club." The club is preparing to develop an environmental protection project in Beijing, so it is recruiting university student volunteers. I felt like Bingbing and I were friends at first sight! Bingbing is Brazilian and quite tall — over 1.7 meters. She has a very open personality. It's no wonder why Zhou Xin says everyone likes Bingbing.

Bingbing often has the opportunity to attend and organize a lot of environmental protection events across China. I think she has such an interesting job! I have decided to join this club and become a volunteer, and work hard with everyone.

What Can You Do?

INTERPRETIVE
- I can name extracurricular activities at school after reading a poster.
- I can identify different aspects of someone's personality after meeting someone.

INTERPERSONAL
- I can exchange information about a person's appearance.
- I can discuss goals related to extracurricular activities.

PRESENTATIONAL
- I can explain what extracurricular activities are available at school.
- I can describe the experience of meeting someone.

ACT IT OUT

Working in groups, compose an original two-minute skit that utilizes the vocabulary and structures introduced in Unit 2. Each of you should assume a role and have a roughly equal number of lines in the skit. Be prepared to perform your skit in class. You can either come up with your own story or choose from one of the following situations:

A) You and your classmates are thinking about studying abroad. Discuss where you would want to go and why.

B) You are applying for a scholarship to study abroad and your professor is writing a recommendation letter. Discuss with your professor why you want to go and your qualifications.

C) You are recruiting members for your school club. Persuade the potential new recruits on why they should join.

CHECK WHAT YOU CAN DO

RECOGNIZE

Adjectives
- 必需
- 地道
- 开朗
- 受欢迎
- 烦恼

Adverbs
- 不见得
- 挺
- 顺便

Conjunctions
- 不过
- 当
- 由于
- 与

Idiomatic Expression
- 一见如故

Measure Words
- 趟
- 段
- 名

Name
- 杨冰冰

Nouns
- 小说
- 知识
- 书本
- 办法
- 资料

- 奖学金
- 主意
- 中国通
- 消息
- 学分
- 成绩
- 日记
- 社
- 地球
- 项目
- 志愿者
- 个子
- 米
- 性格
- 成员

- 爱好
- 巴西
- 报告
- 保护

Preposition
- 为了

Resultative Complements
- 变成
- 碰见
- 超过

Verbs
- 选修
- 主修
- 查

- 申请
- 留学
- 辅修
- 招募
- 加入
- 举办
- 负责
- 讨论
- 发展
- 决定
- 邀请

Verb-Object Compound
- 填表格

WRITE
- 讨
- 论
- 报
- 主
- 修
- 趟
- 段
- 挺
- 查
- 资
- 料
- 申
- 奖
- 通

- 社
- 欢
- 招
- 入
- 负
- 责
- 由
- 于
- 护
- 目
- 与
- 性
- 格
- 举
- 杨

USE

- Use 只要A就B(了) to indicate A is the only condition necessary for B to occur.
- Use 为了…(就)… to explain the purpose of doing something.
- Use 不过 to say "but" to indicate a contrast to the previous statement.
- Use 变得/变成 to describe transformation in state or from one thing to another.
- Use 等等 to indicate "and so on" at the end of a list.
- Use 当……的时候 to formally indicate when something happened.
- Use 由于 to indicate a reason or cause.
- Use 与 to join two nouns in formal writing.

住

Housing

Communication Goals

Lesson 1: 住校与租房 **Living On-Campus vs. Off-Campus**
- Talk about elements of living in rental housing.
- Talk about living with a roommate.
- Describe a roommate's habits.
- Discuss common housekeeping chores.

Lesson 2: 找公寓 **Apartment Hunting**
- Describe steps involved in locating housing, including looking for housing and contract signing.
- Recognize common criteria for selecting housing.
- Express satisfaction and contentment in a situation.

大东，想不到你们的宿舍这么乱！你看床上都是衣服，桌上还有吃剩的东西。

这些都是祥安的，他常常乱放东西。

那你为什么还要跟他住？

因为他很好相处，又会照顾人。上次安娜生病就是祥安带她去看了医生。再说，住宿舍也有很多好处。

住宿舍的好处确实挺多，但是一点隐私都没有，房租还很贵。

校内外的房租都不便宜，我平时
也很忙，会忘了付水电费（shuǐ diàn fèi）。住在
宿舍费用全包（fèi yong bāo），省心又省力（shěng xīn shěng lì）。

不过我已经习惯和祥
安一起住了。你去中
国留学的时候想找什
么样的室友合租（hé zū）呢？

你只要找一个
细心（xì xīn）的室友就
不用担心啦！

到了北京以后，我想租一套（zū tào）三室一厅的公寓。
我的室友一定要细心（xì xīn）、爱干净、会做饭和做
家务（jiā wù）。这样的室友很"理想"（lǐ xiǎng）吧？

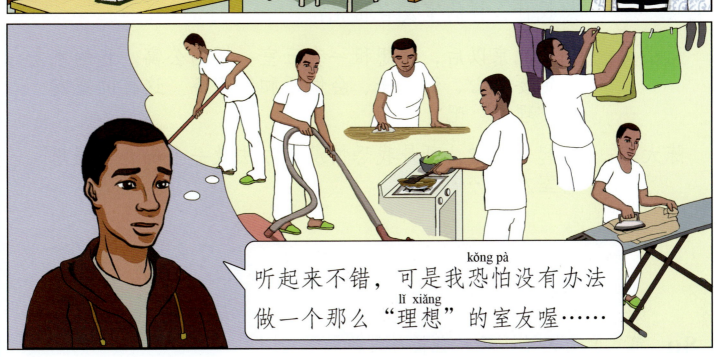

听起来不错，可是我恐怕（kǒng pà）没有办法
做一个那么"理想"（lǐ xiǎng）的室友喔……

LESSON TEXT 3.1

Living On-Campus vs. Off-Campus 住校与租房

Xiaomei visits Dadong and Xiang'an's dorm room. Xiaomei and Dadong talk about roommates as well as the pros and cons of living on-campus and off-campus.

王小美： 大东，想不到你们的宿舍这么乱！你看床上都是衣服，桌上还有吃剩的东西。

陈大东： 这些都是祥安的，他常常乱放东西。

王小美： 那你为什么还要跟他住？

陈大东： 因为他很好相处，又会照顾人。上次安娜生病就是祥安带她去看了医生。再说，住宿舍也有很多好处。

王小美： 住宿舍的好处确实挺多，但是一点隐私都没有，房租还很贵。

陈大东： 校内外的房租都不便宜，我平时也很忙，会忘了付水电费。住在宿舍费用全包，省心又省力。

王小美： 你只要找一个细心的室友就不用担心啦！

陈大东： 不过我已经习惯和祥安一起住了。你去中国留学的时候想找什么样的室友合租呢？

王小美： 到了北京以后，我想租一套三室一厅的公寓。我的室友一定要细心、爱干净、会做饭和做家务。这样的室友很"理想"吧？

陈大东： 听起来不错，可是我恐怕没有办法做一个那么"理想"的室友喔……

Language Tip

| 想不到 (xiǎngbudào) |
| 没想到 (méixiǎngdào) |

In the Lesson Text, Xiaomei uses 想不到 to indicate that she is surprised about how messy Dadong and Xiang'an's dorm was. 想不到 literally means "couldn't think of." Xiaomei can also use 没想到 to express "I never would have thought." Although the two expressions are mostly equivalent, 想不到 is more likely to be used when an event is more surprising, as in "I couldn't have imagined."

Examples:

想不到教授也有不懂的地方。
Who would have thought that there were also things the professor didn't understand.

我没想到他会买这件毛衣。
I never would have thought he would buy that sweater.

字 词 VOCABULARY

LESSON VOCABULARY 3.1

	SIMPLIFIED	TRADITIONAL	PINYIN	WORD CATEGORY	DEFINITION
1.	乱	亂	luàn	adj	disorderly, messy
2.	剩		shèng	v, adj	to be left; surplus
3.	相处	相處	xiāngchǔ	v	to get along with
4.	再说	再說	zàishuō	cj	what's more, besides
5.	好处	好處	hǎochu	n	advantage, benefit
6.	确实	確實	quèshí	adv	really, definitely, indeed
7.	隐私	隱私	yǐnsī	n	privacy
8.	房租		fángzū	n	rent
9.	内外		nèiwài	n	inside and outside
10.	平时	平時	píngshí	adv	ordinarily, in ordinary or normal times
11.	水电费	水電費	shuǐdiànfèi	n	water and electricity bills
	电	電	diàn	n	electricity
	费	費	fèi	n	bill, cost, fee
12.	费用	費用	fèiyong	n	cost, expenses, charges
13.	包		bāo	v	to include, to contain
14.	省心省力		shěngxīn shěnglì	vo	to avoid worry and save effort
	省		shěng	v	to save
	力		lì	n	strength, power
15.	细心	細心	xìxīn	adj	considerate, careful, attentive
16.	合租		hézū	v	to rent together
	租		zū	v	to rent
17.	套		tào	mw	(used to indicate a series or sets of things)
18.	家务	家務	jiāwù	n	household chores, household duties
19.	理想		lǐxiǎng	adj, n	ideal
20.	恐怕		kǒngpà	v	to be afraid, to fear

Simplified	Traditional	Pinyin	Word Category	Definition
21. 坏处	壞處	huàichu	*n*	disadvantage
22. 粗心		cūxīn	*adj*	careless
23. 签合同	簽合同	qiān hétong	*vo*	to sign a contract
签	簽	qiān	*v*	to sign
合同		hétong	*n*	contract
24. 地点	地點	dìdiǎn	*n*	place, site, locale
25. 交通		jiāotōng	*n*	traffic

Idiomatic Expression

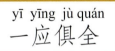

yī yīng jù quán
一应俱全

一应 means "everything" and 俱 means "all" or "complete." 一应俱全 means "everything needed is provided."

This expression appears in the novel *The Gallant Maid* (《儿女英雄传》: *Érnǚ Yīngxióng Zhuàn*), which was written during the Qing Dynasty (1644 – 1912 AD). In the book, Wen Kang used this phrase to express that all of the cooking ingredients needed were available on a table. This expression mostly refers to physical materials and not people.

Example:
这个商店里什么都有，真是一应俱全！
One can find all one needs at this store; it really does have everything!

Alternative Ways of Addressing People in Chinese

In China, there are many different ways to address people. For example, people use the surname or the whole name with Mister (先生: xiānsheng) or Miss (女士: nǚshì), particularly in business and more formal situations (e.g., 陈先生, 孙玛丽女士). Compared with this formal manner of addressing others, there are even more ways to address people on a personal level for both adults and children — all of which are dependent on relationships between people.

The following are ways that people may address each other:

1. Similar to English, it is common for people to address others they know well by using only the given name when it consists of two characters. For example, in the Lesson Text, Mali writes "冰冰" instead of "杨冰冰" in her diary.

2. People frequently address others by duplicating the last character of a given name, whether there are one or two characters. For example, Mali's nickname could be 丽丽. This method of creating a nickname is usually for kids — girls and boys — or young women to reflect a close relationship.

3. Depending on their relationship, people may also address others by adding 阿 (A: Ā), 大, and 小 before a surname or the last character of a given name. Adding 阿 is common in Southern China and considered a term of endearment. For example, 黄祥安 could become 阿黄, 大安, or 小安.

4. Close friends may give each other nicknames unrelated with a person's name. For instance, it is common to create nicknames if people share personality trait with animals. Although an insult in English, you might call someone 阿牛 (Ā Niú: Cow) as cows are known for their strength and patience.

5. It is now a common trend to give oneself an English name, especially when living in an English-speaking environment. The name can sound similar to a person's Chinese name, or it can simply be a name a person likes.

People and Occupations

In *Modern Chinese* Textbook Vol. 1B, Unit 13, Lesson 2, Language Note, occupations were introduced. To create words that describe kinds of people and occupations, specific characters are added on at the end of a word.

家 Used after a noun to indicate a person who is a specialist in a certain field		
科学家	kēxuéjiā	scientist
艺术家	yìshùjiā	artist
舞蹈家	wǔdǎojiā	dancer
作家	zuòjiā	writer
画家	huàjiā	painter
师 Used for a person in a certain profession or trade		
老师	lǎoshī	teacher
魔术师	móshùshī	magician
厨师	chúshī	chef
工程师	gōngchéngshī	engineer
会计师	kuàijìshī	accountant
员 Used for staff member or worker		
演员	yǎnyuán	actor or actress
职员	zhíyuán	staff member, clerk
售货员	shòuhuòyuán	salesclerk
公务员	gōngwùyuán	civil servant

ONLINE RESOURCES
Visit *http://college.betterchinese.com* for more examples of words describing people and occupations.

Structure Note 3.1
Use 再说 *to bring up additional points*

The phrase 再说 *(zàishuō) literally means "to continue speaking." It appears with this meaning in the expression,* 不要再说了 *"don't discuss this further."* 再说 *also functions as a connecting phrase, meaning "moreover"* *or "furthermore." It is used like these English expressions to bring up additional supporting or related points.*

再说，+ Sentence

From the Lesson Text:

再说，住宿舍也有很多好处。
Zài shuō, zhù sùshè yě yǒu hěnduō hǎochu.
Furthermore, living in a dorm has many advantages.

Other Examples:

住校外不见得能省钱，再说也不一定会安全。
Zhù xiàowài bújiàndé néng shěngqián, zàishuō yě bù yídìng huì ānquán.
You won't necessarily save money by living off campus. Furthermore, your safety isn't guaranteed.

现在太晚了，别去他家了，再说他也不一定在家。
Xiànzài tài wǎn le, bié qù tā jiā le, zàishuō tā yě bù yídìng zài jiā.
It's too late now. Don't go to his house. Besides, he may not even be at home.

Practice: Complete each sentence using 再说 to bring up additional supporting or related points.

Example: 你已经选了四门课，不要再选文学课了……
→ 你已经选了四门课，不要再选文学课了，再说你对文学也没有兴趣。

1. 这套公寓太小了，房租还挺贵……
   _____

2. 去中国留学我可以多了解中国文化……
   _____

3. 和我一起去看电影吧，这部电影很有意思……
   _____

Structure Note 3.2
Use 确实 to say "indeed" or "really"

确实 (quèshí) *is used to emphasize that the speaker is confident that a particular assessment of a situation is correct. Like "indeed" and "really" in English,* 确实 *can either be used before the verb or adjective phrase.*

> Subject + 确实 + Verb/Adjective Phrase

From the Lesson Text:

住宿舍的好处确实挺多，但是一点隐私都没有，房租还很贵。

Zhù sùshè de hǎochù quèshí tǐng duō, dànshì yìdiǎn yǐnsī dōu méiyǒu, fángzū hái hěn guì.

There definitely are a lot of advantages to living in a dorm, but there's no privacy at all and the rent is also very expensive.

Other Examples:

他确实很喜欢中国书法。

Tā quèshí hěn xǐhuan Zhōngguó shūfǎ.

He really likes Chinese calligraphy.

天气预报没说错，今天确实很冷。

Tiānqì yùbào méi shuō cuò, jīntiān quèshí hěn lěng.

The weather report was correct, today is indeed very cold.

Practice: Rewrite the sentences using 确实.

Example: 汉字很难写。→汉字确实很难写。

1. 她是一个很好相处的人。

   _____

2. 祥安的宿舍很乱。

   _____

3. 这个地方的环境很好。

   _____

4. 大东对中国的历史很了解。

   _____

5. 云南的气候很舒服。

   _____

Structure Note 3.3
Use 一点(儿)都没/不 *to emphasize "not at all"*

The phrase 一点(儿)都没/不 *is placed before an adjective or verb phrase to emphasize that something is not the case, not even a little bit. This pattern is like the expression, "not at all," with the relevant object placed between* 一点(儿) *and* 都. *As in other expressions using* 一点, 一点儿 *is an optional colloquial variant used in Northern China.*

Subject + 一点(儿) + 都 + 没/不 + Adjective / Verb Phrase

Subject + 一点(儿) + Noun Phrase + 都 + 没/不 + Adjective / Verb Phrase

---

From the Lesson Text:

但是一点隐私都没有。
Dànshì yìdiǎn yǐnsī dōu méiyǒu.
But there's no privacy at all.

Other Examples:

他生病了，一点儿饭都没吃。
Ta shēngbìngle, yìdiǎnr fàn dōu méi chī.
He got sick and didn't eat anything.

你已经不是小孩子了，怎么一点都不会照顾自已呢？
Nǐ yǐjīng bú shì xiǎoháizi le, zěnme yìdiǎn dōu búhuì zhàogù zìjǐ ne?
You are not a child anymore. How can you not know how to take care of yourself at all?

Practice: Create complete sentences using 一点(儿)都没有/不 or 一点(儿)……都没有/不 and the words provided.

Example: 厨房里/食物→厨房里一点食物都没有。

1. 钱包里/钱

   _____

2. 他/愿意学大提琴

   _____

3. 这些衣服/便宜

   _____

4. 他/喜欢坐火车

   _____

5. 她/空

   _____

Structure Note 3.4
Use 恐怕 *to express doubt over an unfortunate situation*

恐怕 *(kǒngpà) means "to be afraid." It is used to predict an unfortunate situation and express regret, much like "I'm afraid" in English* 恐怕 *most often appears without a subject implying that it is the speaker who is regretting something.*

恐怕 + Sentence

Subject + 恐怕 + Verb Phrase

From the Lesson Text:

听起来不错，可是我恐怕没有办法做那么 "理想" 的室友喔……

Tīng qǐlai búcuò, kěshì wǒ kǒngpà méiyǒu bànfǎ zuò nàme "lǐxiǎng" de shìyǒu o ……

It sounds good, but I'm afraid I would not be able to be such an "ideal" roommate . . .

Other Examples:

我还没有做完今天的作业，恐怕不能跟你一起打球了。

Wǒ hái méiyǒu zuòwán jīntiān de zuòyè, kǒngpà bù néng gēn nǐ yìqǐ dǎqiú le.

I haven't finished today's homework yet; I'm afraid I won't be able to play ball with you as planned.

我恐怕不能跟你出国旅游了，这个暑假我要去公司实习。

Wǒ kǒngpà bù néng gēn nǐ chūguó lǚyóu le, zhè ge shǔjià wǒ yào qù gōngsī shíxí.

I'm afraid I won't be able to travel abroad with you as planned. I have an internship with a company this summer.

Practice: Complete the following sentences using 恐怕 and the words provided.

Example:　小美生病了，(上课) ……
　　　　　→小美生病了，恐怕不能去上课了。

1.　他太忙了，（参加比赛）……

_____

2.　我的中文不好，（帮忙）……

_____

3.　大东要上班，（去旅游）……

_____

4.　我周末要和朋友去公园，（看电影）……

_____

练习 3.1: 课文理解

Paired Activity: Discuss the following questions based on the Lesson Text. Be prepared to share your thoughts with the class.

1. 为什么大东的宿舍会这么乱？

2. 小美为什么不喜欢住宿舍？

3. 小美的理想室友是怎么样的？你的呢？

练习 3.2: 你负责做什么家务？

Individual Activity: Dadong and Xiang'an decide its time to split up household chores. Fill out the calendar with at least three chores that each person would do during a single month.

——月						
星期日	星期一	星期二	星期三	星期四	星期五	星期六
23 Example: 做饭 （大东）						

✏️ 练习 **3.3** (上): 住校内还是校外？

Individual Activity: Consider your own housing and roommate preferences and complete the sentences below.

> 1. 你想住校内还是校外？
> 2. 你希望公寓/宿舍会包什么？
> 3. 你希望室友是什么样的人？

💬 练习 **3.4** (中): 住校内外的优缺点

Paired Activity: Working with a classmate, discuss the advantages (优点: yōudiǎn) and disadvantages (缺点: quēdiǎn) of the two housing options and fill out the chart below.

住校内	住校外
Example: 去校园比较方便	去餐厅比较方便

💬 练习 **3.5** (下): 理想的房子

Group Activity: You and your classmates are planning to rent a place together. Working with your group, determine your ideal housing situation and have each person pick one room to describe.

练习 3.6

	Radical	Stroke Order
乱	舌 shé tongue	⼁ 二 千 千 舌 舌 乱
剩	刂(刀) dāo knife	一 厂 厅 乐 成 成 成 成 盛 盛 盛
处	夂 zhǐ walk slowly	丿 夕 夂 处 处
确	石 shí stone	一 丆 不 石 石 石 矿 矿 矿 确 确 确
私	广 yǎn shelter	一 二 千 千 禾 私 私
租	禾 hè grain	一 二 千 千 禾 利 和 和 和 租
内	冂 jiōng wide	⼁ 冂 内 内
省	目 mù eye	⼁ ⼩ ⼩ 少 少 省 省 省 省
细	纟(糸) sī silk	⼄ 纟 纟 纟 纺 纺 细 细
粗	米 mǐ rice	丶 丷 丷 半 半 米 籼 籼 粗 粗
隐	阝 fù hill	阝 阝 阝 阝 阷 阷 隐 隐 隐 隐
套	大 dà big	一 广 大 大 本 本 本 套 套 套
签	竹(竹) zhú bamboo	丿 竹 竹 竹 竹 竹 竹 笒 笒 笒 笒 笒 签
理	玉 yù jade	一 二 千 王 玉 玑 玑 玑 理 理
恐	心 xīn heart	一 工 工 玑 巩 巩 巩 恐 恐 恐

Online chat: Working with a classmate, discuss whether you would rather live alone or with a roommate. Provide reasons to support your preferences.

练习 3.8: 阅读理解

> 　　大东和祥安有很多不同的地方：大东喜欢看书和做运动；祥安喜欢美食和音乐。大东比较细心，也爱干净；祥安有点粗心，会乱放东西。但是为什么大东和祥安会变成朋友和室友呢？大东说，虽然祥安有时候会很粗心，但他是一个善良的人，和他相处很开心。这样的朋友，谁会不喜欢和他在一起住呢？

Read the passage and answer the following questions.
1. What are the differences between Dadong and Xiang'an?
2. Why does Dadong like being friends and roommates with Xiang'an?
3. Compare and contrast the differences between you and a friend, and explain why you like your friend.

练习 3.9: 阅读理解

找室友合租

> 　　我是语言大学的学生，在学校附近租了一间两室一厅的公寓，想找一名室友跟我合租。房租每个月1500元，家电家具一应俱全，包水电费。希望室友也是学生，喜欢安静，爱干净。
>
> 　　具体情况可面谈。有意合租的朋友请找小李，电话是13856908---。谢谢！

Notes:
具体 (jùtǐ): *n.* details
面谈 (miàntán): *v.* to talk with someone face-to-face
有意 (yǒuyì): *v.* to be interested in

Read the roommate ad and answer the following questions.
1. Describe the apartment for rent.
2. What are the renter's requirements for a potential roommate?
3. How would you advertise your place to find a roommate?

Unique Chinese Dwellings

China has developed numerous types of housing, many of which can still be seen today. In addition to traditional courtyard homes (siheyuan), some of the most architecturally unique types of housing include *yaodong* (窑洞: yáodòng), Hakka walled villages (客家围屋: Kèjiā wéiwū), and *shikumen* (石库门: shíkùmén). These styles of homes are major tourist destinations, not to be missed when visiting their respective regions.

Yaodong of the Huangtu Plateau

Cave dwellings in China are concentrated in the Huangtu Plateau (黄土高原: Huángtǔ Gāoyuán). The use of cave dwellings, or yaodong, began in the prehistoric era and has continued to the present day. Cave dwellings are ecologically sustainable, as the earthen walls act as insulation, keeping the house relatively cool in the hot, humid summers and warm in the bitterly cold, dry winters.

Yaodong come in several forms, with three main categories. The first type of yaodong is carved into the sides of cliffs, typically facing south. The second type features a sunken courtyard created in areas without hills, and rooms are then excavated from the sides. The third type covers partially or entirely freestanding structures, built where construction of underground yaodong has been discouraged.

Yaodong structures remain popular, particularly in Shaanxi province. Even now, around 40 million people still reside in yaodong on the plateau.

Hakka Walled Villages

A Hakka walled village is a large fortified building designed to accommodate several families and provide defense against intruders. According to some scholars, the Hakka people developed these structures after migrating to southern China. With resources being scarce, locals in the south responded badly to the migrants. During particularly difficult times, the tension escalated into open warfare. As a result, the Hakka people built up walled structures to house entire villages and guard against neighboring groups and wandering bandits.

While these walled villages had many forms, one of the most common and distinctive was a round, rammed-earth structure known as a *tulou* (土楼: tǔlóu, meaning "earthen building"). These structures are mostly located in the Fujian province. In addition to protection, the thick, earth-based walls of the tulou provide insulation and earthquake resistance. For safety reasons, they have no windows at ground level and only one heavily fortified entrance containing multiple levels of internal defenses if breached. In addition, the structures vary greatly in size, with some reaching areas of over 430,000 ft² and heights of over three stories.

Shikumen of Shanghai

Shikumen are a distinctive type of housing found only in Shanghai that date back to the 1860s. Known as "stone gate" houses, they fused Anglo-American townhouses with traditional Chinese courtyard homes. A shikumen is two to three stories tall, usually enclosed by a brick wall. The name comes from the doorframes made of long stone bars, giving shikumen their unique look.

The shikumen were developed when refugees from southern Jiangsu and northern Zhejiang fled the Taiping Rebellion in 1860 and settled in Shanghai. With the arrival of many migrants, new homes were built to house the influx of people. While they were originally meant for one family, many landlords divided up floors into several rooms and rented out rooms to tenants.

At the height of their popularity, shikumen made up 60 percent of the housing in the city. Today, many shikumen have given way to large apartment buildings or have been turned into fashionable restaurants and boutiques. However, they are still a popular sight to see in Shanghai.

Pinyin

Wáng Xiǎoměi: Dàdōng, xiǎngbudào nǐmen de sùshè zhème luàn! Nǐ kàn chuángshang dōu shì yīfu, zhuōshang hái yǒu chīshèng de dōngxi.

Chén Dàdōng: Zhèxiē dōu shì Xiáng'ān de, tā chángcháng luàn fàng dōngxi.

Wáng Xiǎoměi: Nà nǐ wèishénme hái yào gēn tā zhù?

Chén Dàdōng: Yīnwèi tā hěn hǎo xiāngchǔ, yòu huì zhàogù rén. Shàngcì Ānnà shēngbìng jiù shì Xiáng'ān dài tā qù kàn le yīshēng. Zàishuō, zhù sùshè yě yǒu hěn duō hǎochu.

Wáng Xiǎoměi: Zhù sùshè de hǎochu quèshí tǐng duō, dànshì yìdiǎn yǐnsī dōu méiyǒu, fángzū hái hěn guì.

Chén Dàdōng: Xiàonèiwài de fángzū dōu bù piányi, wǒ píngshí yě hěn máng, huì wàngle fù shuǐdiànfèi. Zhù zài sùshè fèiyòng quánbāo, shěngxīn yòu shěnglì.

Wáng Xiǎoměi: Nǐ zhǐyào zhǎo yí ge xìxīn de shìyǒu jiù bú yòng dānxīn la!

Chén Dàdōng: Búguò wǒ yǐjīng xíguàn hé Xiáng'ān yìqǐ zhù le. Nǐ qù Zhōngguó liúxué de shíhou xiǎng zhǎo shénme yàng de shìyǒu hézū ne?

English

Dadong, I didn't expect your dormitory to be this messy! Look at all the clothes on the bed and the leftovers on the table.

These are all Xiang'an's things. He often leaves things all over the place.

Then why are you still living with him?

Because he is easy to get along with and is very good at taking care of others. Last time when Anna was sick, it was Xiang'an who took her to see the doctor. Furthermore, living in a dorm has many advantages.

There definitely are a lot of advantages to living in a dorm, but there's no privacy at all and the rent is also very expensive.

Neither on-campus housing nor off-campus housing is cheap. I also tend to be very busy and am likely to forget to pay utility bills. Dorm fees are all-inclusive, which saves time and energy.

You won't have to worry if you just find a considerate roommate!

But I'm already used to living with Xiang'an. When you go to study abroad in China, what kind of roommate will you look for?

Wáng Xiǎoměi:	Dàole Běijīng yǐhòu, wǒxiǎng zū yí tào sān shì yì tīng de gōngyù. Wǒ de shìyǒu yídìng yào xìxīn, ài gānjìng, huì zuòfàn hé zuò jiāwù. Zhèyàng de shìyǒu hěn "lǐxiǎng" ba?	After I arrive in Beijing, I would like to rent a three-bedroom apartment with a living room. My roommate must be careful and attentive, love clean conditions, know how to cook, and do household chores with everyone. Isn't this kind of roommate "ideal"?
Chén Dàdōng:	Tīng qǐlai búcuò, kěshì wǒ kǒngpà méiyǒu bànfǎ zuò yí ge nàme "lǐxiǎng" de shìyǒu o......	It sounds good, but I'm afraid I would not be able to be such an "ideal" roommate . . .

What Can You Do?

INTERPRETIVE
- I can name different types of apartments after I see different rental ads.
- I can identify different qualities wanted in a roommate after hearing about others talk about their roommates.

INTERPERSONAL
- I can discuss housing preferences.
- I can compare pros and cons of a housing situation with others.

PRESENTATIONAL
- I can talk about housing situations.
- I can describe ideal living conditions.

找公寓
Apartment Hunting

昨天，玛丽收到了房东的通知，说合同到期之后不想再出租了，
fáng dōng　tōng zhī　dào qī　zhī hòu　chū zū

要收回公寓。玛丽必须在一个月之内搬家，所以她急着找公寓。
bì xū　zhī nèi bān jiā　jí

周信说他对北京的情况比较了解，要玛丽看房的时候叫上他。

玛丽在报纸上看到
bào zhǐ
了一个租房广告，
guǎng gào

和周信一起去看了以后发现那套公寓
fā xiàn
又脏又旧，还没有空调和洗衣机。
zāng　jiù　kōng tiáo　xǐ yī jī

然后他们去看了一套比较新的公寓，房租很便宜
而且还有家具，但可惜离马路近，太吵了。
jiā jù　kě xī　mǎ lù

后来，他们在学校碰到了冰冰。冰冰告诉玛丽她的室友刚搬走，有一个房间空（kōng）了出来。

公寓的家用电器（jiā yòng diàn qì）包括（bāo kuò）电视和冰箱在内（bīng xiāng zài nèi），而且在学校附近（fù jìn），环境非常好，也很安静。

玛丽看了以后对这个公寓很满意（mǎn yì），

也很高兴能跟朋友做室友，觉得自己很幸运（xìng yùn）。

LESSON TEXT 3.2

Apartment Hunting 找公寓

Mali receives a notice from her landlord that she must move out within a month. Zhou Xin accompanies her as she searches for a new apartment.

　　昨天，玛丽收到了房东的通知，说合同到期之后不想再出租了，要收回公寓。玛丽必须在一个月之内搬家，所以她急着找公寓。周信说他对北京的情况比较了解，要玛丽看房的时候叫上他。玛丽在报纸上看到一个租房广告，和周信一起去看了以后发现那套公寓又脏又旧，还没有空调和洗衣机。然后他们去看了一套比较新的公寓，房租很便宜而且还有家具，但可惜离马路很近，太吵了。

　　后来，他们在学校碰到了冰冰。冰冰告诉玛丽她的室友刚搬走，有一个房间空了出来。公寓的家用电器包括电视和冰箱在内，而且在学校附近，环境非常好，也很安静。玛丽看了以后对这个公寓很满意，也很高兴能跟朋友做室友，觉得自己很幸运。

Language Tip

空 (kōng / kòng)

In the Lesson Text, 空 is used to indicate that Bingbing has an empty room. The word 空 has two tones: kōng and kòng. It is pronounced as kōng when used as a noun to mean "air" or as an adjective to mean "empty". It is pronounced as kòng when used as a noun to mean "spare time," and verb to mean "to leave (something) empty."

Examples:

他搬家了，现在房间空着。
He just moved out, and now his room is empty.

我今天没有空。
I don't have time today.

他把房间空出来租给朋友。
He emptied a room to rent to his friend.

字词 VOCABULARY

LESSON VOCABULARY 3.2

	SIMPLIFIED	TRADITIONAL	PINYIN	WORD CATEGORY	DEFINITION
1.	房东	房東	fángdōng	*n*	landlord
2.	通知		tōngzhī	*n*	notification
3.	到期		dàoqī	*vo*	to become due; to expire
	期		qī	*n, mw*	period of time; (used for an issue or term)
4.	之后	之後	zhīhòu	*prep*	after, later
5.	出租		chūzū	*v*	to rent, to let
6.	必须	必須	bìxū	*av*	must
7.	之内		zhīnèi	*prep*	within
8.	搬家		bānjiā	*vo*	to move house
	搬		bān	*v*	to move
9.	急		jí	*adj*	anxious, worry
10.	报纸	報紙	bàozhǐ	*n*	newspaper
11.	广告	廣告	guǎnggào	*n*	advertisement
12.	发现	發現	fāxiàn	*v*	to find, to discover
13.	脏	臟	zāng	*adj*	dirty
14.	旧	舊	jiù	*adj*	old
15.	空调	空調	kōngtiáo	*n*	air-conditioner
16.	洗衣机	洗衣機	xǐyījī	*n*	washing machine
	洗		xǐ	*v*	to wash
17.	家具		jiājù	*n*	furniture
18.	可惜		kěxī	*adj, adv*	unfortunate; unfortunately
19.	马路	馬路	mǎlù	*n*	road
20.	空		kōng, kòng	*v, adj, n*	to leave . . . empty; empty; spare time
21.	家用电器	家用電器	jiāyòng diànqì	*n*	household electrical appliance
	电器	電器	diànqì	*n*	electrical appliance
22.	包括		bāokuò	*v*	to include

LESSON VOCABULARY 3.2 (continued)

	SIMPLIFIED	TRADITIONAL	PINYIN	WORD CATEGORY	DEFINITION
23.	冰箱		bīngxiāng	*n*	refrigerator
	冰		bīng	*n, v*	ice; to be freezing
	箱		xiāng	*n*	box, chest
24.	在内		zàinèi	*prep*	to be included, including
25.	附近		fùjìn	*adv*	nearby
26.	满意	滿意	mǎnyì	*adj*	satisfied
	满	滿	mǎn	*adj, adv*	full; entirely
27.	幸运	幸運	xìngyùn	*adj, n*	lucky; good luck

REQUIRED VOCABULARY 3.2

28.	家庭		jiātíng	*n*	family; household

ONLINE RESOURCES

Visit *http://college.betterchinese.com* for more vocabulary related to household electrical appliances.

Idiomatic Expression

ān jiā luò hù
安家落户

安家落户 means "to settle in a new place."

This expression appears the script of the movie *Zheng Chenggong* (《郑成功》: *Zhèng Chénggōng*). A quote from the script says, "In Taiwan, crops can be harvested two or three times each year; we will be able to settle down after we work hard for several months." The expression is often used when people move to a new place.

Example:
他很喜欢在中国的留学生活，打算在中国安家落户。
He really enjoyed the student life in China, so he plans to settle in China.

Reading a Rental Advertisement

To find housing, being able to read a rental advertisement is essential. While price is a key factor, location, the number of rooms, amenities, and nearby transportation options are also important considerations.

Notice that the rental is in a housing complex, which is where the majority of urban dwellers live.

Below is a typical rental ad found in China:

出租广告

大华小区C栋二层有两室一厅一卫，面积一百平。公寓内有全新家具和家电 。租金是3000元/月（包水电费，押一付三）。公寓干净整洁，交通方便，有17、28路车。有意者面谈。
联络人：陈先生 电话：15811243---

The following terms are commonly used when looking for housing:

Chinese	Pinyin	English Definition
Location:		
小区	xiǎoqū	apartment complex
栋	dòng	(used for buildings)
层	céng	(used for floors or stories)
Number of Rooms:		
两室一厅一卫	liǎngshì yìtīng yíwèi	two bedrooms, one living room, one bathroom
室	shì	room(s)
厅	tīng	living room(s)
卫	wèi	(short for 卫生间) bathroom(s)
Measurements:		
面积	miànji	area
平方米	píngfāngmǐ	square meters
Transportation:		
公交车 / 公共汽车	gōngjiāo chē / gōnggòng qìchē	buses / public bus
地铁	dìtiě	subway
火车	huǒchē	train
Rental terms:		
押一付三	yā yī fù sān	first month's deposit, three months rent
签合同	qiān hétong	to sign a contract
People:		
联络人	liánluòrén	contact person
有意者	yǒuyìzhě	interested party
房东	fángdōng	landlord
合租人	hézūrén	co-tenant

STRUCTURE NOTE 3.5

Use 之内/外/前/后 *to indicate that things are within or outside of scope*

之 *(zhī) is a particle commonly seen in written Chinese that serves a number of functions. It replaces the more casual* 以 *in location phrases like* 之内 *(zhīnèi) and* 之外 *to create the meanings "within" and "outside." These phrases are often used in reference to some quantity of time or space, as in* 两个月之内, *"within two months," but can also be used in a more abstract way, as in* 想象之外, *"beyond imagination." Similarly,* 之前 *and* 之后 *(zhīhòu) are equivalent to the more casual* 以前, *"before" and* 以后, *"after".*

> Noun Phrase + 之内 / 外 / 前 / 后

From the Lesson Text:

玛丽必须在一个月之内搬家。
Mǎlì bìxū zài yí ge yuè zhīnèi bānjiā.
Mali has to move out within a month.

Other examples:

这里的房租不太贵，一千块钱之内就能租到很好的公寓。
Zhèlǐ de fángzū bú tài guì, yì qiān kuài qián zhīnèi jiù néng zūdào hěn hǎo de gōngyù.
The rent here is not too expensive; a very good apartment can be rented for under 1,000 dollars.

除了法国和英国之外，他还去了很多其他的欧洲国家旅游。
Chúle Fǎguó hé Yīngguó zhīwài, tā hái qùle hěn duō qítā de Ōuzhōu guójiā lǚyóu.
Besides France and England, he has also traveled to other European countries.

Practice: Choose the correct words to fill in the blanks.

> 之前　之内　之外　之后

1. 老师要我在两天_____把作业全都交给他。
2. 回宿舍_____，她就没再出去了。
3. 你要记得在三天_____再去看一次医生。
4. 除了他_____，我们还请了很多人。
5. 房东让我在这个星期_____交房租，要不然就要让我搬家了。

STRUCTURE NOTE 3.6
Use 可惜 *to express regret over an unfortunate situation*

可惜 *(kěxī) can be used as an adjective meaning "unfortunate" and as an adverb meaning "unfortunately." Like the English "unfortunately,"* 可惜 *can introduce a sentence in which the speaker describes a regrettable situation.*

可惜 + Sentence

From the Lesson Text:

但可惜离马路很近，太吵了。
Dàn kěxī lí mǎlù hěn jìn, tài chǎo le.
But unfortunately, the apartment was too close to the road and was very noisy.

Other examples:

昨天的活动非常有意思，可惜你没有来。
Zuótiān de huódòng fēicháng yǒu yìsi, kěxī nǐ méiyǒu lái.
The event yesterday was very interesting; it's a pity you didn't come.

我也想和你一起去看表演，可惜我要上班。
Wǒ yě xiǎng hé nǐ yìqǐ qù kàn biǎoyǎn, kěxī wǒ yào shàngbān.
I would like to go to the performance with you, but unfortunately I have to go to work.

Practice: Create complete sentences using 可惜.

Example:　我特别想参加学校的游泳比赛，可惜……
→ 我特别想参加学校的游泳比赛，可惜我生病了。

1.　我想买那件红色的毛衣，……

_____

2.　这学期我只能选英国文学，……

_____

3.　我们想去中国旅游，……

_____

4.　旅游的时候我想给大家寄明信片，……

_____

STRUCTURE NOTE 3.7

Use 包括……(在内) **to list included items or examples within a category**

包括 (bāokuò) can express "to include," "including," and "to be included." 包括 is often used to introduce a list of things that are included in a category. The phrase 在内 (zàinèi), "within," is optionally added at the end.

包括 + A, + B . . . + (在内)

From the Lesson Text:

公寓的家用电器包括电视和冰箱在内。
Gōngyù de jiāyòng diànqì bāokuò diànshì hé bīngxiāng zàinèi.
The apartment's household appliances include a television and refrigerator.

Other Examples:

包括英国、美国、中国在内的很多国家都支持这个环境保护活动。
Bāokuò Yīngguó, Měiguó, Zhōngguó zàinèi de hěn duō guójiā dōu zhīchí zhè ge huánjìng bǎohù huódòng.
Many countries including England, America, and China support this environmental protection activity.

很多人，包括你和我在内，都不太了解中国文化。
Hěnduō rén, bāokuò nǐ hé wǒ zàinèi, dōu bú tài liǎojiě Zhōngguó wénhuà.
Many people, including you and I, do not really understand Chinese culture.

Practice: Rewrite the following sentences using 包括……在内.

Example: 他买了很多书，比如中文、英语和法语书。
→ 他买了包括中文、英语和法语在内的很多书。

1.   我喜欢很多运动，比如跑步、游泳和打太极。

_____

2.   我很喜欢中国的文化，比如中国武术和京剧。

_____

3.   我去过很多地方旅行，比如北京、巴黎和伦敦。

_____

4.   我们可以用电脑做很多事情，比如收电子邮件、玩游戏和找资料。

_____

STRUCTURE NOTE 3.8
Use 对……(不)满意 *to express satisfaction or dissatisfaction with something*

While in English we talk about being satisfied "with" something, in Chinese the preposition 对, *"to" or "toward," is used to create the equivalent expression. To indicate that the subject is dissatisfied,* 不 *is placed before* 满意 *(mǎnyì).*

Subject + 对 + Object (+ 不) + 满意

From the Lesson Text:
玛丽对这个公寓很满意。
Mǎlì duì zhè ge gōngyù hěn mǎnyì.
Mali is very satisfied with this apartment.

Other Examples:
我对我的新手机很满意。
Wǒ duì wǒ de xīn shǒujī hěn mǎnyì.
I am very satisfied with my new cellphone.

教授对这个学生写的报告不太满意。
Jiàoshòu duì zhè ge xuésheng xiě de bàogào bú tài mǎnyì.
The professor is not very satisfied with the report this student wrote.

Practice: Create complete sentences using 对……满意 and the information provided below.

Example:　老师 / 我的作业 / 很
　　　　　→ 老师对我的作业很满意。

1. 她 / 新的飞机场 / 很

　　_____

2. 妈妈 / 我的家教 / 非常 / 不

　　_____

3. 他 / 学校附近的环境 / 很

　　_____

4. 我 / 你选的颜色 / 很

　　_____

5. 朋友 / 我拍的照片 / 特别 / 不

　　_____

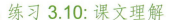

练习 3.10: 课文理解

Paired Activity: Discuss the following questions based on the Lesson Text. Be prepared to share your thoughts with the class.

> 1. 玛丽为什么急着找房子?
>
> 2. 冰冰的公寓怎么样?
>
> 3. 你觉得找房子的时候要注意什么?

练习 3.11: 玛丽看房

Paired Activity: Working with a classmate, explain why Mali was not satisfied with the two housing options she viewed with Zhou Xin. Provide at least two reasons for each.

练习 3.12 (上): 客户需求表

Individual Activity: You and a friend decide to live off-campus. You go to a housing agency and the housing agent asks you to fill out the client preferences form below.

客户需求表			
姓名		性别	
电话		电邮地址	
房间要求			
家电、家具要求	Example: 电器		
附近环境			
交通			
合同（时间）		费用	

Notes:
客户需求表 (kèhù xūqiú biǎo): *n.* client preferecne form
性别 (xìngbié): *n.* gender   要求 (yāoqiú): *n.* requirement

Paired Activity: After receiving the form, the housing agent presents two apartments that are available. Using the information below, discuss the two options with your partner and reach a conclusion.

Example: 这套公寓交通比较方便，可惜不能合租。

公寓 A

- 两室一厅
- 包家具、电视和冰箱，但没有洗衣机
- 不包水电费
- 开车二十分钟到学校
- 不用签合同，而且可以合租
- 房租：3000元/月

公寓 B

- 一室一厅
- 包家具、电器
- 包水电费、网费
- 五分钟走到学校
- 要签合同，不能合租
- 房租：1800元/月

练习 **3.14**（下）: 分租广告

Group Activity: Looking at the images below, discuss what issues you would have with each living situation.

	Radical	Stroke Order
之	丶 diǎn dot	丶 亠 之
纸	纟(糸) sī silk	纟 纟 纟 纟 纩 纸 纸
广	广 yǎn shelter	丶 亠 广
调	讠(言) yán speech	丶 讠 讠 讱 讱 调 调 调 调
洗	氵(水) shuǐ water	丶 冫 氵 汁 汫 汫 洗 洗
器	口 kǒu mouth	丨 吅 吅 吅 吅 吅 哭 哭 哭 哭 哭 哭 器 器 器 器
具	八 bā eight	丨 冂 冂 月 月 且 具 具
惜	忄(心) xīn heart	丶 丷 忄 忄 忄 忄 忄 惜 惜 惜
庭	广 yǎn shelter	丶 亠 广 广 庐 庄 庭 庭
旧	丨 shù line	丨 丨丨 丨丨 旧 旧
括	扌(手) shǒu hand	一 十 扌 扩 扩 抇 括 括
箱	竹(竹) zhú bamboo	丿 丿 竹 竹 竹 竹 竿 竿 笨 箱 箱 箱 箱 箱
附	阝 fù hill	了 阝 阝 阝 阶 附 附
满	氵(水) shuǐ water	丶 冫 氵 汇 汻 泸 泩 滿 满 满 满
幸	干 gān dry	一 十 土 去 圭 幸 幸 幸

Online chat: Working with a classmate, discuss where you live and your current housing situation. Describe your general feelings about your home and your environment.

练习 3.17: 阅读理解

To:	王小美
From:	孙玛丽
Subject:	找公寓

小美：

　　我最近找房的时候学到一些经验：看到不错的租房广告之后，不要马上去看房，要先打电话问清楚公寓的情况；看房的时候最好带上一个朋友。你还要考虑房东好不好相处，室友怎么样。找理想的公寓不是一件容易的事情，看房的时候要很细心。我很喜欢这里的生活，说不定有一天我会在中国安家落户！

玛丽

Read the e-mail and answer the following questions.
1. What should Xiaomei do before looking for an apartment?
2. What are important considerations for Xiaomei when looking at housing?
3. What are important considerations for you when looking at housing?

练习 3.18: 阅读理解

租房广告

　　大学附近一套四室两厅的公寓有两个空房出租。房间有书桌、衣柜、床。客厅有电视、冰箱、空调和洗衣机，家电齐全。大房1200元一个月，有阳台和洗手间。小房每个月900元。室友是两个女孩子，都在附近上班。欢迎好相处、喜欢干净的学生和上班族入住。

联系人：刘女士　　电话：13944508---

Notes:
齐全 (qíquán): *adj.* complete
阳台 (yángtái): *n.* balcony
洗手间 (xǐshǒujiān): *n.* restroom
上班族 (shàngbānzú): *n.* someone who works and leaves the office at fixed times
联系人 (liánxìrén): *n.* contact person

Read the advertisement and answer the following questions.
1. What basic amenities are included?
2. What kind of renter is Ms. Liu looking for?
3. What kinds of renters would you look for when renting out an apartment?

Beijing City Planning and Influence

China has a long and varied history of urban planning, especially with regards to its capitals. This can be seen in the way some of its oldest cities are laid out in a symmetrical grid pattern. Two well-known cities planned in this way are Xi'an (西安: Xī'ān) and Beijing.

Xi'an

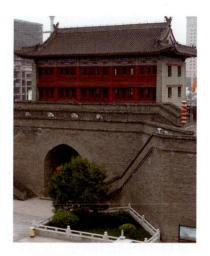

Xi'an was the capital of China during several dynasties and considered one of the Four Great Ancient Capitals of China. During the Tang Dynasty (618 – 907 AD), it was one of the largest cities in the world. Then known as Chang'an, or "Perpetual Peace," the ancient city is laid out in a symmetrical grid enclosed by a city wall for defense. This design would come to influence city planning for many dynasties to come.

As the imperial capital, Chang'an was designed to emphasize the legitimacy of the emperor through urban planning. The *Rites of Zhou* (《周礼》: *Zhōulǐ*), a classic from the Zhou Dynasty, (1046 – 256 BC) lays out several key guidelines, incorporating a north-south axis and feng shui elements into the planning of the city itself. The symmetry of the city also reflects ancient Chinese values of harmony: many ancient palaces are built on sites thought to be particularly harmonious within the overall structure of the city.

Xi'an is one of the few cities in China with its city walls still extant. Xi'an's symmetrical grid pattern is also extremely influential: not only did it shape the design of Beijing and other Chinese cities, but also that of other major Asian cities that were imperial capitals, including Seoul and Kyoto.

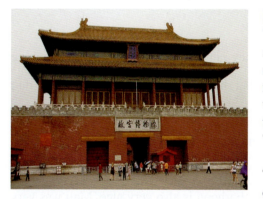

Beijing

With the Forbidden City at its heart, Beijing is organized on a north-south axis that reflected the belief that China — and the emperor — was at the center of the world. Along this imperial axis running through the city are major sites essential to imperial life, including many of the key gates into what was then a walled city. Directly south of the Forbidden City is Qianmen, then the first entry point into Beijing. To the North lies the Drum and Bell Tower, the official timekeeper for imperial China.

The perfect meridian and the city's symmetry are also further reflected in the placement of important sites in accordance with feng shui principles. Yin elements such as the ancestral temple, considered more oriented towards history, were built on the left (west). Yang elements such as the Alter of the Grains and Soils, oriented towards present activity and growth, were on the right (east).

The imperial axis holds particular importance even in modern times: for the Beijing Olympics in 2008, the imperial axis was further extended to the Olympic Park, built directly north of the Forbidden City and the Drum and Bell Towers. Even as the city has outgrown its traditional boundaries, expansions of the city have led to a pattern of concentric ring roads that encircle modern Beijing, preserving its symmetry. Visitors can even walk the imperial axis themselves through walking tours that take them from the Forbidden City to the Drum and Bell Towers.

Pinyin

Zuótiān, Mǎlì shōudàole fángdōng de tōngzhī, shuō hétong dàoqī zhīhòu bù xiǎng zài chūzū le, yào shōuhuí gōngyù. Mǎlì bìxū zài yí ge yuè zhīnèi bānjiā, suǒyǐ tā jízhe zhǎo gōngyù. Zhōu Xīn shuō tā duì Běijīng de qíngkuàng bǐjiao liǎojiě, yào Mǎlì kànfáng de shíhou jiàoshang tā. Mǎlì zài bàozhǐ shang kàndàole yí ge zūfáng guǎnggào, hé Zhōu Xīn yìqǐ qù kànle yǐhòu fāxiàn nà tào gōngyù yòu zāng yòu jiù, hái méiyǒu kōngtiáo hé xǐyījī. Ránhòu tāmen qù kànle yí tào bǐjiao xīn de gōngyù, fángzū hěn piányi érqiě háiyǒu jiājù, dàn kěxī lí mǎlù hěn jìn, tài chǎo le.

Hòulái, tāmen zài xuéxiào pèngdao le Bīngbīng. Bīngbīng gàosu Mǎlì tā de shìyǒu gāng bānzǒu, yǒu yí ge fángjiān kōngle chūlái. Gōngyù de jiāyòng diànqì bāokuò diànshì hé bīngxiāng zàinèi, érqiě zài xuéxiào fùjìn, jiāotōng hěn fāngbiàn, huánjìng yě fēicháng hǎo. Mǎlì kàn le yǐhòu duì zhè ge gōngyù hěn mǎnyì, yě hěn gāoxìng néng gēn péngyou zuò shìyǒu, juéde zìjǐ hěn xìngyùn.

English

Yesterday, Mali received a notice from her landlord saying that upon expiration of her contract, he does not wish to continue leasing out the apartment and plans to take it back. Mali has to move out within a month, so she's urgently looking for a new apartment. Zhou Xin said he's very familiar with Beijing and told Mali to let him know when she goes for viewings. Mali saw a rental ad in the newspaper. When she went with Zhou Xin to look at the apartment, they found it dirty and old. Furthermore, it didn't even include an air conditioner or washing machine. After that, they saw a newer apartment that was very cheap and includes furniture. But unfortunately, the apartment was too close to the road and was very noisy.

In the end, they ran into Bingbing at school. Bingbing told Mali that her roommate had just moved out, so she had a free room. The apartment's household appliances include a television and refrigerator. It is also close to school, the transportation is convenient, and the neighborhood is also very nice. Mali was very satisfied with this apartment after taking a look, and she was happy that she could room with a friend. She considered herself very lucky.

What Can You Do?

INTERPRETIVE

- I can identify a rental ad in printed and digital media.
- I can list housing amenities after seeing a rental ad.

INTERPERSONAL

- I can discuss my preferences for a rental.
- I can compare housing options with others.

PRESENTATIONAL

- I can talk about the process of looking for an apartment.
- I can present information about an apartment and its surroundings.

ACT IT OUT

Working in groups, compose an original two-minute skit that utilizes the vocabulary and structures introduced in Unit 3. Each of you should assume a role and have a roughly equal number of lines in the skit. Be prepared to perform your skit in class. You can either come up with your own story or choose from one of the following situations:

A) Your roommate wants to move out and into the school dormitory, but you would like him/her to stay. Convince your roommate to continue living with you.

B) You went apartment hunting today. Afterwards, you meet up with your friends, and they ask you about the apartments you saw and what they offered.

C) You are subletting your apartment for the summer while you travel abroad. Convince a good friend to rent the apartment while you are gone, explaining all the benefits of your place including any appliances you have.

CHECK WHAT YOU CAN DO

RECOGNIZE

Adjectives
- □ 乱
- □ 细心
- □ 粗心
- □ 急
- □ 脏
- □ 旧
- □ 满意
- □ 可惜
- □ 理想
- □ 幸运

Adverbs
- □ 确实
- □ 平时

□ 附近

Auxiliary Verb
- □ 必须

Conjunction
- □ 再说

Measure Word
- □ 套

Nouns
- □ 好处
- □ 隐私
- □ 房租
- □ 内外
- □ 水电费

- □ 费用
- □ 家务
- □ 坏处
- □ 地点
- □ 交通
- □ 房东
- □ 通知
- □ 报纸
- □ 广告
- □ 空调
- □ 洗衣机
- □ 家具
- □ 马路
- □ 家用电器
- □ 冰箱

□ 家庭

Prepositions
- □ 之后
- □ 之内
- □ 在内

Verbs
- □ 相处
- □ 包
- □ 合租
- □ 恐怕
- □ 出租
- □ 发现
- □ 包括
- □ 剩

□ 空

Verb-Object Compounds
- □ 省心省力
- □ 签合同
- □ 到期
- □ 搬家

WRITE

- □ 乱
- □ 剩
- □ 处
- □ 确
- □ 私
- □ 租
- □ 内
- □ 省
- □ 细
- □ 粗
- □ 隐
- □ 套
- □ 签
- □ 理
- □ 恐

- □ 之
- □ 纸
- □ 广
- □ 调
- □ 洗
- □ 器
- □ 具
- □ 惜
- □ 庭
- □ 旧
- □ 括
- □ 箱
- □ 附
- □ 满
- □ 幸

USE

- □ Use 再说 to bring up additional points.
- □ Use 确实 to say "indeed" or "really."
- □ Use 一点(儿)都没/不 to emphasize not at all.
- □ Use 恐怕 to express doubt over an unfortunate situation.

- □ Use 之内/外/前/后 to indicate that things are within or outside of scope.
- □ Use 可惜 to express pity at an unfortunate situation.
- □ Use 包括……(在内) to list included items or examples within a category.
- □ Use 对……(不)满意 to express satisfaction or dissatisfaction with something.

Shopping

第四单元
UNIT 4

Communication Goals

Lesson 1: 网上购物 **Shopping Online**
- Describe the basic elements of shopping online.
- Use common terms related to sales promotions and warranty periods accurately.
- Discuss sales offers and state reasons for purchasing decisions.

Lesson 2: 退货 **Returning Merchandise**
- Express apologies and frustrations.
- Talk about household items.
- Demonstrate understanding of terms related to a store's return policy.

网上购物
Shopping Online

祥安一向很喜欢美
食、摄影和写博客。
最近，他想用博客
给朋友们介绍和分
享中国美食，让大
家都有机会了解中
国的饮食文化。

祥安打算买一个比较专
业的数码相机来拍照。

大东建议祥安在网上买，
因为商店的价格常常不
如网上的划算，并且网
上有很多的打折活动。

但中平提醒祥安注意网络安全，他
在报纸上常看到网络购物的投诉。

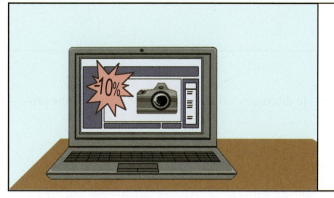

祥安找到一个卖新kuǎn xiàng jī相机的wǎng zhàn网站，既dǎ zhé打折又miǎn fèi sòng huò免费送货，但不bǎo xiū保修。他决定在网上gòu wù购物之前，先去附近的商店比较一下。

中平陪祥安去了一家电器商店，那里有很多dǎ zhé打折的míng pái shù mǎ xiàng jī名牌数码相机，chǎn pǐn产品有一年的bǎo xiū qī保修期，还可以用yōu huì quàn优惠券在这家商店的wǎng zhàn网站上gòu wù购物。

后来，祥安看中了一kuǎn款黑白色的xiàng jī相机，jì既便yòu宜又好用。中平说xiàng jī相机的颜色和yàng zi样子让他想起dà xióng māo大熊猫。祥安觉得买这个xiàng jī相机真是最合适不过了，因为这样他的bó kè博客就可以叫"yáng xióng māo洋熊猫游中国"！

LESSON TEXT 4.1

Shopping Online 网上购物

Xiang'an is looking to buy a new digital camera for his food blog. He discusses with Dadong and Zhongping the pros and cons of buying a camera online.

祥安一向很喜欢美食、摄影和写博客。最近，他想用博客给朋友们介绍和分享中国美食，让大家都有机会了解中国的饮食文化。

祥安打算买一个比较专业的数码相机来拍照。大东建议祥安在网上买，因为商店的价格常常不如网上的划算，并且网上有很多的打折活动。但中平提醒祥安注意网络安全，他在报纸上常看到网络购物的投诉。祥安找到了一个卖新款相机的网站，既打折又免费送货，但不保修。他决定在网上购物之前，先去附近的商店比较一下。

中平陪祥安去了一家电器商店，那里有很多打折的名牌数码相机，产品有一年的保修期，还可以用优惠券在这家商店的网站上购物。后来，祥安看中了一款黑白色的相机，既便宜又好用。中平说相机的颜色和样子让他想起大熊猫。祥安觉得买这个相机真是最合适不过了，因为这样他的博客就可以叫"洋熊猫游中国"！

Language Tips

博客 (bókè)

In the Lesson Text, Xiang'an uses a 博客 to share and introduce delicious food with others. 博客, alternatively called 网络日志 (wǎngluò rìzhì: Internet diary), comes from the English word "blog." In Taiwan, the terms 部落格 (bùluògé) and 网志 (wǎngzhì) are used to refer to a blog.

Example:

为什么越来越多的人喜欢用博客？

Why do more and more people like to use blogs?

看中 (kànzhòng)

In the Lesson Text, when Xiang'an is shopping for a camera at an electronics store, he uses 看中 to indicate that he has taken a liking to a black and white camera that he sees. The word 中 (zhòng) can literally mean "to hit (a target)." Together with 看, the phrase 看中 means "to take a liking to somebody or something."

Example:

老板看中了他的努力和善良，打算给他这个工作机会。

The boss likes that he works hard and likes his kindheartedness; he plans to offer him this job opportunity.

字 词 VOCABULARY

LESSON VOCABULARY 4.1

SIMPLIFIED	TRADITIONAL	PINYIN	WORD CATEGORY	DEFINITION
1. 一向		yíxiàng	*adv*	consistently, up to now, all along
2. 美食		měishí	*n*	delicious food
3. 摄影	攝影	shèyǐng	*vo, n*	to take a photograph; photography
4. 博客		bókè	*n*	blog
5. 分享		fēnxiǎng	*v*	to share
6. 饮食文化	飲食文化	yǐnshí wénhuà	*n*	cuisine culture, food culture
饮食	飲食	yǐnshí	*n*	cuisine, food
7. 数码相机	數碼相機	shùmǎ xiàngjī	*n*	digital camera
数码	數碼	shùmǎ	*n, adj*	numeral; digital
相机	相機	xiàngjī	*n*	camera
8. 价格	價格	jiàgé	*n*	price
9. 不如		bùrú	*v*	to be inferior to, not as good as
10. 划算		huásuàn	*adj*	to be worth the price
11. 并且	並且	bìngqiě	*cj*	and, besides, moreover
12. 打折		dǎzhé	*v*	to discount
13. 提醒		tíxǐng	*v*	to remind, to warn
14. 购物	購物	gòuwù	*n, vo*	shopping; to go shopping
15. 投诉	投訴	tóusù	*n*	complaint
16. 款		kuǎn	*n*	style, type
17. 网站	網站	wǎngzhàn	*n*	website
18. 免费	免費	miǎnfèi	*adj*	free of charge, free, gratis
19. 送货	送貨	sònghuò	*vo*	to deliver goods
货	貨	huò	*n*	goods
20. 名牌		míngpái	*n*	famous brand
21. 产品	産品	chǎnpǐn	*n*	product

LESSON VOCABULARY 4.1 (continued)

Simplified	Traditional	Pinyin	Word Category	Definition
22. 保修期		bǎoxiū qī	*n*	guarantee period, warranty period
修		xiū	*v*	to repair
23. 优惠券	優惠券	yōuhuìquàn	*n*	coupon
优惠	優惠	yōuhuì	*adj*	preferential, favorable
券		quàn	*n*	ticket, coupon
24. 既…又…		jì…yòu…	*prep*	both . . . and . . .
25. 样子	樣子	yàngzi	*n*	appearance
26. 大熊猫	大熊貓	dàxióngmāo	*n*	giant panda
27. 洋		yáng	*adj*	foreign

REQUIRED VOCABULARY 4.1

Simplified	Traditional	Pinyin	Word Category	Definition
28. 原价	原價	yuánjià	*n*	original price
29. 税		shuì	*n*	tax
30. 质量	質量	zhìliàng	*n*	quality

Idiomatic Expression

yì fēn qián　　yì fēn huò
一分钱，一分货

一分钱，一分货 means "you get what you pay for."

Example:
一分钱，一分货。大商场卖的电器虽然贵，但是质量有保证。
You get what you pay for. Although the electric appliances sold at the department store are expensive, their quality is guaranteed.

Shopping Promotions

Discounts

Discounts are expressed with a number + 折 (zhé). If an item is marked 9折 or 九折 (jiǔ zhé), it means that it can be purchased for 90 percent of its regular price, or at a 10 percent discount. In contrast to how discounts are typically represented in Western cultures, the lower the number, the greater the discount.

Examples: 7折 / 七折 = 30% off   2.5折 / 二点五折 = 75% off

Other terms commonly associated with shopping promotions involve bargaining. There are various ways to ask, "Is there a discount?" to find out if an item is on sale or not. For example, 打折吗? 打不打折? If you would like to ask how much is the discount, you can ask 打几折?

Promotions

The following are common terms related to promotions:

Promotions Terms	Pinyin	Meaning
半价	bànjià	half price
特价	tèjià	special price (特: special)
免费	miǎnfèi	free of charge
卖完为止	màiwán wéizhǐ	offer good as long as item is in stock
买一送/赠一	mǎi yī sòng/zèng yī	buy one, get one free
满300送100优惠券	mǎn 300 (sānbǎi) song 100 (yībǎi) yōuhuì quàn	buy 300, receive 100 store credits
大甩卖	dà shuǎimài	a fire sale (甩: throwing away or giving something up)
跳楼价	tiàolóujià	blowout sale (跳楼: to jump off a building, indicating a price that jumps from high to low)
削价	xuējià	to cut the price (削: to cut)

Special Sales Terms	Pinyin	Meaning
隆重开业	lóngzhòng kāiyè	grand opening
周年店庆	zhōunián diànqìng	anniversary sale
结业促销	jiéyè cùxiāo	closing sale

STRUCTURE NOTE 4.1

Use A 不如 B to indicate A is not as good as B

The expression A + 比 + B + Adjective indicates that A is more (adjective) than B. The phrase 不如 (bùrú) expresses the opposite, meaning that A is not as good as B. Unlike 比, A 不如 B can either be used with an adjective, indicating that A is not as good as B in some respect, or it can be used with no adjective, simply meaning that A is not as good as B in general.

A + 不如 + B (+ Adjective)

From the Lesson Text:

商店的价格常常不如网上的划算。
Shāngdiàn de jiàgé chángcháng bùrú wǎngshang de huásuàn.
Store prices usually aren't as good as online prices.

Other examples:

我的中文不如她的好。　　住宿舍不如住家里舒服。
Wǒ de Zhōngwén bùrú tā de hǎo.　Zhù sùshè bùrú zhù jiāli shūfu.
My Chinese is not as good as hers.　Living in the dorm isn't as comfortable
　　　　　　　　　　　　　　　　as living at home.

Practice: Rewrite the following sentences using 不如.

Example: 住校内比住校外方便。→ 住校外不如住校内方便。

1. 昆明的夏天比北京的舒服。

　　_____

2. 这家医院附近的环境没有那家的好。

　　_____

3. 我的实习经历没有他的多。

　　_____

4. 我家离飞机场比她家离飞机场远。

　　_____

5. 我觉得历史比数学有意思。

　　_____

STRUCTURE NOTES

语法

STRUCTURE NOTE 4.2
Use 并且 to mean "also" to connect words or clauses in formal contexts

While 和 *is the most common conjunction used in casual contexts, it is not considered very formal.* 并且 *(bìngqiě) is a more formal word that joins words or phrases together. Unlike* 和, *which is used to join nouns and other short elements,* 并且 *is usually used to join longer phrases as well as introduce clauses, similar to the English expressions "as well as" or "and furthermore."*

```
Clause, + 并且 + Clause
```

From the Lesson Text:

商店的价格常常不如网上的划算，并且网上有很多的打折活动。

Shāngdiàn de jiàgé chángcháng bùrú wǎngshàng de huásuàn, bìngqiě wǎngshàng yǒu hěnduō de dǎzhé huódòng.

Store prices usually aren't as good as online prices. Furthermore, online sites often have sales promotions.

Other examples:

他是一个很细心的人，并且非常好相处。

Tā shì yí ge hěn xìxīn de rén, bìngqiě fēicháng hǎo xiāngchǔ.

He is a very considerate person and extremely easy to get along with.

他要我陪他去美国，可是我怕坐飞机，并且我也不会说英语。

Tā yào wǒ péi tā qù Měiguó, kěshì wǒ pà zuò fēijī, bìngqiě wǒ yě bú huì shuō Yīngyǔ.

He wants me to go to America with him, but I am afraid of riding on planes. Furthermore, I don't know how to speak English.

Practice: Combine the two sentences together using 并且.

Example: 姐姐的宠物爱吃很多东西／很爱玩。
→姐姐的宠物爱吃很多东西，并且很爱玩。

1. 我的公寓有各种家电／在学校附近。

   _____

2. 今年夏天的气温一般在37度左右／有一点闷热。

   _____

3. 她的性格活泼开朗／对人很热情。

   _____

STRUCTURE NOTE 4.3
Use 既 *A* 又 *B* as a formal way to express "both A and B"

既 (jì) *is a conjunction generally used in more formal contexts, such as writing.* 既 *A* 又 *B expresses the same meaning as* 又 *A* 又 *B, meaning having both A attribute and B attribute.*

> Subject + 既 + Adjective / Verb Phrase + 又 + Adjective / Verb Phrase

From the Lesson Text:

祥安找到了一个卖新款相机的网站，既打折又免费送货。

Xiáng'ān zhǎodàole yí ge mài xīn kuǎn xiàngjī de wǎngzhàn, jì dǎzhé yòu miǎnfèi sònghuò.

Xiang'an found a site selling new camera models, with discounts and free shipping.

Other examples:

老师的儿子既聪明又可爱。

Lǎoshī de érzi jì cōngming yòu kě'ài.

The teacher's son is both clever and cute.

大家都说他既尊敬长辈又会照顾晚辈，是个很有礼貌的人。

Dàjiā dōu shuō tā jì zūnjìng zhǎngbèi yòu huì zhàogù wǎnbèi, shì ge hěn yǒu lǐmào de rén.

Everyone says that he both respects his elders and looks after the younger generation — he's a very well-mannered person.

Practice: Create complete sentences using 既…又… and the information provided.

Example: 他 / 会说英语 / 汉语 → 他既会说英语又会说汉语。

1. 我的室友 / 爱去健身房运动 / 图书馆看书

   _____

2. 出去旅游的时候我们 / 要玩得开心 / 注意安全

   _____

3. 她穿那条裙子 / 看起来漂亮 / 可爱

   _____

4. 开车去机场 / 快 / 方便

   _____

5. 酸辣汤 / 好喝 / 不贵

   _____

STRUCTURE NOTE 4.4
Use 最……不过了 *to emphasize superlatives*

The pattern 最 *+ Adjective +* 不过了 *indicates that one cannot find something that exceeds the current subject in some attribute. The attribute can be either good, such as* 好, 美丽, *etc., or negative, such as* 差 *or* 坏.

最 + Adjective + 不过了

From the Lesson Text:　　祥安觉得买这个相机真是最合适不过了。
Xiáng'ān juéde mǎi zhè ge xiàngjī zhēn shì zuì héshì búguò le.
Xiang'an believes this is his ideal camera.

Other examples:　　小孩子穿这样的衣服最可爱不过了。
Xiǎoháizi chuān zhè yàng de yīfu zuì kě'ài búguò le.
Little kids wearing this kind of clothing are the cutest.

我觉得参加保护环境的活动最有意思不过了。
Wǒ juéde cānjiā bǎohù huánjìng de huódòng zuì yǒuyìsi búguò le.
I think participating in events on environmental protection is most interesting.

Practice: Express the following statements in Chinese by applying the 最……不过了 structure and using the information provided below.

Example:　　This is the best way to write emails.
→ 这样写电邮最好不过了。

1.　　Taking this road to school is the fastest.

　　_____

2.　　Being able to be with family during the Spring Festival is the best.

　　_____

3.　　The girl wearing the pink skirt is the cutest.

　　_____

4.　　Taking a nap on a rainy day is the most comfortable thing.

　　_____

5.　　It is most common for him to catch a cold in the summer.

　　_____

练习 4.1: 课文理解

Paired Activity: Discuss the following questions based on the Lesson Text. Be prepared to share your thoughts with the class.

1. 祥安为什么要买数码相机？

2. 为什么祥安后来去了电器商店？

3. 如果你是祥安，你会在网上买数码相机吗？为什么？

练习 4.2 (上): 产品比较

Paired Activity: Xiang'an would also like to buy a new computer for school and for blogging. Working with a classmate, use the word bank to compare the options below and help Xiang'an make a decision.

既…又…　不如　并且　最……不过

Example: 新款笔记本R7的荧幕尺寸不如名牌笔记本BC9的大。

新款笔记本R7	名牌笔记本BC9	减价笔记本TX28
荧幕尺寸：12英寸	荧幕尺寸：16英寸	荧幕尺寸：10英寸
价格：3866元	价格：4199元	价格：2299元
送货：加100元	送货：免费	送货：加50元
保修期：2年	保修期：1年	保修期：不包保修

Notes:

荧幕尺寸 (yíngmù chǐcùn): *n.* screen size　　英寸 (yīngcùn): *n.* inch

练习 4.3 (下): 在网络还是商店购物?

Paired Activity: Based on your discussion in Practice Exercise 4.2 in the previous page, the next step is helping Xiang'an decide where to purchase the computer. Below are the differences between purchasing at a store and on a website. Discuss where Xiang'an should purchase the computer and why.

	网络	商店
价格	比商店便宜300元	比网络贵300元
保修期	1年保修期	2年保修期
送货	送货加50元	有现货
送货时间	1星期	有现货
优惠	多送1年保修期	送200元优惠券

练习 4.4: 购物经验

Individual Activity: Think about your own experience and preferences when buying a computer. Describe why these factors are important to you.

	你觉得重要吗?	为什么?
服务	我觉得买电脑的时候，店员的服务很重要。	我去过一家商店，店员的服务很差。她既不给我介绍新款的电脑，又不给我试用，这让我很不满意。
价格		
质量		
保修		

练习 4.5: 卖东西

Group Activity: Find an item that your group would like to sell. Write a description of the product and the terms of sale.

	Radical	Stroke Order
享	亠 tóu lid	丶 亠 宀 亡 吂 亨 享
饮	饣 shí food	丿 𠂆 饣 饣 饮 饮 饮
数	攵(攴) pū knock	丶 丷 丷 半 半 米 米 娄 娄 娄 数 数 数
码	石 shí rock	一 丆 石 石 石 码 码
相	木 mù wood	一 十 十 木 相 相 相 相 相
并	八 bā eight	丶 丷 兰 关 并
折	扌(手) shǒu hand	一 扌 扌 扌 折 折 折
投	扌(手) shǒu hand	一 扌 扌 扌 扖 投 投
款	欠 qiàn yawn	一 十 士 圭 圭 圭 耂 耂 耂 款 款
站	立 lì stand	丶 亠 亠 立 立 刬 站 站 站
免	刀 dāo knife	丿 𠂊 免 免 免 免 免
货	贝 bèi shell	丿 亻 亻 化 化 货 货 货
牌	片 piàn slice	丿 丬 片 片 片 牌 牌 牌 牌 牌 牌
产	亠 tóu lid	丶 亠 亠 产 产 产
既	无 wú without	𡤃 𡤃 𡤃 𣌘 𣌘 既 既 既

练习 4.7: 线上聊天

Online chat: Working with a classmate, discuss whether you prefer shopping online or in a store. Provide reasons to support your preferences.

练习 4.8: 阅读理解

　　回家以后，祥安在电器商店的网站上买了他之前看中的数码相机。虽然这款相机不是最便宜的，但是一分钱一分货。祥安对相机非常满意，走到哪里都带着。

　　有一天下大雨，祥安忘了带雨伞，相机进水了以后就不能用了。祥安很担心，不知道应该怎么办。中平让祥安给电器商店打电话问能不能修。因为相机有一年的保修期，商店很快就把相机修好了，祥安非常高兴。

Read the passage and answer the following questions.
1. What happened to Xiang'an's digital camera?
2. What did Xiang'an do about the situation?
3. Describe a similar problem you or someone you know has had in the past.

练习 4.9: 阅读理解

店庆活动
　　为了感谢顾客对我店的支持，在12月7日店庆日，各款包括电脑（4000 - 8500元）、数码相机（2000 - 8000元）、电视（3000 - 8000元）在内的家电全都六折。买满1500元，送150元优惠券；满8000元，送一部手机；满1万元，送一台名牌洗衣机。网络购物也有一样的优惠，并且免费送货！

　　欢迎您的光临！

Notes:
店庆 (diànqìng): *n.* store celebration
顾客 (gùkè): n. customer
感谢 (gǎnxiè): *v.* to thank
支持 (zhīchí): *v.* to support
满 (mǎn): *adj.* complete

Read the advertisement and answer the following questions.
1. What is the price range of the items sold in the store?
2. What promotions are currently available?
3. You have a budget of ¥5000. What can you buy and why?

Neighborhood Boutiques in China

As China modernizes, a new homegrown design aesthetic can be found as a generation begins to explore the possibilities within Chinese design. Not only can this new, distinctive Chinese look be found in hip T-shirts and other fashionable trends, it can also be found in neighborhoods in the major cities of China.

Tianzifang (田子坊: Tiánzǐfāng)

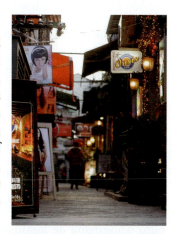

Nestled within an old Shikumen neighborhood in the French Concession quarter of Shanghai is Tianzifang, an area that contains art studios, international restaurants, and craft stores. The area was slated for destruction, until an outcry led to its preservation and its new life as a major destination for both visitors and residents alike. A major part of Tianzifang's appeal lies in the residents themselves, who continue to lead a traditional Shanghainese lifestyle amongst the new restaurants and stores that have sprung up.

798

The popular artist district of 798 in Beijing was once home to several military factory complexes. After the factories became obsolete and vacant, they were discovered by Beijing's Central Academy of Fine Arts as a potential workshop space. Artists started trickling in, attracted to both cheap rent and the large, empty spaces. 798 now boasts a thriving art scene with museums, galleries, bookstores, boutiques, and nightclubs that attract young Beijingers, artists, and visitors. However, with old political slogans preserved in the spaces, its former past as a factory complex can still be seen.

Nanluoguxiang (南锣鼓巷: Nán Luógǔ Xiàng)

Located in the historic hutongs of old Beijing in the Drum and Bell Tower district, the narrow alleyway of Nanluoguxiang is one of the epicenters of a hip and modern Chinese youth culture that is simultaneously international yet distinctly Chinese. Vintage shops, cafes, bars, and boutiques line the streets, selling everything from traditional folk art with a modern twist to quirky shops specializing in designer matchboxes. Many of China's up-and-coming designers make their home here, catering to a generation of young Chinese that is developing its own aesthetic tastes.

Pinyin

Xiáng'ān yíxiàng hěn xǐhuan měishí, shèyǐng hé xiě bókè. Zuìjìn, tā xiǎng yòng bókè gěi péngyoumen jièshào hé fēnxiǎng Zhōngguó měishí, ràng dàjiā dōu yǒu jīhuì liǎojiě Zhōngguó de yǐnshí wénhuà.

Xiáng'ān dǎsuan mǎi yí ge bǐjiao zhuānyè de shùmǎ xiàngjī lái pāizhào. Dàdōng jiànyì Xiáng'ān zài wǎngshàng mǎi, yīnwèi shāngdiàn de jiàgé chángcháng bùrú wǎngshàng de huásuàn, bìngqiě wǎngshàng yǒu hěnduō de dǎzhé huódòng. Dàn Zhōngpíng tíxǐng Xiáng'ān zhùyì wǎngluò ānquán, tā zài bàozhǐshàng cháng kàndào wǎngluò gòuwù de tóusù. Xiáng'ān zhǎodàole yí ge mài xīn kuǎn xiàngjī de wǎngzhàn, jì dǎzhé yòu miǎnfèi sònghuò, dàn bù bǎoxiū. Tā juédìng zài wǎngshàng gòuwù zhīqián, xiān qù fùjìn de shāngdiàn bǐjiào yí xià.

Zhōngpíng péi Xiáng'ān qùle yì jiā diànqì shāngdiàn, nàlǐ yǒu hěn duō dǎzhé de míngpái shùmǎ xiàngjī, chǎnpǐn yǒu yì nián de bǎoxiūqī, hái kěyǐ yòng yōuhuìquàn zài zhè jiā shāngdiàn de wǎngzhàn shàng gòuwù. Hòulái, Xiáng'ān kànzhòngle yì kuǎn hēibáisè de xiàngjī, jì piányi yòu hǎoyòng. Zhōngpíng shuō xiàngjī de yánsè hé yàngzi ràng tā xiǎngqǐ dàxióngmāo. Xiáng'ān juéde mǎi zhè ge xiàngjī zhēn shì zuì héshì búguò le, yīnwèi zhèyàng tā de bókè jiù kěyǐ jiào "yáng xióngmāo yóu Zhōngguó"!

English

Xiang'an has always enjoyed the culinary arts, photography, and blogging. Recently, he has been thinking about using his blog to introduce Chinese cuisine to his friends. This way, he can provide others with the opportunity to understand Chinese cuisine and culture.

Xiang'an plans to buy a more professional digital camera to take pictures. Dadong recommends that Xiang'an buy the camera online because the store prices usually aren't as good as online prices. Furthermore, online sites often have sales promotions. Zhongping reminds Xiang'an to pay attention to Internet safety and tells him that he has seen a lot of complaints in the news about making purchases online. Xiang'an found a site selling new camera models, with discounts and free shipping, but they do not offer a warranty. He decides that before making an online purchase, he will do some comparison shopping at a local store.

Zhongping accompanied Xiang'an to an electronics store, where there were a lot of brand-name cameras at discounted prices. The products come with a one-year warranty and there is also a coupon for items purchased through the store's online site. In the end, Xiang'an decided on a black and white camera that was both cheap and user-friendly. Zhongping said the camera's color scheme and shape reminded him of a panda. Xiang'an believes this is his ideal camera, because this way he can call his blog site "The Western Panda Touring China"!

What Can You Do?

INTERPRETIVE
- I can list different kinds of shopping promotions after seeing them online and in-store.
- I can compare different products after seeing them online.

INTERPERSONAL
- I can discuss shopping recommendations with someone else.
- I can exchange information about shopping promotions.

PRESENTATIONAL
- I can summarize the pros and cons of shopping online versus shopping in-store.
- I can talk about my preferences for shopping online or offline.

退货
Returning Merchandise

不好意思，这台
电暖器（diàn nuǎn qì）才用了两
次就用不了了，
能退货（tuì huò）吗？

你是什么时候买
的？有收据（shōu jù）吗？

我是两个星期前
买的，这是收据（shōu jù）。

真的很抱
歉（bào qiàn），商品（shāng pǐn）
只能在一
周之内退（tuì）
货（huò）。

什么？可是卖的时候你没有告诉我啊。

你看收据（shōu jù）上写得很
清楚（qīng chu），不好意思。

那么确实是没办法退了。玛丽，别不
开心。我带你去大商场（shāng chǎng）买一台（tái）新的。

^{shāng chǎng}
可是大商场会比小
商店的价钱贵吧？

^{rèn wéi} ^{máo jīn} ^{yá gāo}
我认为像毛巾和牙膏这样
的日用品，在小商店买会
^{rì yòng pǐn}
比较划算，但是买电器还
^{shāng chǎng} ^{bǎo zhèng}
是在大商场更有保证。我
^{bǎi huò gōng sī}
家附近那家百货公司就挺
不错的，还能在一个月之
^{tuì huò}
内退货。

^{qí shí bù guǎn}
好吧，我们去看看。其实不管买什
^{dōu} ^{tuì huò tiáo jiàn}
么东西，我都应该先看退货条件。

你先看看退货须知，
^{tuì huò xū zhī}
有不懂的地方就问
我吧。

^{tuì huò xū zhī}
退货须知
^{shāng pǐn} ^{shòu}
一、商品可以在售后
^{huàn}
三十天之内退换。
^{huàn} ^{chū shì}
二、退换时必须出示
^{shōu jù}
收据。
^{shāng pǐn} ^{bāo zhuāng}
三、商品和包装不能有
^{sǔn huài}
损坏。

LESSON TEXT 4.2

Returning Merchandise 退货

Zhou Xin and Mali attempt to return a heater to a small shop where it was recently purchased. but are unsuccessful after learning about the store's return policy. The two go to a larger store in search of another heater.

孙玛丽： 不好意思，这台电暖器才用了两次就用不了了，能退货吗？

店员： 你是什么时候买的？有收据吗？

孙玛丽： 我是两个星期前买的，这是收据。

店员： 真的很抱歉，商品只能在一周之内退货。

孙玛丽： 什么？可是卖的时候你没有告诉我啊。

店员： 你看收据上写得很清楚，不好意思。

周信： 那么确实是没办法退了。玛丽，别不开心。我带你去大商场买一台新的。

孙玛丽： 可是大商场会比小商店的价钱贵吧？

周信： 我认为像毛巾和牙膏这样的日用品，在小商店买会比较划算，但是买电器还是在大商场更有保证。我家附近那家百货公司就挺不错的，还能在一个月之内退货。

孙玛丽： 好吧，我们去看看。其实不管买什么东西，我都应该先看退货条件。

周信： 你先看看退货须知，有不懂的地方就问我吧。

退货须知

一、商品可以在售后三十天之内退换。
二、退换时必须出示收据。
三、商品和包装不能有损坏。

Language Tips

必须 (bìxū)

In the Lesson Text, the return policy uses 必须 to state that a receipt must be presented to make an exchange. 必须 precedes the main verb to express that an action is required. When 必需 is normally used as an adjective, indicating that something is necessary or essential.

必需 (bìxū)

Examples:

每个学生都必须带自己的课本。
Each student must bring his/her own textbook.

毛巾和牙膏是必需的日用品。
Towels and toothpaste are essential articles for daily use.

价格 (jiàgé)

Both 价格 and 价钱 mean "price." However, 价格 is more formal and primarily used in writing, as in the Lesson Text "商店的价格常常不如网上的划算" from *Modern Chinese* Textbook Vol. 2A, Unit 4, Lesson 1, while 价钱 is more often used in speech, as in this Lesson Text when Mali asks Zhou Xin, "可是大商场会比小商店的价钱贵吧？"

价钱 (jiàqián)

Examples:

购物的时候不能只看商品的价格，还要注意退货条件。
When shopping, don't only look at the price; you should also pay attention to the return policy.

我觉得小商店的价钱不见得都比大商场的便宜。
I don't think all the prices at small stores are necessarily cheaper than the ones at large stores.

LESSON VOCABULARY 4.2

	SIMPLIFIED	TRADITIONAL	PINYIN	WORD CATEGORY	DEFINITION
1.	台	臺	tái	*mw*	(used for appliances, instruments, etc.)
2.	电暖器	電暖器	diànnuǎnqì	*n*	heater
3.	用不了		yòngbuliǎo	*v*	can't be used
4.	退货	退貨	tuìhuò	*vo*	to return merchandise/goods
	退		tuì	*v*	to return
5.	收据	收據	shōujù	*n*	receipt
6.	抱歉		bàoqiàn	*v*	to be sorry, to be apologetic
7.	商品		shāngpǐn	*n*	merchandise, goods, commodity
8.	清楚		qīngchu	*adj*	clear
9.	商场	商場	shāngchǎng	*n*	market
10.	认为	認爲	rènwéi	*v*	to think/believe that
11.	毛巾		máojīn	*n*	towel
12.	牙膏	牙膏	yágāo	*n*	toothpaste
13.	日用品		rìyòngpǐn	*n*	daily necessities
14.	保证	保證	bǎozhèng	*n, v*	guarantee, warranty; to guarantee; to warrant
15.	百货公司	百貨公司	bǎihuò gōngsī	*n*	department store
16.	其实	其實	qíshí	*adv*	as a matter of fact, actually
17.	不管……都		bùguǎn……dōu	*prep*	no matter . . .all, regardless of . . . all
18.	条件	條件	tiáojiàn	*n*	policy, conditions
19.	须知	須知	xūzhī	*n*	notice
20.	售		shòu	*v*	to sell
21.	换	換	huàn	*v*	to exchange
22.	出示		chūshì	*v*	to show
23.	包装	包裝	bāozhuāng	*n*	packaging
24.	损坏	損壞	sǔnhuài	*n, v*	damage; to damage
	坏	壞	huài	*adj*	broken

Simplified	Traditional	Pinyin	Word Category	Definition
25. 付款		fù kuǎn	*vo*	to pay money
26. 牌子		páizi	*n*	brand
27. 部分		bùfen	*n*	part
28. 所有		suǒyǒu	*adj*	all
29. 顾客	顧客	gùkè	*n*	customer

ONLINE RESOURCES

Visit *http://college.betterchinese.com* for more vocabulary on different types of daily necessities.

Idiomatic Expression

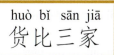

huò bǐ sān jiā
货比三家

货比三家 means "to compare the price of an item at three different stores." It is also often used in a longer expression: 货比三家不吃亏 (chīkuī: to take a loss), which means it does not hurt to shop around in order to make a decision you will not regret. It describes a situation where people compare a certain item in various stores before purchasing the one that best meets their needs and expectations.

Example:
如果想要省钱，买东西前最好去不同的商店看一下，货比三家不吃亏嘛！
If you want to save money, you should shop around before making a purchase in order to get the best one!

Reading a Return Policy

Returns can be tricky, as Mali and Zhou Xin discovered in this chapter. Many smaller stores and markets in China do not allow customers to return or exchange a purchase.

Here is what a typical return policy might look like:

退货须知：

商品售后七天之内保证无条件退货。
如有质量或配件问题，十四天内退换，半年保修。

退货时商品和包装不能有损坏或拆封。
特价商品不得退换。退货时必须出示收据。

The following terms are commonly used in return and exchange policies:

Chinese	Pinyin	Meaning
Time-related Terms		
无条件	wú tiáojiàn	unconditional; without exceptions
之内	zhīnèi	within
超过	chāoguò	to exceed
售后	shòuhòu	after purchase
Verbs		
拆封	chāifēng	to remove the seal; to open
保证	bǎozhèng	guarantee, warranty
保修	bǎoxiū	a guarantee to keep something in working condition
退货	tuìhuò	to return merchandise/goods
出示	chūshì	to show
换	huàn	to exchange

Chinese	Pinyin	Meaning
Other terms associated with returns and exchanges:		
不得	bùdé	must not; may not; not be allowed
必须	bìxū	must
配件	pèijiàn	accessory; attachment; component
收据	shōujù	receipt
保证	bǎozhèng	guarantee; to guarantee
商品	shāngpǐn	commodity, goods
损坏	sǔnhuài	damage; to damage
包装	bāozhuāng	packaging
退货须知	tuìhuò xūzhī	return notice

STRUCTURE NOTE 4.5

Use 得了/不了 to express ability or inability to complete certain actions

In compounds containing resultative complements, such as 找到, 得 and 不 may be inserted between the verb and the complement to indicate that the result can or cannot be achieved. For example, 找得到 means "can find," and 找不到 means "cannot find." The resultative complement 了 (liǎo) is used only in these 得/不 phrases and can appear following many verbs, including 用, 做, 办, and 受. In these contexts, Verb + 得了 means to be able to successfully complete that action, and Verb + 不了 means unable to do so.

For 得/不 resultative compounds, to ask a question about whether the subject is able to successfully complete this action, 吗 may be added to the end of the sentence as usual, or a special affirmative-negative pattern may be used: Verb-得-Result + Verb-不-Result, as in, "用得了用不了?"

Verb + 得/不 + 了 (+ Object)

From the Lesson Text:　这台电暖器才用了两次就用不了了。
Zhè tái diànnuǎnqì cái yòngle liǎng cì jiù yòngbuliǎo le.
I only used this heater twice and it's broken now.

Other examples:

他太忙了，去不了你的生日派对。
Tā tài máng le, qùbuliǎo nǐ de shēngrì pàiduì.
He is too busy, so he can't go to your birthday party.

这么多的菜，你吃得了吗?
Zhème duō de cài, nǐ chīdeliǎo ma?
There is so much food, can you really eat it all?

Practice: Answer the following questions using 得了 or 不了 and the words provided.

Example:　这些作业你能做吗?（太难了）
→这些作业太难了，我做不了。

1.　这些工作你能做吗?（很简单）
_____

2.　你现在要走回家吗?（外面下雨）
_____

3.　你明天会去图书馆吗?（太忙了）
_____

4.　这个菜你能吃吗?（太辣了）
_____

5.　这台电脑能用吗?（坏了）
_____

语法

STRUCTURE NOTES

STRUCTURE NOTE 4.6
Use 像…这 / 那样的… to describe categories using comparisons

像+A+这 / 那样的+B expresses the meaning, "Bs that are similar to A," or "those kind of Bs that are like A." As in the Lesson Text, A can be a list of items, or just a single item.

像 + Noun Phrase + 这 / 那样的 + Noun Phrase

From the Lesson Text:
我认为像毛巾和牙膏这样的日用品，在小商店买会比较划算。

Wǒ rènwéi xiàng máojīn hé yágāo zhèyàng de rìyòngpǐn, zài xiǎo shāngdiàn mǎi huì bǐjiao huásuàn.

I think that it's a better deal to buy daily necessities like towels and toothpaste at smaller stores.

Other examples:
我很喜欢像她那样活泼开朗的人。

Wǒ hěn xǐhuan xiàng tā nàyàng huópo kāilǎng de rén.

I like people who are lively and cheerful like she is.

生病的时候可以做像跑步、打球这样的运动吗？

Shēngbìng de shíhou kéyǐ zuò xiàng pǎobù, dǎqiú zhèyàng de yùndòng ma?

When you are sick, can you do sports activities like running or playing ball?

Practice: Change the following sentences into Chinese by applying the 像……这样的 structure and using the information provided below.

Example: I think home appliances like air-conditioning and washing machines should be provided with the apartments people rent.

→ 我认为出租的公寓应该有像空调、洗衣机这样的家电。

1. I like to go to the student store to buy some things like pens, notebooks, and so on.

   _____

2. I like traditional festivals like the Spring Festival.

   _____

3. He likes to visit places like hutongs.

   _____

4. She thinks that having more good food such as green vegetables is very healthy.

   _____

5. I like to take pictures in places like gardens.

   _____

STRUCTURE NOTE 4.7
Use 其实 *to say "actually"*

其实 *(qíshí) is similar to "actually," and introduces information that is contrary to what was said before.* 其实 *is also used by some Chinese speakers as a pause-filler an expression commonly used in conversation when the speaker cannot think of what to say, much like speakers use "actually" in English.*

其实 + Sentences

From the Lesson Text:

其实不管买什么东西，我都应该先看退货条件。
Qíshí bùguǎn mǎi shénme dōngxi, wǒ dōu yīnggāi xiān kàn tuìhuò tiáojiàn.
Actually, no matter what I buy, I should be sure to first take a look at the return policy.

Other Examples:

很多人觉得中文比较难学，其实多练习就能学好。
Hěn duō rén jué de Zhōngwén bǐjiao nán xué, qíshí duō liànxí jiù néng xué hǎo.
A lot of people think Chinese is hard to learn, but actually you learn Chinese well by practicing.

别看他很年轻，其实他已经有很多年的工作经验。
Bié kàn tā hěn niánqīng, qíshí tā yǐjīng yǒu hěnduō nián de gōngzuò jīngyàn.
He may look very young, but he actually has many years of work experience.

Practice: Change the following sentences by using 其实.

Example: 这家餐厅看起来很贵……（不贵…好吃）
→其实这家餐厅不贵，而且菜很好吃。

1.   这个公寓看上去附近环境不错……（很不安全）

   _____

2.   住在学校宿舍听起来很方便……（一点隐私都没有）

   _____

3.   很多人认为小商店的东西一定会比大商场的便宜……（不一定）

   _____

STRUCTURE NOTE 4.8
Use 不管…都/还… *to express that something does not matter*

In the sentence pattern "It doesn't matter whether he wants to go or not, I will still go," there are two key parts: the condition that doesn't matter, and the result that will still take place. To express this in Chinese, use 不管 *(bùguǎn) to introduce the condition clause, and place* 都 *or* 还 *following the subject in the result clause to indicate "still." The condition clause is generally phrased as a question, either using the affirmative-negative pattern or a question word like* 什么. *In English, the word "if" can be used instead of "whether," as in "it doesn't matter if you believe me or not." In Chinese, however,* 如果, 要是, *and other "if" words are never used in this way — never say "*不管 如果*."*

> 不管 + Condition Clause + , + Subject + 都/还 + Verb Phrase

From the Lesson Text: 其实不管买什么东西，我都应该先看退货条件。
Qíshí bùguǎn mǎi shénme dōngxi, wǒ dōu yīnggāi xiān kàn tuì huò tiáojiàn.
Actually, no matter what I buy, I should be sure to take a look at the return policy.

Other Examples:
不管什么时候，他对人都非常客气。
Bùguǎn shénme shíhou, tā duì rén dōu fēicháng kèqi.
No matter what the occasion, he is always extremely polite.

不管她去哪里旅游，她都会给朋友们寄明信片。
Bùguǎn tā qù nǎlǐ lǚyóu, tā dōu huì gěi péngyoumen jì míngxìnpiàn.
No matter where she is traveling, she always sends postcards to her friends.

Practice: Rewrite the following sentences using 不管…都….

Example: 约会很多次/我会紧张
→ 不管约会多少次，我都会紧张。

1. 她穿什么/很漂亮

_____

2. 去那家饭馆多少次/我觉得很好吃

_____

3. 什么时候/我不爱出去逛街

_____

4. 饿的时候，酸的、甜的、苦的、辣的/我能吃

_____

5. 从一月到十二月/我在旅行

_____

练习 4.10: 课文理解

Paired Activity: Discuss the following questions based on the Lesson Text. Be prepared to share your thoughts with the class.

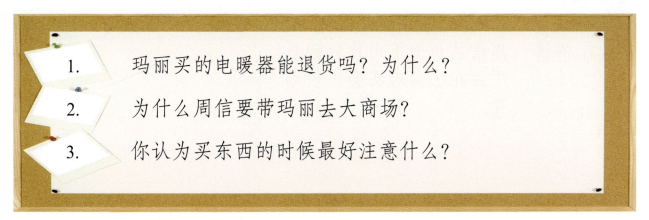

1. 玛丽买的电暖器能退货吗？为什么？

2. 为什么周信要带玛丽去大商场？

3. 你认为买东西的时候最好注意什么？

练习 4.11 (上): 退货须知

Individual Activity: Learning from Mali and Zhou Xin's experiences in this lesson, make sure you understand a store's return policy before making a purchase. Look at the signs below illustrating the return policy and describe each condition next to its respective sign.

Example: 退换时必须出示收据

练习 **4.12** (下): 大商场还是小商店

Paired Activity: Think about Mali and Zhou Xin's experience shopping and making returns in this lesson. Compare the shopping experience between the two stores.

	小商店	大商场
Example: 价格	周信认为像毛巾这样的日用品在小商店买会比较划算。	

练习 **4.13**: 讨论退货条件

Paired Activity: Most of us have experienced problems in returning items to a store. Think of three questions to ask your classmate and take turns answering them.

	Questions	Answers
Example:	你买了什么？	我买了一台电脑。
1.		
2.		
3.		

练习 **4.14**: 比较各店的退货条件

Group Activity: Have each group member choose a store with an online shopping website. Choose a product, then research and compare the prices and return policies among the different websites.

	Radical	Stroke Order
台	厶 sī self	厶 厶 台 台 台
退	辶 chuò walk	コ ヨ ヨ 艮 艮 艮 艮 退 退
据	扌(手) shǒu hand	一 扌 扌 扌 护 护 护 据 据 据
抱	扌(手) shǒu hand	一 扌 扌 扌 扚 扚 扚 抱
楚	木 mù wood	一 十 才 木 术 杧 林 林 林 梺 梺 梺 楚
牙	牙 yá teeth	一 二 于 牙
证	讠(言) yán speech	丶 讠 讠 订 证 证 证
其	八 bā eight	一 十 廿 廿 甘 其 其 其
须	彡 shān hair	丿 彡 彡 彡 彡 须 须 须
售	口 kǒu mouth	丿 亻 亻 亻 佇 佇 佳 佳 售 售
换	扌(手) shǒu hand	一 扌 扌 扌 护 护 换 换 换
示	一 yī one	一 二 于 示 示
损	扌(手) shǒu hand	一 扌 扌 扌 护 护 损 损 损
坏	土 tǔ earth	一 十 土 圤 坏 坏
付	亻(人) rén person	丿 亻 亻 付 付

Online chat: Working with a classmate, discuss your preferences regarding shopping at a small shop and a large store. Provide reasons to support your preferences.

练习 4.17: 阅读理解

玛丽上星期四在大商场买的暖气机又坏了。这已经是第二台了，这让玛丽很生气，想去退货。玛丽记得退货须知上写着退换时必须出示收据，但是她找不到收据。玛丽只好带着电暖器去商场问能不能退货。店员告诉玛丽，要是退货的话必须有收据，但是因为电暖器还在保修期之内，商场可以负责免费保修。玛丽听了很高兴，还好买之前货比三家，挑了这家服务有保证的商店。

Read the passage and answer the following questions.
1. Why is Mali unable to return the heater?
2. What suggestion does the salesclerk offer Mali?
3. Mali has been asked to take a customer survey. Write a few comments about her experience.

练习 4.18: 阅读理解

产品召回通知

因产品质量问题，我公司需要召回美心牌暖气机。请购买了美心电暖器的商店在10月31日前把电暖器退回公司，并且办理退货手续。如果商店已经把产品售出，我们会免费为顾客办理保修或者退货。非常抱歉！

地址：北京市武术街33号
电话：010-64248---

美心公司

10月20日

Notes:
召回 (zhàohuí): *v.* to recall
售出 (shòuchū): *v.* to dispense
办理 (bànlǐ): *v.* to handle
手续 (shǒuxù): *n.* procedure

Read the notice and answer the following questions.
1. What are the stores, selling Meixin heaters, supposed to do with the product?
2. If the stores have already sold the heaters to customers, what compensation will the customers receive?
3. Your company has discovered a defective merchandise. Write a notice to Mali on how to return her heater.

Time-Honored Chinese Brands

In Chinese, brands that have withstood the test of time are those that were established before 1956 and offer products that are unique. These bands are awarded the distinguished title of 老字号 (Lǎo Zìhào: Time-Honored Brand) by China's Ministry of Commerce. Three such time-tested brands, ranging from over 300 to about 70 years old, include Tongrentang (同仁堂: Tóngréntáng), a traditional Chinese medicine company, Quanjude (全聚德: Quánjùdé), a Peking Duck restaurant, and White Rabbit Creamy Candy (大白兔奶糖: Dàbáitù Nǎitáng), a brand of sweets.

Tongrentang

First established in 1669 by a senior physician to the Qing court, Tongrentang is known for its high-quality traditional Chinese herbal medicines. The company became the only supplier to the Qing imperial court in 1723, and remained so until the end of the Qing Dynasty in 1911. Tongrentang's original mission was to share with the public prescriptions and medicines that were previously only available to the imperial court.

Now in business for over 300 years and with 800 branches around the world, Tongrentang has become an institution for Chinese communities. The original shop in Beijing, still located in the same spot near the Forbidden City, is even featured in many tourist itineraries. There, visitors can be seen by a doctor and purchase prescriptions to improve their health.

Quanjude

In China, Quanjude is a name synonymous with Peking Duck. The restaurant chain was first founded in 1864. Roast duck was a delicacy mostly enjoyed by the imperial court and the aristocracy, and Quanjude's recipe was developed from a chef who had worked at the Forbidden City. In particular, the restaurant's trademark technique of roasting duck with wood from fruit trees to impart a subtle fruit flavor was first reserved primarily for the imperial family.

The dish was originally meant for the emperors but quickly became popular amongst the public. Even as other restaurants developed their own recipes, Quanjude's has remained the gold standard. The company has now established branches around China and overseas, and the restaurants have become a standard destination for tourists and residents alike. The original branch in Beijing has a counter to show how many roast ducks have been served over the years. When customers finished their meals, they receive a ticket to indicate the number of the duck they have eaten. So far, over 2 million roast ducks and counting have been served.

White Rabbit Creamy Candy

Beloved by generations of Chinese children, White Rabbit Creamy Candy was first created in 1943 in Shanghai. Made of cream, this sticky confectionary (with a texture that is similar to a nougat) is unusual in that it includes a thin translucent edible wrapping made of sticky rice. The wrapping is eaten with the candy instead of removed. Because of its milky taste, the candy was seen as nutritious, and the company claimed that "seven White Rabbit candies are equal to one glass of milk."

In the past, many Chinese could not afford milk, so White Rabbit candies were often given and received as gifts, especially during Chinese New Year and weddings, displaying the host's wealth and generosity. In fact, when US President Richard Nixon went to China in a historic 1972 visit, then-Premier Zhou Enlai presented him with a gift of White Rabbit candies. Today, White Rabbit candies can be found around the world, with many other flavors beyond the iconic milky original.

Pinyin	English
Sūn Mǎlì: Bùhǎoyìsi, zhè tái diànnuǎnqì cái yòngle liǎng cì jiù yòngbuliǎo le, néng tuìhuò ma?	Excuse me. I only used this heater twice and it's broken now. Can I be return it?
Diànyuán: Nǐ shì shénme shíhou mǎi de? Yǒu shōujù ma?	When did you buy it? Do you have a receipt?
Sūn Mǎlì: Wǒ shì liǎng ge xīngqī qián mǎi de, zhè shì shōujù.	I bought it two weeks ago. Here is the receipt.
Diànyuán: Zhēn de hěn bàoqiàn, shāngpǐn zhǐ néng zài yì zhōu zhīnèi tuìhuò.	I'm very sorry, but we only accept returns for items purchased within one week.
Sūn Mǎlì: Shénme? Kěshì mài de shíhou nǐ méiyǒu gàosu wǒ a.	What? But you didn't tell me that when you were selling it.
Diànyuán: Nǐ kàn shōujùshang xiě de hěn qīngchu, bùhǎoyìsi.	If you look on the receipt, it clearly states this. I'm sorry.
Zhōu Xìn: Nàme quèshí shì méi bànfǎ tuì le. Mǎlì, bié bù kāixīn. Wǒ dài nǐ qù dà shāngchǎng mǎi yì tái xīn de.	Then we definitely can't return it now. Mali, don't be upset. I'll take you to a large store to buy a new one.
Sūn Mǎlì: Kěshì dà shāngchǎng huì bǐ xiǎo shāngdiàn de jiàqián guì ba?	But the items sold at large stores are more expensive than in small stores, aren't they?
Zhōu Xìn: Wǒ rènwéi xiàng máojīn hé yágāo zhèyàng de rìyòngpǐn zài xiǎo shāngdiàn mǎi huì bǐjiao huásuàn, dànshì mǎi diànqì háishì zài dà shāngchǎng gèng yǒu bǎozhèng. Wǒ jiā fùjìn nà jiā bǎihuò gōngsī jiù tǐng búcuò de, hái néng zài yí ge yuè zhīnèi tuìhuò.	I think that it's a better deal to buy daily necessities like towels and toothpaste at smaller stores. However, it's safer to buy electronics at a larger store. There is a pretty good department store near my home that also has a one month return policy.

Sūn Mǎlì:	Hǎo ba, wǒmen qù kànkan. Qíshí bùguǎn mǎi shénme dōngxi, wǒ dōu yīnggāi xiān kàn tuìhuò tiáojiàn.	Okay, let's go check it out. Actually, no matter what I buy, I should be sure to first take a look at the return policy.
Zhōu Xìn:	Nǐ xiān kànkan tuìhuò xūzhī, yǒu bù dǒng de dìfang jiù wèn wǒ ba.	Take a look at the return policy. If there is anything you don't understand, feel free to ask me.

Tuìhuò xūzhī

Yī, Shāngpǐn kěyǐ zài shòuhòu sānshí tiān zhīnèi tuìhuàn.

Èr, Tuìhuàn shí bìxū chūshì shōujù.

Sān, Shāngpǐn hé bāozhuāng bù néng yǒu sǔnhuài.

Return Policy:

1) Store goods can be exchanged within 30 days from the date of purchase.

2) Receipts must be presented when making a return.

3) Merchandise and packaging must not be damaged.

What Can You Do?

INTERPRETIVE
- I can list what types of items a store carries after visiting it.
- I can identify a store's return policy after reviewing it.

INTERPERSONAL
- I can exchange information on how to make a return at a store.
- I can discuss the differences between a small privately-owned store and a large chain store.

PRESENTATIONAL
- I can convey regret and apologies when having to exchange an item.
- I can summarize a store's return policy and its conditions for return.

ACT IT OUT

Working in groups, compose an original two-minute skit that utilizes the vocabulary and structures introduced in Unit 4. Each of you should assume a role and have a roughly equal number of lines in the skit. Be prepared to perform your skit in class. You can either come up with your own story or choose from one of the following situations:

A) You and your siblings are buying a birthday gift online for your mom. Discuss the benefits of purchasing from different websites and decide which site you are going to buy the gift.

B) At the department store, you and your classmate want to return a shirt he/she recently purchased. Discuss the return policies with the store clerk and if your classmate is able to make the return.

C) While you were at the department store yesterday, your cousin had a bad shopping experience. She calls customer service the next day to complain about the bad service she received.

CHECK WHAT YOU CAN DO

RECOGNIZE

Adjectives
- ☐ 划算
- ☐ 洋
- ☐ 清楚
- ☐ 所有

Adverbs
- ☐ 一向
- ☐ 其实

Conjunction
- ☐ 并且

Measure Word
- ☐ 台

Nouns
- ☐ 美食
- ☐ 博客
- ☐ 饮食文化
- ☐ 数码相机
- ☐ 价格
- ☐ 投诉
- ☐ 款
- ☐ 网站
- ☐ 名牌
- ☐ 产品
- ☐ 保修期
- ☐ 优惠券
- ☐ 样子
- ☐ 大熊猫
- ☐ 原价
- ☐ 税
- ☐ 质量
- ☐ 电暖器
- ☐ 收据
- ☐ 商品
- ☐ 商场
- ☐ 毛巾
- ☐ 牙膏
- ☐ 日用品
- ☐ 百货公司
- ☐ 条件
- ☐ 须知
- ☐ 包装
- ☐ 牌子
- ☐ 部分
- ☐ 顾客
- ☐ 保证
- ☐ 损坏
- ☐ 购物

Prepositions
- ☐ 既…又…
- ☐ 不管……都

Verbs
- ☐ 分享
- ☐ 不如
- ☐ 打折
- ☐ 提醒
- ☐ 用不了
- ☐ 抱歉
- ☐ 认为
- ☐ 售
- ☐ 换
- ☐ 出示

Verb-Object Compound
- ☐ 免费
- ☐ 送货
- ☐ 退货
- ☐ 付款
- ☐ 摄影

WRITE

- ☐ 享
- ☐ 饮
- ☐ 数
- ☐ 码
- ☐ 相
- ☐ 并
- ☐ 折
- ☐ 投
- ☐ 款
- ☐ 站
- ☐ 免
- ☐ 货
- ☐ 牌
- ☐ 产
- ☐ 既
- ☐ 台
- ☐ 退
- ☐ 据
- ☐ 抱
- ☐ 楚
- ☐ 牙
- ☐ 证
- ☐ 其
- ☐ 须
- ☐ 售
- ☐ 换
- ☐ 示
- ☐ 损
- ☐ 坏
- ☐ 付

USE

- ☐ Use A 不如 B to indicate A is not as good as B.
- ☐ Use 并且 to mean "also" to connect words or clauses in formal contexts.
- ☐ Use 既 A 又 B as a formal way to express "both A and B."
- ☐ Use 最……不过了 to emphasize superlatives.
- ☐ Use 得了 / 不了 to express ability or inability to complete certain actions.
- ☐ Use 像…这 / 那样的… to describe categories using comparisons.
- ☐ Use 其实 to say "actually."
- ☐ Use 不管…都 / 还… to express that something does not matter.

娱

Hobbies

第五单元
UNIT 5

Communication Goals

Lesson 1: 篮球比赛 **At a Basketball Game**
- Talk about a recent athletic event.
- Express opinions about athletes, sports stars, and their teams.
- Discuss the results of a sporting event.

Lesson 2: 采访 **An Interview**
- Talk about a musical competition.
- Discuss musical performances that include traditional Chinese instruments.
- Express inspirations and aspirations for giving a musical performance.
- Express gratitude for encouragement received.

篮球比赛
At A Basketball Game

你们觉得这场比赛哪个队会赢？山猫还是飞鱼？

当然是山猫！山猫队球员的都像山猫一样厉害，跑得快、跳得高，一定能赢！

可是你别忘了飞鱼队除了队长的实力非常强以外，另外还有两个球员是篮球明星。这次飞鱼赢定了！

祥安，小心飞鱼会被山猫吃掉喔！

小美，想不到你这么迷山猫队（shān māo）。比赛要开始了，我们看球吧。

山猫对（duì）飞鱼最后的比分（bǐ fēn）是99比（bǐ）101。

山猫　飞鱼
99　4　101

哈哈，小美，没想到飞鱼（fēi yú）比山猫（shān māo）厉害吧！

这场比赛一点儿也不公平（gōng píng）！有几次飞鱼犯规（fēi yú fàn guī）了，可是裁判（cái pàn）都没有吹哨（chuī shào）！

山猫队（shān māo）不过（bú guò）输了两分而已（ér yǐ）。与其（yǔ qí）说裁判（cái pàn）不公平（gōng píng），倒不如（dào bù rú）说山猫（shān māo）的运气（yùn qi）不好！

依（yī）我看，打篮球重视的就是团队精神（tuán duì jīng shén）。这次飞鱼（fēi yú）队配合（pèi hé）得比山猫（shān māo）队好。不过赛季（sài jì）才刚开始，谁是最后（zuì hòu）的冠军（guàn jūn）还说不定呢！

LESSON TEXT 5.1

At A Basketball Game 篮球比赛

Basketball season is here! Xiang'an, Dadong, and Xiaomei are watching the basketball game between the Mountain Lions and the Flying Fish.

陈大东：　你们觉得这场比赛哪个队会赢？山猫还是飞鱼？

王小美：　当然是山猫！山猫队的球员都像山猫一样厉害，跑得快、跳得高，一定能赢！

黄祥安：　可是你别忘了飞鱼队除了队长的实力非常强以外，另外还有两个球员是篮球明星。这次飞鱼赢定了！

王小美：　祥安，小心飞鱼会被山猫吃掉喔！

陈大东：　小美，想不到你这么迷山猫队。比赛要开始了，我们看球吧。

山猫对飞鱼最后的比分是99比101。

黄祥安：　哈哈！小美，没想到飞鱼比山猫厉害吧！

王小美：　这场比赛一点儿也不公平！有几次飞鱼犯规了，可是裁判都没有吹哨！

黄祥安：　山猫队不过输了两分而已。与其说裁判不公平，倒不如说山猫的运气不好！

陈大东：　依我看，打篮球重视的就是团队精神。这次飞鱼队配合得比山猫队好。不过赛季才刚开始，谁是最后的冠军还说不定呢！

Language Tips

像……一样(xiàng……yíyàng)

In the Lesson Text, Xiaomei uses "像……一样" to describe that the players are like mountain lions. 像 can be used to replace 跟 in the pattern A 跟 B 一样 (adj.) with the same meaning as "A is as Adj. as B" or "A is like B."

Example:

他跳得像山猫一样高。
He jumps as high as a mountain lion.

赢定 (yíng dìng)

In the debate between Xiaomei and Xiang'an about which basketball team would win, Xiang'an uses "这次飞鱼赢定了!" to express his confidence that the Flying Fish would be the winner. The word 定 literally means "certainly, definitely." Thus, 赢定 means "someone or something will definitely win." On the contrary, 输定 indicates that "someone or something will definitely lose."

Example:

他很有实力，这次武术比赛赢定了！
He is very strong, and he will definitely win this martial arts match.

字 词 VOCABULARY

LESSON VOCABULARY 5.1

	SIMPLIFIED	TRADITIONAL	PINYIN	WORD CATEGORY	DEFINITION
1.	场	場	chǎng	mw, n	(used for recreational or sports activities); field
2.	队	隊	duì	n	team
3.	赢	贏	yíng	v	to win
4.	球员	球員	qiúyuán	n	ball-team member
5.	厉害	屬害	lìhai	adj	fierce
6.	队长	隊長	duìzhǎng	n	captain
7.	实力	實力	shílì	n	strength
8.	强	強	qiáng	adj	powerful
9.	另外		lìngwài	adv, adj	in addition; other
10.	篮球明星	籃球明星	lánqiú míngxīng	n	basketball star
	篮球	籃球	lánqiú	n	basketball
	明星		míngxīng	n	star
11.	吃掉		chīdiào	rv	to eat up
12.	对	對	duì	v	versus
13.	比分		bǐfēn	n	score
	比		bǐ	n	ratio
14.	公平		gōngpíng	adj	fair
15.	犯规	犯規	fànguī	vo	to foul, to break the rules
16.	裁判		cáipàn	n	referee
17.	吹哨		chuīshào	vo	to blow a whistle
	吹		chuī	v	to blow
	哨		shào	n	whistle
18.	不过……而已	不過……而已	búguò……éryǐ	cj	only, merely, nothing more than
19.	输	輸	shū	v	to lose
20.	与其…倒不如	與其…倒不如	yǔqí……dàoburú	cj	rather than . . . it would be better to

SIMPLIFIED	TRADITIONAL	PINYIN	WORD CATEGORY	DEFINITION
21. 运气	運氣	yùnqi	*n*	fortune, luck
22. 依		yī	*prep*	according to
23. 团队精神	團隊精神	tuánduì jīngshén	*n*	team spirit
团队	團隊	tuánduì	*n*	team, group
精神		jīngshén	*n*	spirit
24. 配合		pèihé	*v*	to coordinate, to cooperate
25. 赛季	賽季	sàijì	*n*	sports competition season
26. 最后	最後	zuìhòu	*adj, adv*	final, last; finally, lastly
27. 冠军	冠軍	guànjūn	*n*	champion

PROPER NOUN

SIMPLIFIED	TRADITIONAL	PINYIN	WORD CATEGORY	DEFINITION
28. 山猫	山貓	Shānmāo	*n*	Mountain Lion
29. 飞鱼	飛魚	Fēiyú	*n*	Flying Fish

REQUIRED VOCABULARY 5.1

SIMPLIFIED	TRADITIONAL	PINYIN	WORD CATEGORY	DEFINITION
30. 教练	教練	jiàoliàn	*n*	coach

Idiomatic Expression

fǎn bài wéi shèng
反败为胜

反败为胜 means "to turn the defeat into a victory."

This expression appears in the *Romance of the Three Kingdoms* (《三国演义》: *Sānguó Yǎnyì*). In the novel, warring states vie to gain control of China and one of the general leads his soldiers to turn a losing battle into victory. This expression is often used to describe a situation where one gains an advantage after being at a disadvantage.

Example:

他的努力让他最终反败为胜，赢得比赛。
His hard work eventually paid off; he turned the tide and won the match.

Terms Related to Sports

In *Modern Chinese* Textbook Vol. 1B, Unit 10, Lesson 2, Language Notes, specific activities that were paired with the verb 打 were introduced. Here, certain verbs are paired with specific words to describe actions that are common in sports. Take note of words with the radical 扌 (shǒu) for verbs involving the hand, 足 for verbs involving the foot or leg, 氵 (shuǐ) for verbs involving water activities, and 马 as a verb for riding actions.

Chinese	Pinyin	English	Chinese	Pinyin	English
Verbs with the 足 radical:					
跑	pǎo	to run	跑步	pǎobù	to run
			短跑	duǎnpǎo	to sprint
跳	tiào	to jump	跳高	tiàogāo	to high jump
			跳远	tiàoyuǎn	to long jump
			跳水	tiàoshuǐ	to dive
			跳绳	tiàoshéng	to jump rope, to skip rope
			跳舞	tiàowǔ	to dance
踢	tī	to kick	踢球	tīqiú	to kick the ball
			踢足球	tī zúqiú	to kick a soccer ball; to play soccer
			踢毽子	tī jiànzi	to kick a hacky sack, to kick a shuttlecock
Verbs with the 扌 radical:					
打	dǎ	to play/hit	打球	dǎqiú	to hit a ball
			打篮球	dǎ lánqiú	to play basketball
			打棒球	dǎ bàngqiú	to play baseball
			打乒乓球	dǎ pīngpāng qiú	to play ping pong
			打网球	dǎ wǎngqiú	to play tennis
			打羽毛球	dǎ yǔmáoqiú	to play badminton
			打橄榄球	dǎ gǎnlǎnqiú	to play rugby; to play American football
			打太极拳	dǎ tàijíquán	to do Tai Chi
拍	pāi	to beat/bounce	拍手	pāishǒu	to clap
			拍球	pāiqiú	to bounce a ball, to dribble
投	tóu	to put in	投篮	tóulán	to shoot a basket
			投球	tóuqiú	to throw a ball
接	jiē	to catch	接球	jiēqiú	to catch a ball
			接力赛	jiēlìsài	relay race
Verbs with the 氵 radical:					
游	yóu	to swim	游泳	yóuyǒng	to swim
滑	huá	to swim	滑雪	huáxuě	to ski
溜	liū	to slide	溜冰	liūbīng	to ice-skate
Verbs with the 马 radical:					
骑	qí	to ride	骑马	qímǎ	to ride a horse
			骑车	qíchē	to ride a bicycle

STRUCTURE NOTE 5.1
Use 另外 to talk about additional items

另外 (lìngwài), meaning "other" or "in addition," is combined with a numeral and a measure word to introduce additional items. Most often, 一 is used, as in 另外一个, "another one." 另外 can also be used without the numeral-classifier to introduce a sentence.

From the Lesson Text:

另外还有两个球员是篮球明星。
Lìngwài háiyǒu liǎng ge qiúyuán shì lánqiú míngxīng.
In addition, there are two players who are basketball stars.

Other examples:

这个公寓有电视和冰箱，另外还有空调和洗衣机。
Zhè ge gōngyù yǒu diànshì hé bīngxiāng, lìngwài háiyǒu kōngtiáo hé xǐyījī.
This house has a television and a refrigerator; in addition, it has an air conditioner and a washing machine.

对不起，我心里已经有另外一个人了。
Duìbuqǐ, wǒ xīnlǐ yǐjīng yǒu lìngwài yí ge rén le.
Sorry, my heart already belongs to another person.

Practice: Rewrite the following sentences using 另外.

Example: 我们今天买了一个比较好看的手机。
→ 我们今天买了另外一个比较好看的手机。

1.   他们昨天看了一场比较有意思的足球比赛。

   _____

2.   她准备明天去参加一个生日派对。

   _____

3.   他们去了一家中国饭馆吃饭。

   _____

4.   他们住在学校附近的一个公寓。

   _____

5.   除了手机之外，我还买了一些书。

   _____

STRUCTURE NOTE 5.2
Use (只)不过……而已 *to minimize the significance of something*

The phrase 不过 *(búguò) literally means, "not more than" or "nothing more than," and* 而已 *(éryǐ) means "that's all." These two phrases can be placed around a statement to emphasize that it is unimportant — "it's just like this, that's all." To make the sentence even more emphatic,* 只 *can be added before the pattern.*

Subject (+只) + 不过 + Verb Phrase + 而已

From the Lesson Text:

山猫队不过输了两分而已。
Shānmāo Duì búguò shūle liǎng fēn éryǐ.
The Mountain Lions lost by only two points.

Other examples:

周末我们没有做什么，只不过是出去看了一场电影而已。
Zhōumò wǒmen méiyǒu zuò shénme, zhǐbuguò shì chūqu kànle yì chǎng diànyǐng éryǐ.
We didn't do much this weekend; we only went out to see a movie.

你不要太担心输赢，这只不过是一个小游戏而已。
Nǐ búyào tài dānxīn shūyíng, zhè zhǐbuguò shì yíge xiǎo yóuxì éryǐ.
Don't worry too much about the result, it is nothing more than a little game.

Practice: Create complete sentences using 不过……而已 and the information provided.

Example: 感冒……
→ 我不过是感冒而已，吃一点儿药就好了。

1. 运气不好……

   _____

2. 太累……

   _____

3. 输了这次比赛……

   _____

4. 误会……

   _____

5. 公寓有点脏……

   _____

STRUCTURE NOTE 5.3

Use 与其…(倒)不如… *to indicate a preferred alternative*

The pattern 与其 *(yǔqí) A,* (倒)不如 *(dàoburú) B means "rather than A, it would be better to do B instead" or "it's not so much A as B." As in the Lesson Text example, this pattern is commonly used with* 说*, meaning "it would be more accurate to say A than B." Rather than* 到*, the character* 倒*, meaning "upside-down" or "reverse," is used in this pattern.*

> 与其 + Clause, (+ 倒) 不如 + Clause

> Subject + 与其 + Verb Phrase, (+ 倒) 不如 + Verb Phrase

From the Lesson Text:

与其说裁判不公平，倒不如说山猫的运气不好！
Yǔqí shuō cáipàn bù gōngpíng, dàoburú shuō Shānmāo de yùnqi bù hǎo!
Rather than say the referees weren't fair, let's just say the Mountain Lions were unlucky!

Other examples:

我们与其在家看电视，倒不如去公园散散步。
Wǒmen yǔqí zài jiā kàn diànshì, dàoburú qù gōngyuán sànsan bù.
Rather than watching television at home, it would be better to go to the park for a walk instead.

与其说考试太难，不如说你准备得不够好。
Yǔqí shuō kǎoshì tài nán, burú shuō nǐ zhǔnbèi de bú gòu hǎo.
Rather than saying the exam was too difficult, it would be more accurate to say you didn't prepare well enough.

Practice: Match the following sentences on this basis of the information given.

与其坐火车到那么远的地方，	不如散步过去。
与其花一个小时到商店看手机，	不如在附近逛逛。
与其每个月花钱租公寓，	不如在网上看好了。
与其写信给妹妹，	不如在网上跟她聊天。
我们与其开车去商店，	不如考虑买一套公寓吧。

STRUCTURE NOTE 5.4
Use 依……看 *to formally express someone's opinion*

The phrase 依 (someone) 看 *means "according to (someone's) view" or "in (someone's) opinion" and is a more formal variant of previously introduced expressions such as* 对 (someone) 来说. *Be sure not to confuse* 依 *with* 衣, *as in* 衣服.

依 + Someone + 看，Sentence

From the Lesson Text:　　依我看，打篮球重视的就是团队精神。
Yī wǒ kàn, dǎ lánqiú zhòngshì de jiù shì tuánduì jīngshen.
In my opinion, the most important aspect of playing basketball is the spirit of teamwork.

Other examples:　　依我看，我们还是去欧洲旅游吧。
Yī wǒ kàn, wǒmen háishì qù Ōuzhōu lǚyóu ba.
In my opinion, it would be better for us travel to Europe.

依她看，和中国朋友聊天是练习中文的好办法。
Yī tā kàn, hé Zhōngguó péngyou liáotiān shì liànxí Zhōngwén de hǎo bànfǎ.
In her opinion, chatting with Chinese friends is a good way to practice Chinese.

Practice: Respond the following questions/sentences by using 依我看 to express your point of view.

Example: 我想买一台电暖器，你觉得应该到哪里买？
→依我看，在大商店买电暖器比较有保证。

1. 你觉得住校内还是校外比较好？

   _____

2. 你觉得理想的生活是什么样的？

   _____

3. 这场球赛真不公平！

   _____

4. 这台电视又坏了！

   _____

5. 你认为在网上付款安全吗？

   _____

练习 5.1: 课文理解

Paired Activity: Discuss the following questions based on the Lesson Text. Be prepared to share your thoughts with the class.

1. 祥安觉得哪一队会赢？为什么？

2. 为什么山猫队会输呢？

3. 你觉得一场公平的比赛应该是怎么样的？

练习 5.2（上）: 看比赛

Individual Activity: Look at the images below and describe what is happening is each one. Use some of the words in the word bank below in your descriptions.

像……一样 厉害 跑 跳 实力 团队精神 配合 犯规

Example: 山猫队的球员都像山猫一样厉害，跑得快、跳得高。

练习 5.3（下）：球队比较

Paired Activity: Using the two profiles below, compare and contrast the two teams.

球员	灰熊队	大猫队
实力	防守非常强，但速度不够快	跑得快、跳得高，但防守一般
投篮命中率	40%	55%
犯规次数	三次	五次

Notes:

防守 (fángshǒu): *n.* defense   速度 (sùdù): *n.* speed   一般 (yìbān): *adj.* ordinary,

投篮命中率 (tóulán mìngzhònglǜ): *n.* shooting average (percentage)   次数 (cìshù): *n.* number of times

练习 5.4（上）：讨论运动

Paired Activity: Working with a classmate, discuss different sports. Think of three questions to ask your classmate about his/her preferences and then record the answers below.

Example: 你最喜欢什么运动？	我最喜欢的运动是……
1.	1.
2.	2.
3.	3.

练习 5.5（下）：计划去看运动比赛

Group Activity: You and your friends would like to attend a sporting event, anywhere in the world. Taking into account the group's preferences, determine what event you will attend. Research the event and plan an outing for the group.

	Radical	Stroke Order
队	阝 fù hill	了 阝 队 队
厉	厂 hǎn cliff	一 厂 厂 厉 厉
吹	口 kǒu mouth	丿 冂 口 口 吩 吹 吹
赢	贝 bèi shell	丶 一 亠 亠 言 言 言 言 亡 月 月 亮 亮 赢 赢 赢 赢 赢 赢
强	弓 gōng bow	丁 弓 弓 弘 弘 弘 弘 弘 弘 强 强
另	口 kǒu mouth	丨 口 口 号 另
犯	犭 quǎn dog	丿 犭 犭 犯 犯
规	见 jiàn see	一 二 主 夫 却 规 规
裁	衣 yī clothes	一 十 土 丰 丰 尹 戋 表 表 裁 裁 裁
输	车 chē cart	一 七 车 车 车 车 轮 轮 输 输 输 输
精	米 mǐ rice	丶 丷 丷 半 米 米 米 米 米 精 精 精 精
神	礻(示) shì show	丶 ㇇ 礻 礻 礻 和 和 神
赛	宀 mián roof	丶 宀 宀 宀 宀 审 审 寒 寒 寒 寒 赛 赛
冠	冖 mì cover	丶 冖 冖 宀 完 完 冠 冠
军	冖 mì cover	丶 冖 冖 军 军 军

练习 5.7: 线上聊天

Online chat: Working with a classmate, discuss what sports you participate in. If you do not participate in sports, describe what other activities you do instead.

练习 5.8: 阅读理解

9月20日

今天，我、中平和大东参加了学校举办的班级篮球赛。一开始我们配合得不好，上半场输了十分。下半场我们都打得很努力，但最后还是输了两分，没能反败为胜。比赛的时候，另外一队有两次犯规裁判都没有吹哨，我觉得裁判特别不公平。然后我想起上次比赛，当小美说裁判不公平的时候，我还说是因为山猫的运气不好。唉！大东说得对，比赛最重要的是团队精神，不是运气。与其说裁判不公平，倒不如说我们的团队精神不够好。希望我们下次比赛能配合得更好！

Read Xiang'an's blog and answer the following questions.
1. Why does Xiang'an think the team lost the game?
2. What does Dadong consider to be the most important aspect of a team?
3. Xiaomei reads Xiang'an's blog and decides to leave a comment. Write a comment describing what she thought about the game.

练习 5.9: 阅读理解

观赛须知

1. 篮球比赛地点：学校体育馆
   比赛时间：9月6日早上10点

2. 请在比赛开始前半个小时凭票入场

3. 入场前请配合安检

3. 比赛时请礼貌观赛

4. 比赛后请带走垃圾

Notes:
凭票 (píngpiào): vo. to use the ticket
安检 (ānjiǎn): n. security
观赛 (guānsài): v. to watch the competition
垃圾 (lājī): n. garbage

Read the notice and answer the following questions.
1. How early should you arrive and what should you do before entering the gymnasium?
2. What should you do after the game?
3. Create your rules for attending an event and include at least three rules.

Popular Sports

Sports are a popular pastime in China. Young people can often be seen playing soccer or basketball in neighborhood parks and on quiet streets. Two other sports that are very popular in China are table tennis and badminton.

Table Tennis (乒乓球: pīngpāngqiú)

Although table tennis was invented in England, it has come to be associated with China. Officially known as ping pong in China, the sport first became popular starting in the 1950s, when China entered the 1959 World Championships and won its first world title in Chinese sporting history.

Ping pong even changed Chinese politics and international relations. At the 1971 World Table Tennis Championships in Nagoya, Japan, the Chinese men's world champion invited an American player onto the Chinese team bus when the American player could not find his own bus. This act of kindness provided an opportunity to ease China-US relations. A few days later, the Chinese invited the American table tennis team for an all-expense paid visit to China. This "ping-pong diplomacy" eventually led to President Nixon's historic trip to China in 1972, thawing out an icy relationship between two formerly hostile countries.

Badminton (羽毛球: yǔmáoqiú)

Badminton was developed in British India and became a major sport in China. Over 100 million people play badminton around the country, and Chinese players often perform extremely well in international competitions. Part of the reason that badminton is so popular in China is because the sport can be played leisurely in open places and is also a highly competitive sport at the professional level.

Badminton, along with table tennis, soccer, and basketball, are televised regularly in China. The stars of this sport enjoy high profile status on and off the court. In China, people can often be seen informally practicing with friends out on the streets and in parks. There are an abundance of badminton courts in universities and local neighborhood parks.

Traditional Chinese Games

One popular pastime in China is playing traditional board games for both fun and mental stimulation. The following are two popular Chinese "mind sports" that anyone can enjoy.

Go (围棋: wéiqí)

Go originated around 2300 BC but has remained popular because of the complex thinking the game requires. Two players, each with his or her set of stones, alternately place stones on a 19 by 19 square grid. A player can remove an opponent's stones by completely surrounding them with his or her own stones. The goal is to have the most stones on the board when all of the squares are filled. While the rules are simple, there are countless strategies, so a game can take as short as 15 minutes or as long as a few days to finish.

Chinese Chess (象棋: xiàngqí)

Playing Chinese Chess is similar to playing Western-style chess, both of which are believed to be part of a family of similar games that originated in India. In these games, two players each begin with an army of pieces at opposite ends of a square board. Every piece has unique movement patterns and players capture enemy pieces by moving their own pieces into their opponents' spaces. The end goal of a player's "army" is to capture the opponent's general.

In recent years, traditional games have seen a resurgence in popularity among Chinese youth. Many children and teens flock to board game cafes, bars, and clubs in their otherwise busy lives. There are also many leagues worldwide (e.g., the China Xiangqi Association) that hold tournaments every year, as well as individual tournaments (e.g., the ING Cup) sponsored by various organizations. These games are not only played by the young; elderly players enjoying board games outdoors are a common sight in China.

Pinyin

Chén Dàdōng: Nǐmen juéde zhè chǎng bǐsài nǎge duì huì yíng? Shānmāo háishì Fēiyú?

Wáng Xiǎoměi: Dāngrán shì Shānmāo! Shānmāo Duì de qiúyuán dōu xiàng Shānmāo yíyàng lìhai, pǎo de kuài, tiào de gāo, yídìng néng yíng!

Huáng Xiáng'ān: Kěshì nǐ bié wàngle Fēiyú Duì chúle duìzhǎng de shílì fēicháng qiáng yǐwài, lìngwài hái yǒu liǎng ge qiúyuán shì lánqiú míngxīng. Zhè cì Fēiyú yíngdìng le!

Wáng Xiǎoměi: Xiáng'ān, xiǎoxīn Fēiyú huì bèi Shānmāo chīdiào ō!

Chén Dàdōng: Xiǎoměi, xiǎngbudào nǐ zhème mí Shānmāo Duì. Bǐsài yào kāishǐ le, wǒmen kànqiú ba.

Shānmāo duì Fēiyú zuìhòu bǐfēn shì 99 bǐ 101.

Huáng Xiáng'ān: Hāha! Xiǎoměi, méi xiǎngdao Fēiyú bǐ Shānmāo lìhai ba!

Wáng Xiǎoměi: Zhè chǎng bǐsài yìdiǎnr yě bù gōngpíng! Yǒu jǐ cì Fēiyú fànguīle, kěshì cáipàn dōu méiyǒu chuīshào!

English

Which team do you think will win this match? The Mountain Lions or the Flying Fish?

Of course it will be the Mountain Lions! The players are strong and quick, just like mountain lions. They will win for sure!

But don't forget that the Flying Fish have a strong team captain; in addition, there are two players who are basketball stars. I think the Flying Fish will win for sure!

Xiang'an, just be careful the Flying Fish don't get eaten alive by the Mountain Lions!

Xiaomei, I never thought you were such a fan of the Mountain Lions. All right, all right, the game is about to start. Let's go watch.

The final score between the Mountain Lions and the Flying Fish is 99-101.

Haha! Xiaomei, bet you never thought the Flying Fish were better than the Mountain Lions?

I don't think this game was fair at all! There were a few times when the Flying Fish committed fouls, but the referees didn't make the calls!

Huáng Xiáng'ān:	Shānmāo Duì búguò shūle liǎng fēn éryǐ. Yǔqí shuō cáipàn bù gōngpíng, dàoburú shuō Shānmāo de yùnqi bù hǎo!	The Mountain Lions lost by only two points. Rather than say the referees weren't fair, let's just say the Mountain Lions were unlucky!
Chén Dàdōng:	Yī wǒ kàn, dǎ lánqiú zhòngshì de jiùshì tuánduì jīngshén. Zhè cì Fēiyú Duì pèihé de bǐ Shānmāo Duì hǎo. Búguò sàijì cái gāng kāishǐ, shéi shì zuìhòu de guànjūn hái shuōbudìng ne!	In my opinion, the most important aspect of playing basketball is the spirit of teamwork. This time around, the Flying Fish displayed better teamwork than the Mountain Lions. However, it's still early in the season and it's hard to say who will be the champions in the end.

What Can You Do?

INTERPRETIVE
- I can identify vocabulary related to a sporting event while watching or listening to it.
- After watching it, I can recognize the results of a sports game after watching it.

INTERPERSONAL
- I can debate a team's performance at a sports event.
- I can discuss with someone else regarding his/her opinion about a sports game.

PRESENTATIONAL
- I can report a sports game and the event's results.
- I can present a description of a sports team's performance using similes.

采访
An Interview

xiào kān
校刊第81期：

wán měi jié hé
中西音乐 完美结合

yuè duì huò dé
上周，我校乐队获得了大
cái yì   jì zhě
学生才艺比赛的第一名。记者
cǎi fǎng   yuè duì
采访了乐队的队长孙玛丽，她
lái zì
是来自美国的留学生。

记　者：恭喜你们赢得冠军。你们的表演能受到评委和观众的喜爱，你认为你们成功的原因是什么？

孙玛丽：我想是因为我们用小提琴和古筝一起演奏，这种中西结合的音乐让观众们觉得很特别。

记　者：你们是怎么想到这样的表演形式呢？

孙玛丽：在美国的时候，我的好朋友小美带我去听过一场中国民乐演奏，里面的古筝演奏令我十分难忘。来中国以后，我交了几个玩民乐的朋友，所以就想试试一起演奏。

记　者：你们乐队以后有什么计划吗？

孙玛丽：希望我们能有机会去更多的地方表演，让更多人欣赏这种中西结合的音乐。

记　者：你现在最想感谢谁呢？

孙玛丽：我要感谢我的音乐伙伴们，是他们帮我实现了演奏中西音乐的理想。我也要谢谢我的好朋友小美，感谢她一直在音乐上支持我，希望我们以后能一起表演！

LESSON TEXT 5.2

An Interview 采访

After Mali and her band win the intercollegiate student talent competition, Mali is interviewed by a reporter from the school magazine.

校刊第81期：

中西音乐完美结合

上周，我校乐队获得了大学生才艺比赛的第一名。记者采访了乐队的队长孙玛丽，她是来自美国的留学生。

记者：　恭喜你们赢得冠军。你们的表演能受到评委和观众的喜爱，你认为你们成功的原因是什么？

孙玛丽：　我想是因为我们用小提琴和古筝一起演奏，这种中西结合的音乐让观众们觉得很特别。

记者：　你们是怎么想到这样的表演形式呢？

孙玛丽：　在美国的时候，我的好朋友小美带我去听过一场中国民乐演奏，里面的古筝演奏令我十分难忘。来中国以后，我交了几个玩民乐的朋友，所以就想试试一起演奏。

记者：　你们乐队以后有什么计划吗？

孙玛丽：　希望我们能有机会去更多的地方表演，让更多人欣赏这种中西结合的音乐。

记者：　你现在最想感谢谁呢？

孙玛丽：　我要感谢我的音乐伙伴们，是他们帮我实现了演奏中西音乐的理想。我也要谢谢我的好朋友小美，感谢她一直在音乐上支持我，希望我们以后能一起表演！

Language Tip

款 (kuǎn)

种 (zhǒng)

In the Lesson Text, 种 is used in "这种中西结合的音乐" as a measure word to point to a type of musical fusion between Chinese and Western instruments. 款 from the Lesson Text in *Modern Chinese* Textbook Vol. 2A, Unit 4, Lesson 1 is used as the measure word for a particular style of 相机. Both 款 and 种 can also be used as measure words for additional types of things. 款 is used for different styles of things, such as clothing, electronic equipment, cars, etc. 种 is used for different types of things, people, or animals.

Examples:

她在网上看到很多款在打折的大衣。
She saw many styles of coats on sale online.

他是工作非常努力的那种人。
He is the type of person who works very hard.

LESSON VOCABULARY 5.2

	SIMPLIFIED	TRADITIONAL	PINYIN	WORD CATEGORY	DEFINITION
1.	校刊		xiàokān	*n*	school magazine
2.	完美		wánměi	*adj*	perfect
3.	结合	結合	jiéhé	*n*	combination, fusion
4.	乐队	樂隊	yuèduì	*n*	band
5.	获得	獲得	huòdé	*v*	to gain, to achieve
	得		dé	*v*	to get
6.	才艺	才藝	cáiyì	*n*	talent and skill
7.	记者	記者	jìzhě	*n*	journalist, reporter
8.	采访	採訪	cǎifǎng	*v*	to cover, to interview
9.	来自	來自	láizì	*v*	come from
10.	评委	評委	píngwěi	*n*	judge, jury
	评	評	píng	*v*	to discuss, to judge
11.	观众	觀眾	guānzhòng	*n*	audience
12.	喜爱	喜愛	xǐ'ài	*n*	like, love
13.	原因		yuányīn	*n*	reason
14.	古筝	古筝	gǔzhēng	*n*	stringed plucked instrument similar to the zither
15.	演奏		yǎnzòu	*n, v*	musical performance; to give a musical performance
16.	种	種	zhǒng	*mw*	(used for style, kind, type, etc.)
17.	形式		xíngshì	*n*	form, shape, format
18.	民乐	民樂	mínyuè	*n*	folk instrumental music
19.	令		lìng	*v*	to make, to cause
20.	十分		shífēn	*adv*	very, fully, utterly
21.	难忘	難忘	nánwàng	*adj*	unforgettable, memorable
22.	欣赏	欣賞	xīnshǎng	*v*	to appreciate, to admire
23.	感谢	感謝	gǎnxiè	*v*	to thank, to be grateful
24.	伙伴		huǒbàn	*n*	partner, companion

LESSON VOCABULARY 5.2 (continued)

SIMPLIFIED	TRADITIONAL	PINYIN	WORD CATEGORY	DEFINITION
25. 实现	實現	shíxiàn	v	to realize, to achieve
26. 支持		zhīchí	v	to support

REQUIRED VOCABULARY 5.2

SIMPLIFIED	TRADITIONAL	PINYIN	WORD CATEGORY	DEFINITION
27. 梦想	夢想	mèngxiǎng	n	dream
梦	夢	mèng	n, v	dream; to dream
28. 放弃	放棄	fàngqì	v	to give up, to let go

Idiomatic Expression

duō cái duō yì
多才多艺

Both 才 and 艺 mean "talents," and 多才多艺 means "(to have) many capabilities and talents."

This expression appears in the *Book of Documents* (《尚书》: *Shàng Shū*), written at least 1,500 years ago. In the book, the king is very sick, and the prime minister writes a letter to the spirits of previously deceased kings, hoping they will take his life instead of the king. The prime minister offers his talents and ability to serve the ghosts and gods in place of the king, who is needed to take care of his people and kingdom. This expression is used to describe people with many talents and is usually a compliment.

Example:
这是一位非常多才多艺的音乐家。她不但会唱歌，还能演奏很多乐器。
This musician is very talented. Not only can she sing, but she can also play many musical instruments.

Playing Instruments

In English, the verb "play" can be used for any instrument. In Chinese, there are specific verbs for playing a particular musical instrument, similar to how sports have specific verbs.

The following are terms commonly used to describe playing a specific musical instrument:

Verb	Pinyin	Meaning	Used for	Instrument
吹	chuī	to blow	wind instruments	黑管 (hēiguǎn): clarinet 笛子 (dízi): flute 喇叭 (lǎba): trumpet 号 (hào): horn 芦笙 (lúshēng): lusheng, a reed-pipe wind instrument 箫 (xiāo): flute
打	dǎ	to beat	percussion instruments	鼓 (gǔ): drum
拉	lā	to pull	bowed instruments	小提琴 (xiǎotíqín): violin 中提琴 (zhōngtíqín): viola 大提琴 (dàtíqín): cello 二胡 (èrhú): erhu, a bowed instrument with two strings
敲	qiāo	to knock or strike	the gong	锣 (luó): gong
弹	tán	to play, to pluck	stringed instruments	钢琴 (gāngqín): piano 吉他 (jítā): guitar 古筝 (gǔzhēng): guzheng, an instrument that today comes most commonly with 21 strings 琵琶 (pípa): pipa, a Chinese lute

笛子

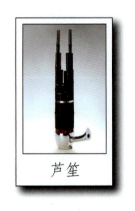

芦笙

二胡

鼓

古筝

琵琶

锣

STRUCTURE NOTE 5.5

Use 来自 *to indicate a place or origin*

The pattern 来自 *(láizì) + Location is a more formal way to express* 从 *+ Location +* 来. *It indicates that the subject comes from a particular place.*

来自 + Location

From the Lesson Text:

她是来自美国的留学生。
Tā shì láizì Měiguó de liúxuésheng.
She is a foreign exchange student from the United States.

Other examples:

来自不同国家的小提琴家都来到这里参加这个比赛。
Láizì bù tóng guójiā de xiǎotíqínjiā dōu láidao zhèlǐ cānjiā zhè ge bǐsài.
Violinists from various countries have all come here to participate in this competition.

这家商店有来自全国各地的产品。
Zhè jiā shāngdiàn yǒu láizì quánguó gè dì de chǎnpǐn.
This store has products from all over the country.

Practice: Respond to the questions using 来自 and the information provided.

Example: 你是从哪里来的？→ 我来自北京。

1. 这位老师是从哪里来的？（加拿大）
   _____

2. 那位留学生是从哪个国家来的？（法国）
   _____

3. 这位球员是从哪所大学来的？（体育大学）
   _____

STRUCTURE NOTE 5.6
Use 收到 *to express obtaining physical objects and* 受到 *to indicate receiving abstract concepts*

The phrases 收到 *(shōudào) and* 受到 *(shòudào) are easily confusable.* 收到 *means "to obtain,"* *"to receive," or "to acquire,"and is used primarily with physical objects, such as* 信, 商品, *and* 钱, *and sometimes with abstract objects such as* 建议. 受到 *has a more passive meaning, and indicates "to receive," "to get," or "to be affected by" an abstract concept, such as* 欢迎 *and* 教育.

> Subject + 收到 + Object

> Subject + 受到 + Object

From the Lesson Text:
你们的表演能受到评委和观众的喜爱……
Nǐmen de biǎoyǎn néng shòudào píngwěi hé guānzhòng de xǐ'ài...
Your performance was acclaimed by both the judges and the audience...

Other examples:
我收到了你的信。
Wǒ shōudàole nǐ de xìn.
I have received your letter.

你觉得这部电影会受到大学生的欢迎吗?
Nǐ juéde zhè bù diànyǐng huì shòudào dàxuésheng de huānyíng ma?
Do you think this film will be well-received by college students?

Practice: Choose the correct phrase to fill in the blanks.

收到　　　受到

1. 他们一出场就_____球迷的欢迎。

2. 我_____了她从加拿大发给我的邮件。

3. 他们的武术表演_____很多观众的喜爱。

4. 周信_____玛丽从云南带来的茶叶。

5. 祥安明天就会_____在网上买的帽子 。

STRUCTURE NOTE 5.7
Use 令 to express making someone feel a certain way

In English, expressions such as "exciting" and "worrying" express that something makes people feel excited and worried. In Chinese, this meaning is conveyed through "make (someone) (adjective)" patterns. 令 (lìng) is one of the more formal terms that can fill the "make" role. To express that something makes people in general feel a certain way, 人 fills the "someone" slot. The appropriate adjective is then added to create common phrases such as 令人满意, "satisfying," 令人羡慕, "exciting," and 令人担心, "worrying." In the Lesson Text example, this 令 pattern makes use of the pronoun 我 and the adjective 难忘 to create 令我十分难忘, meaning "absolutely unforgettable to me."

> 令 + Someone + Feeling Adjective

From the Lesson Text:

里面的古筝演奏令我十分难忘。
Lǐmiàn de gǔzhēng yǎnzòu lìng wǒ shífēn nánwàng.
The group included a traditional zither performance, which I found to be unforgettable.

Other Examples:

有没有最令你难忘的事？
Yǒuméiyǒu zuì lìng nǐ nánwàng de shì?
Do you have a most unforgettable moment?

这是一首令人快乐的歌。
Zhè shì yì shǒu lìng rén kuàilè de gē.
This is a song that makes people happy.

Practice: Rewrite the following sentences using 令 without changing the meaning of the sentence.

Example:　我很担心妈妈的病。→ 妈妈的病令我很担心。

1.　大家都很羡慕她在音乐上的成功。

　　_____

2.　玛丽很高兴可以申请到奖学金。

　　_____

3.　妈妈不放心妹妹一个人去公园。

　　_____

4.　跟他分手我非常难过。

　　_____

5.　她对这个公寓很满意。

　　_____

STRUCTURE NOTE 5.8
Use (在) ……上 to introduce topics

在……上 expresses "on the subject of" and can be used with or without the 在. As with other 在 phrases, it can either precede the sentence as an introductory clause or follow the subject.

$$\boxed{(在 +) \text{Topic} + 上 + , + \text{Sentence}}$$

$$\boxed{\text{Subject} (+ 在) + \text{Topic} + 上 + \text{Phrase}}$$

From the Lesson Text:

感谢她一直在音乐上支持我。
Gǎnxiè tā yìzhí zài yīnyuèshang zhīchí wǒ.
Thank her for continually supporting me in the area of music.

Other Examples:

很多人在留学的问题上有自己的想法。
Hěn duō rén zài liúxué de wèntíshang yǒu zìjǐ de xiǎngfǎ.
Many people have their own thoughts on the question of study abroad.

老师，请给大家一些学习上的建议。
Lǎoshī, qǐng gěi dàjiā yìxiē xuéxíshang de jiànyì.
Teacher, please give everyone a few recommendations regarding study.

Practice: Create complete sentences by using the 在……上 structure and putting the words provided in the correct order.

Example:　天才/小美/音乐→小美在音乐上是个天才。

1. 聪明/我/赚钱

   _____

2. 爸爸妈妈/很放心/学习/对我

   _____

3. 工作/非常努力/他

   _____

4. 做得非常好/飞鱼队/球员配合

   _____

5. 志愿者招募/比我做得好/她

   _____

练习 5.10: 课文理解

Paired Activity: Discuss the following questions based on the Lesson Text. Be prepared to share your thoughts with the class.

1. 乐队的表演为什么能让观众和评委感觉很特别？

2. 玛丽为什么能实现她的音乐理想？

3. 你喜欢这种中西结合的音乐吗？为什么？

练习 5.11: 音乐学校报名

Individual Activity: You want to learn a musical instrument. Using the advertisement below, write down what instrument(s) you would like to learn and what class(es) you would take.

课程表	
初级古筝	周一，三 6:00-7:00 下午
初级琵琶、中级琵琶	周二，四 8:30-9:30 下午
初级钢琴、中级钢琴	周六 10:00-11:00 上午
初级小提琴	周日 2:30-3:30 下午

Additional Vocabulary:
课程表 (kèchéngbiǎo): *n.* timetable
初级 (chūjí): *adj.* elementary, beginning
琵琶 (pípa): *n.* Chinese lute
中级 (zhōngjí): *n.* intermediate

Example: 我想学古筝，所以我会选初级古筝。

练习 5.12 (上): 你的爱好

Individual Activity: In the first row, provide your name, hobby(ies), and activities related to your interest(s) that you have attended or participated in. Then ask two other classmates about their hobbies and events.

名字	爱好	活动
Example: 玛丽	喜欢拉小提琴	参加音乐演奏

练习 5.13 (中): 采访

Paired Activity: Interview your classmate about an event that he or she recently attended. Think up four questions about the event, then interview your classmates for the answers.

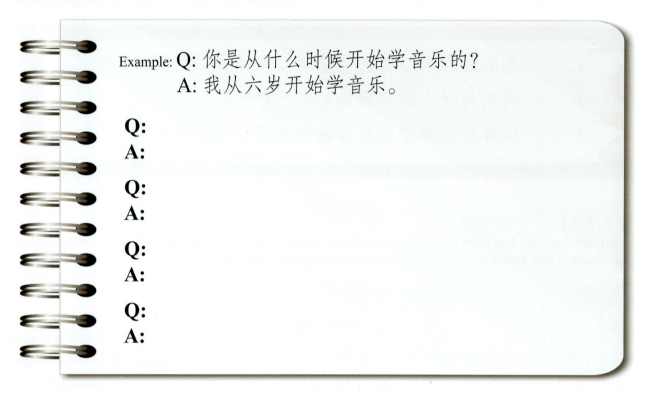

Example: Q: 你是从什么时候开始学音乐的?
A: 我从六岁开始学音乐。

Q:
A:

Q:
A:

Q:
A:

Q:
A:

练习 5.14 (下): 音乐会活动

Group Activity: Working with your group, have each member find and research a group event to attend. Then, have each person introduce his/her event to the group. Discuss and choose one to go to and explain why.

Your choice:

时间:

地点:

活动介绍:

Group decision:

活动:

选择原因:

	Radical	Stroke Order
刊	刂(刀) dāo knife	一 二 干 开 刊
获	艹(草) cǎo grass	一 十 艹 艹 芬 茅 茏 获 获 获
艺	艹(草) cǎo grass	一 十 艹 艺
采	爫(爪) zhǎo claw	丿 爫 爫 爫 平 平 采 采
访	讠(言) yán speech	丶 讠 讠 讠 访 访
评	讠(言) yán speech	丶 讠 讠 讠 讠 评
委	禾 hé grain	丿 二 千 禾 禾 禾 委 委
众	人 rén person	丿 人 亼 众 众
种	禾 hé grain	丿 二 千 禾 禾 禾 和 和 种
形	彡 shān hair	一 二 于 开 开 形 形
式	弋 yì catch	一 二 三 王 式 式
民	乙 yǐ second	一 一 尸 尸 民
令	人 rén person	丿 人 亼 今 令
忘	心 xīn heart	丶 一 亡 亡 忘 忘 忘
支	支 zhī branch	一 十 岁 支

Online chat: Working with a classmate, discuss your personal hobbies and interests. Provide the reasons for your preferences.

练习 5.17: 阅读理解

To:	孙玛丽
From:	王娜
Subject:	感谢你们的表演！

玛丽：

　　你好！我叫王娜。你们乐队在大学生才艺比赛上的演出让我非常难忘，我觉得你真是多才多艺。我对音乐不太了解，但读了校刊对你的采访以后，我对生活有了新的认识。我很羡慕你能有自己的计划，希望像你一样，能努力去实现自己的梦想。我会一直支持你们的乐队！加油！

王娜

Read the e-mail and answer the following questions.
1. How does Wang Na know Mali?
2. Why does Wang Na write to Mali?
3. Write about someone you admire and explain why.

练习 5.18: 阅读理解

"舞在校园" 等着你

　　喜爱跳舞的朋友们注意啦！第四届"舞在校园"比赛的报名开始了。这次比赛和去年一样，你只要登录学校的网站就可以报名。

　　如果你想跳舞、爱跳舞，也会跳舞，就快来参加吧。我们等着你！

比赛地点：活动中心
报名时间：9月18日~9月21日

Notes:
届 (jiè): *mw.* used for competition
报名 (bàomíng): *vo.* to sign up
登录 (dēnglù): *v.* to log in

Read the poster and answer the following questions.
1. What kind of students are likely to sign up?
2. How should people sign up for the competition?
3. Write a blog entry describing your feelings about the competition after attending it.

Traditional Chinese Instruments

By about 1000 BC, China already had a rich musical tradition, complete with a sophisticated theory system and many different instruments. Propriety and music constituted the two pillars of the ancient rituals of an honored and educated man. Traditional Chinese instruments that remain popular today include the guzheng (古筝: gǔzhēng), the pipa (琵琶: pípa), and the erhu (二胡: èrhú). Not only are these instruments heard in traditional Chinese music, but they are also integrated in different genres of music, both inside and outside China.

Guzheng

The guzheng was invented over 2500 years ago, during the Warring States Period. A large, plucked zither that first had five strings, the guzheng now has between 12 to 23 strings. By the time of the Tang Dynasty (618 – 907 AD), it was the most widely played instrument in China, and strongly associated with the imperial court. The guzheng has fallen in and out of favor over the years, with a folk music revival in the 1960s bringing it back into fashion again. Because of the guzheng's reputation as a prestigious instrument, it remains a common instrument for young children to learn.

Pipa

The pipa was first mentioned in Chinese texts from the Han Dynasty (206 BC – 220 AD). This lute started out being played much like a guitar, horizontally and plucked with a pick. However, this changed during the Tang Dynasty as musicians started using their fingernails instead of the pick and positioned the pipa upright to play. This provided for a broader range of techniques among Chinese plucked-string instruments. For centuries, the pipa was renowned as the king of Chinese instruments, and it featured in many classic Tang Dynasty poems. With an electric version of the instrument recently developed, it is still widely played today.

Erhu

Also called "the Chinese violin," the erhu dates back to the tenth century. It differs from a violin since the instrument has just two strings. Originally used as musical accompaniment, the erhu is now often played as a solo instrument, especially as it is thought to sound like the human voice. Today, not only is the erhu used for traditional Chinese music, but because of its versatility, it has also been incorporated into contemporary music. Because it is small and easily carried, the erhu is popular with street musicians and can be seen and heard in parks around China.

Many singers, bands, and composers today combine various Chinese instruments with Western instruments and music. Chinese singers and musicians often use Chinese instruments in rock, pop, and hip-hop songs to provide a distinctly Chinese tone to Western music genres.

The guzheng, pipa, and erhu have also found their way into Western classical music, where composers are drawn to

these instruments because of the contrast they provide to traditional Western instruments. One renowned international music ensemble even uses traditional Chinese instruments to explore the music and traditions of the Silk Road, combining and exchanging ideas across cultures through music.

Pinyin

Xiàokān Dì-bāshíyī (81) qī:

Zhōngxī Yīnyuè Wánměi Jiéhé

Shàngzhōu, wǒ xiào yuèduì huòdéle dàxuéshēng cáiyì bǐsài de dìyī míng. Jìzhě cǎifǎngle yuèduì de duìzhǎng Sūn Mǎlì, tā shì láizì Měiguó de liúxuéshēng.

Jìzhě: Gōngxǐ nǐmen yíngdé guànjūn. Nǐmen de biǎoyǎn néng shòudào píngwěi hé guānzhòng de xǐài, nǐ rènwéi nǐmen chénggōng de yuányīn shì shénme?

Sūn Mǎlì: Wǒ xiǎng shì yīnwèi wǒmen yòng xiǎotíqín hé gǔzhēng yìqǐ yǎnzòu, zhè zhǒng zhōngxī jiéhé de yīnyuè ràng guānzhòngmen juéde hěn tèbié.

Jìzhě: Nǐmen shì zěnme xiǎngdào zhèyang de biǎoyǎn xíngshì ne?

Sūn Mǎlì: Zài Měiguó de shíhou, wǒ de hǎo péngyǒu Xiǎoměi dài wǒ qù tīngguo yì chǎng Zhōngguó mínyuè yǎnzòu, lǐmiàn de gǔzhēng yǎnzòu lìng wǒ shífēn nánwàng. Lái Zhōngguó yǐhòu, wǒ jiāole jǐ ge wán mínyuè de péngyǒu, suǒyǐ jiù xiǎng shìshi yìqǐ yǎnzòu.

English

School Magazine Issue #81:

A Perfect Fusion of Chinese and Western Music:

Last week, a band from our school won first place at the Intercollegiate Student Talent Competition. Our reporter interviewed the leader of the band, Sun Mali, a foreign exchange student from the United States.

Congratulations on winning the championship. Your performance was acclaimed by both the judges and the audience. For what reason do you think you were successful?

I think it's because we incorporated the violin and zither in the performance. This type of fusion of Chinese and Western music was very unique from the audience's perspective.

How did you come up with this performance format?

When I was in America, my good friend, Xiaomei, once took me to a Chinese folk instrumental performance. The group included a traditional zither, which I found to be unforgettable. After coming to China, I met a few friends who played traditional folk instruments so we decided to experiment with such performances.

Jìzhě:	Nǐmen yuèduì yǐhòu yǒu shénme jìhuà ma?

What plans does the group have for the future?

Sūn Mǎlì:	Xīwàng wǒmen néng yǒu jīhuì qù gèng duō de dìfang biǎoyǎn, ràng gèng duō rén xīnshǎng zhè zhǒng zhōngxī jiéhé de yīnyuè.

We hope to have the opportunity to perform at more venues, allowing more people to experience this fusion of Chinese and Western music.

Jìzhě:	Nǐ xiànzài zuì xiǎng gǎnxiè shéi ne?

Who would you like to thank most right now?

Sūn Mǎlì:	Wǒ yào gǎnxiè wǒ de yīnyuè huǒbànmen, shì tāmen bāng wǒ shíxiànle yǎnzòu zhōngxī yīnyuè de lǐxiǎng. Wǒ yě yào xièxie wǒde hǎo péngyou Xiǎoměi, gǎnxiè tā yìzhí zài yīnyuè shàng zhīchí wǒ, xīwàng wǒmen yǐhòu néng yìqǐ biǎoyǎn!

I would like to thank my partners in the band. They helped make this fusion performance possible. I would also like to thank my good friend, Xiaomei, for continually supporting me in the area of music. I hope we will have the opportunity to perform together in the future!

What Can You Do?

INTERPRETIVE
- I can recognize different kinds of Chinese and Western musical instruments and genres after listening to them.
- I can identify a media article based on media-related vocabulary after reading it.

INTERPERSONAL
- I can discuss preferences about music to someone else.
- I can conduct an interview, either as a journalist or the person being interviewed.

PRESENTATIONAL
- I can describe something that happened during childhood.
- I can talk about a musical performance from the perspective of a performer or a member of the audience.

ACT IT OUT

Working in groups, compose an original two-minute skit that utilizes the vocabulary and structures introduced in Unit 5. Each of you should assume a role and have a roughly equal number of lines in the skit. Be prepared to perform your skit in class. You can either come up with your own story or choose from one of the following situations:

A) Your uncle is visiting for the weekend and wants to see a sporting event. Discuss what games you can go to and decide which event you will attend.

B) You and your friends just came from a wonderful concert. Discuss what portion of the performance you each enjoyed.

C) You meet up with your dad after running into your favorite athlete at the mall. Describe the experience to your dad, including what the athlete looked like, and why that person is your favorite athlete.

CHECK WHAT YOU CAN DO

RECOGNIZE

Adjectives
- □ 厉害
- □ 强
- □ 公平
- □ 完美
- □ 难忘
- □ 最后

Adverbs
- □ 十分
- □ 另外

Conjunctions
- □ 不过…而已
- □ 与其…倒不如

Measure Words
- □ 场
- □ 种

Nouns
- □ 队
- □ 球员
- □ 队长
- □ 实力
- □ 篮球明星
- □ 比分
- □ 裁判
- □ 运气
- □ 团队精神
- □ 赛季
- □ 冠军
- □ 山猫
- □ 飞鱼
- □ 教练
- □ 校刊
- □ 结合
- □ 乐队

- □ 才艺
- □ 记者
- □ 评委
- □ 观众
- □ 喜爱
- □ 原因
- □ 古筝
- □ 形式
- □ 民乐
- □ 伙伴
- □ 梦想
- □ 演奏

Preposition
- □ 依

Verbs
- □ 赢
- □ 对

- □ 输
- □ 配合
- □ 获得
- □ 采访
- □ 来自
- □ 令
- □ 欣赏
- □ 感谢
- □ 实现
- □ 支持
- □ 放弃

Verb-Object Compounds
- □ 犯规
- □ 吹哨

WRITE

- □ 队
- □ 厉
- □ 吹
- □ 赢
- □ 强
- □ 另
- □ 犯
- □ 规
- □ 裁
- □ 输
- □ 精
- □ 神
- □ 赛
- □ 冠
- □ 军

- □ 刊
- □ 获
- □ 艺
- □ 采
- □ 访
- □ 评
- □ 委
- □ 众
- □ 种
- □ 形
- □ 式
- □ 民
- □ 令
- □ 忘
- □ 支

USE

- □ Use 另外 to talk about additional items.
- □ Use (只)不过……而已 to minimize the significance of something.
- □ Use 与其…(倒)不如… to indicate a preferred alternative.
- □ Use 依……看 to formally express someone's opinion.

- □ Use 来自 to indicate a place of origin.
- □ Use 收到 to express obtaining physical objects and 受到 for receiving abstract concepts.
- □ Use 令 to express making someone feel a certain way.
- □ Use (在)……上 to introduce topics.

Cuisine

食

第六单元
UNIT 6

Communication Goals

Lesson 1: 学做中国菜 **Learning Chinese Cooking**
- Identify commonly-used Chinese cooking ingredients.
- Follow a recipe to make a Chinese dish.
- Use idiomatic expressions to describe the appearance and flavor of food.

Lesson 2: 逛超市 **Going to the Supermarket**
- Talk about necessary ingredients for making a dish.
- Discuss freshness and expiration dates of food.
- Use idiomatic expressions to make compliments about food.
- Talk about the authenticity of dishes.

学做中国菜
Learning Chinese Cooking

发件人	玛丽 ▼
收件人	小美
主 题	宫保鸡丁食谱

B *I* U 14px ▼ A 🔗 🖼 😊 信纸

亲爱的小美：

　　恭喜你们申请到了奖学金！你想好下周的中国美食比赛
做什么菜了吗？你可以试试做宫保鸡丁（gōng bǎo jī dīng）。我一直以为（yǐ wéi）这道（dào）菜
会很难做，上星期和周信一起做了宫保鸡丁（gōng bǎo jī dīng）之后，才知道其
实做法（zuò fǎ）很简单。这是我们的食谱（shí pǔ）：
材料（cái liào）：鸡肉（jī ròu）400克（kè），葱（cōng）15克（kè），辣椒（là jiāo）20克（kè），花生米（huā shēng mǐ）50克（kè），油（yóu）500
克（kè），盐（yán）1小匙，糖（táng）1小匙，淀粉（diàn fěn）25克（kè），料酒（liào jiǔ）1大匙（chí），酱油（jiàng yóu）
1/2大匙（chí）

🖂 发送　　存草稿　　取消

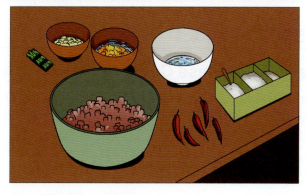

第一，把鸡肉、葱和辣椒切丁。

第二，鸡丁里放入盐、料酒和淀粉后拌匀。

第三，把鸡丁和油放进锅里；鸡丁炒熟后盛出来。

第四，先将葱和辣椒丁大火炒一会儿，然后放入炒好的鸡丁和酱油、糖、盐；最后加入花生米炒一会儿，这道家常菜就做好了！无论在哪里，宫保鸡丁都十分受欢迎。

对了，你看到安娜发给我们的邮件了吗？她说明年春天会跟俄罗斯舞蹈团来北京表演，我已经收到了她寄来的票。安娜打算表演结束之后留在北京和我们一起念书，实在是太好了！很高兴你们下学期都能来中国留学，我很想念大家！

玛丽

恭 喜

发送　存草稿　取消

LESSON TEXT 6.1

Learning Chinese Cooking 学做中国菜

Over in Beijing, Mali writes a letter to Xiaomei asking how her preparations for the Chinese Cooking Competition are going. Mali includes Zhou Xin's recipe for Kung Pao Chicken and tips on how to make it.

亲爱的小美：

恭喜你们申请到了奖学金！你想好下周的中国美食比赛做什么菜了吗？你可以试试做宫保鸡丁。我一直以为这道菜会很难做，上星期和周信一起做了宫保鸡丁之后，才知道其实做法很简单。这是我们的食谱：

材料：鸡肉400克，葱15克，辣椒20克，花生米50克，油500克，盐1小匙，糖1小匙，淀粉25克，料酒1大匙，酱油1/2大匙

第一，把鸡肉、葱和辣椒切丁。
第二，鸡丁里放入盐、料酒和淀粉后拌匀。
第三，把鸡丁和油放进锅里；鸡丁炒熟后盛出来。
第四，先将葱和辣椒丁大火炒一会儿，然后放入炒好的鸡丁和酱油、糖、盐；最后加入花生米炒一会儿，这道家常菜就做好了！无论在哪里，宫保鸡丁都十分受欢迎。

对了，你看到安娜发给我们的邮件了吗？她说明年春天会跟俄罗斯舞蹈团来北京表演，我已经收到了她寄来的票。安娜打算表演结束之后留在北京和我们一起念书，实在是太好了！很高兴你们下学期都能来中国留学，我很想念大家！

玛丽

Language Tip

大匙 (dàchí)

小匙 (xiǎochí)

Mali uses 小匙 and 大匙 in her Kung Pao Chicken recipe. Both 小匙 and 大匙 are used in cooking recipes as measurements. 小匙 means "teaspoon" and 大匙 means "tablespoon." The terms 茶匙 and 汤匙 can also be used to mean teaspoon and tablespoon, as well as referring to the actual spoons used for tea and soup.

Example:

做这道菜的时候要放一小匙盐和两大匙糖。
When making this dish, add one teaspoon of salt and two tablespoons of sugar.

字 词 VOCABULARY

LESSON VOCABULARY 6.1

	SIMPLIFIED	TRADITIONAL	PINYIN	WORD CATEGORY	DEFINITION
1.	以为	以爲	yǐwéi	v	to think, to believe (mistakenly)
2.	道		dào	mw	(used for a course of food)
3.	做法		zuòfǎ	n	method, way of doing/making something
4.	食谱	食譜	shípǔ	n	recipe, cookbook
5.	材料		cáiliào	n	material, ingredients
6.	鸡肉	鷄肉	jīròu	n	chicken meat
7.	克		kè	n	gram
8.	葱		cōng	n	green onion, scallion
9.	辣椒		làjiāo	n	hot pepper
10.	花生米		huāshēngmǐ	n	shelled peanut
11.	油		yóu	n	oil
12.	盐	鹽	yán	n	salt
13.	匙		chí	n	spoon
14.	糖		táng	n	sugar
15.	淀粉	澱粉	diànfěn	n	starch
16.	料酒		liàojiǔ	n	cooking wine
17.	酱油	醬油	jiàngyóu	n	soy sauce
18.	切丁		qiēdīng	v	to dice
	切		qiē	v	to cut
	丁		dīng	v	to dice (in cooking)
19.	拌匀		bànyún	v	to mix evenly
	拌		bàn	v	to mix
	匀		yún	adj	even
20.	锅	鍋	guō	n	wok
21.	炒熟		chǎo shú	v	to stir-fry until the food is cooked
	炒		chǎo	v	to stir-fry, to sauté

LESSON VOCABULARY 6.1 (continued)

SIMPLIFIED	TRADITIONAL	PINYIN	WORD CATEGORY	DEFINITION
熟		shú	*adj*	cooked
22. 盛		chéng	*v*	to scoop out, to fill
23. 将	將	jiāng	*prep*	(used to introduce the object before a verb)
24. 大火		dàhuǒ	*n*	high heat
火		huǒ	*n*	fire
25. 家常菜		jiāchángcài	*n*	home cooking
家常		jiācháng	*adj*	family routine
26. 无论……都	無論……都	wúlùn……dōu	*cj*	no matter what . . . all; regardless of . . . all
27. 实在	實在	shízài	*adv*	so; really; honestly

PROPER NOUN

28. 宫保鸡丁	宮保鷄丁	Gōngbǎojīdīng	*n*	Kung Pao Chicken (spicy fried diced chicken)

REQUIRED VOCABULARY 6.1

29. 适量	適量	shìliàng	*adj*	appropriate amount
量		liàng	*n*	quantity
30. 少许	少許	shǎoxǔ	*adj*	a little

 ONLINE RESOURCES

Visit *http://college.betterchinese.com* for more vocabulary on ingredients.

Idiomatic Expression

jīn jīn yǒu wèi
津津有味

津津有味 means "to eat with a good appetite." By itself, 津 means "saliva," but 津津 means "with great interest," which is used to connote "with gusto," "with relish," or "with keen pleasure."

This phrase appears in the collected writings of Zhu Shunshui in *Zhu Shunshui's Collection* (《朱舜水集》: *Zhū Shùnshuǐ Jí*), written during the Ming Dynasty (1368 - 1644 AD). In the book, Zhu wrote, "The more I read the masterpiece, the more interesting it became; I found the principles behind the piece more important than the beautiful language it was written in." This expression is often used to modify an action so that the action is done with great interest, such as eating with great relish or listening with great interest.

Examples:

这道菜很好吃，大家都吃得津津有味。
This dish is very delicious; everyone is enjoying it very much.

他看书看得津津有味。
He is attentively reading a book.

Reading a Recipe

The following are terms commonly used in recipes (食谱):

Common styles of preparing dishes:

Character	Pinyin	Meaning
炒	chǎo	to stir-fry
炖	dùn	to stew; to braise
红烧	hóngshāo	to "red braise": to braise in a marinade of soy sauce, rice wine, and caramelized sugar
煎	jiān	to fry in shallow oil or to simmer in water
烤	kǎo	to roast; to bake; to toast; to warm
清炒	qīngchǎo	to stir-fry without any sauce
水煮	shuǐzhǔ	to boil in water
炸	zhá	to deep fry
蒸	zhēng	to steam

Cooking Measurements

The following are terms commonly used in cooking measurements:

Character	Pinyin	Meaning	Character	Pinyin	Meaning
杯	bēi	cup	克	kè	gram
小匙	xiǎochí	teaspoon	斤	jīn	measure word: 500 grams
大匙	dàchí	tablespoon	毫升	háoshēng	milliliter

Vocabulary Related to 吃

Chinese people often greet each other with 你吃了吗? (Have you eaten?), indicating the important role that food has in the language itself. The word 吃 also features prominently in metaphors.

The following are commonly used metaphors using 吃:

Chinese	Pinyin	Literal explanation	Meaning	Example
吃不消	chībuxiāo	to eat what is not needed	to be unable to bear (exertion, fatigue, etc.)	太多的报告和论文让学生们吃不消。
吃醋	chīcù	to eat vinegar	to be jealous (usually of a romantic rival)	她很容易吃醋，如果看到男朋友和别的女孩子聊天就会很生气。
吃苦	chīkǔ	to eat bitterness	to deal with difficult times	他很怕吃苦，常常没有办法做完自己的工作。
吃亏	chīkuī	to eat loss	to lose out, to be at a disadvantage	不听老人言，吃亏在眼前。
吃香	chīxiāng	to eat delicious (food)	to be popular, to be well-liked	他毕业之后想找一个钱赚得多，而且很吃香的工作。

STRUCTURE NOTE 6.1
Use 以为 *to express mistaken belief*
In English, the verb "thought" is most often used to indicate a mistaken belief, as in, "I thought you were already home." Similarly, the verb 以为 *(yǐwéi) generally indicates that the subject is mistaken.*

> Subject + 以为 + Clause

From the Lesson Text:

我一直以为这道菜会很难做。
Wǒ yìzhí yǐwéi zhè dào cài huì hěn nánzuò.
I always thought this was a difficult dish to prepare.

Other examples:

我以为你不爱吃麻婆豆腐，没想到你这么喜欢吃。
Wǒ yǐwéi nǐ bú ài chī Mápódòufu, méi xiǎngdào nǐ zhème xǐhuan chī.
I thought you didn't like to eat Mapo Tofu; I didn't expect that you would like eating this so much.

我一直都以为你住校内。
Wǒ yìzhí dōu yǐwéi nǐ zhù xiàonèi.
I always thought you lived on campus.

Practice: Complete the sentences using 以为.

Example:
没想到你爱吃辣的东西，我……
→ 没想到你爱吃辣的东西，我以为你不能吃辣。

1. 原来你住的离我这么近，我……
   _____

2. 这条裙子要500块！我……
   _____

3. 他已经工作了吗？我……
   _____

4. 没想到你中文只学了一年，我……
   _____

5. 你从来没有听过音乐会啊！我……
   _____

STRUCTURE NOTE 6.2
Use 将 to indicate an action performed on a specific object in formal contexts

In formal writing, 将 (jiāng) is used as a particle to replace 把 in sentences where the object is placed before the verb, known as 把 construction sentences. Remember that these constructions are used to describe a situation in which a subject takes an object and does something with it, and that the final verb phrase must contain some additional material following the verb, such as a resultative complement.

Subject + 将 + Object + Verb Phrase

From the Lesson Text:

先将葱和辣椒丁大火炒一会儿。
Xiān jiāng cōng hé làjiāo dīng dàhuǒ chǎo yìhuǐr.
Pour the diced green onions and chili peppers into the wok, stir-fry briefly at high heat.

Other examples:

她将课本借给了我。
Tā jiāng kèběn jiè gěi le wǒ.
She lent me her textbook.

你们可以帮我将家具搬进公寓吗?
Nǐmen kěyǐ bāng wǒ jiāng jiājù bānjìn gōngyù ma?
Can you all help me move the furniture into the house?

Practice: Use 将 to transform the following sentences.

Example: 水倒进杯子里。→ 将水倒进杯子里。

1. 你要准备好烹饪材料。

   _____

2. 他的表演结合了中国民乐和西方音乐。

   _____

3. 十五天之内,把报告发给王教授。

   _____

STRUCTURE NOTE 6.3

Use 无论⋯都⋯ to express "no matter what" something is always the case

无论 (wúlùn) *is a more formal way to express* 不管. *It is used in the same way to indicate that some condition does not matter, and that an event will take place anyway.*

> 无论 + Question / Phrase, + Subject + 都 + Verb Phrase

From the Lesson Text:

无论在哪里，宫保鸡丁都十分受欢迎。
Wúlùn zài nǎlǐ, Gōngbǎojīdīng dōu shífēn shòu huānyíng.
No matter where you are, Kung Pao Chicken is an extremely popular dish.

Other Examples:

无论到哪里旅行，你都要注意安全。
Wúlùn dào nǎlǐ lǚxíng, nǐ dōu yào zhùyì ānquán.
No matter where you travel, you have to pay attention to your safety.

无论这场比赛会不会赢，我都会一直支持你。
Wúlùn zhè chǎng bǐsài huì bu huì yíng, wǒ dōu huì yìzhí zhīchí nǐ.
It doesn't matter whether you win this match or not, I will always support you.

Practice: Create complete sentences using 无论⋯都⋯ and the information provided below.

Example: 明天天气怎么样 / 我要去打球
→ 无论明天天气怎么样，我都要去打球。

1. 我怎么说 / 他不相信我
   _____

2. 她怎样努力 / 得不到观众的喜爱
   _____

3. 作业多简单 / 你要认真做
   _____

4. 你租哪个公寓 / 要签合同
   _____

5. 在哪里买东西 / 看清楚退货条件
   _____

STRUCTURE NOTE 6.4
Use 实在 to mean "really" and "honestly"
实在 *(shízài) can be used as an adverb expressing "really" and "honestly" to emphasize the statement, similarly to* 真的. 真的 *is primarily used in spoken Chinese, while* 实在 *is used primarily in written Chinese.* 实在 *occurs before a verb or an adjective phrase.*

Subject + 实在 + Adjective / Verb Phrase

From the Lesson Text:

实在是太好了！
Shízài shì tài hǎo le!
This is so great!

Other Examples:

他觉得这场球赛实在不公平。
Tā juéde zhè chǎng qiúsài shízài bù gōngpíng.
He thought this match was really unfair.

我的工作很忙，实在没有时间去旅游。
Wǒ de gōngzuò hěn máng, shízài méiyǒu shíjiān qù lǚyóu.
My job is really busy. I honestly don't have any time to go on vacation.

Practice: Rewrite the sentences using 实在.

Example: 我读不懂这本书。→ 我实在读不懂这本书。

1.   他的宿舍太乱了。

_____

2.   我不记得昨天发生什么了。

_____

3.   打篮球的时候团队精神很重要。

_____

4.   没有收据我们不能帮你退货。

_____

5.   这一场中国民乐表演令人十分难忘。

_____

练习 PRACTICE

练习 6.1: 课文理解

Paired Activity: Discuss the following questions based on the Lesson Text. Be prepared to share your thoughts with the class.

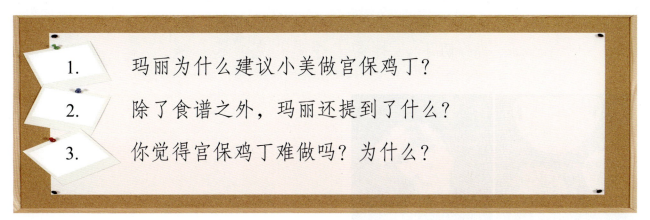

1. 玛丽为什么建议小美做宫保鸡丁？

2. 除了食谱之外，玛丽还提到了什么？

3. 你觉得宫保鸡丁难做吗？为什么？

练习 6.2 (上): 朋友来做客

Paired Activity: Dadong, Zhongping, Xiaomei, and Xiang'an are going to have a dinner party. Below are their food preferences and a list of dishes they know how to cook. Discuss what each character likes and create a menu for tonight's meal. Explain your reasoning for selecting the dishes.

	大东	中平	小美	祥安
牛肉	✓	✕	✓	✓
鸡肉	✓	✕	✓	✓
海鲜	✕	✕	✓	✓
猪肉	✓	✕	✕	✓
豆腐	✕	✓	✓	✓
鱼	✕	✕	✓	✓
辣的菜	✕	✓	✓	✓
米饭	✓	✓	✓	✓
饺子	✓	✓	✓	✓

大家会做的菜

菜:	青菜炒牛肉	汤:	酸辣汤
	宫保鸡丁		鸡汤
	水煮鱼		豆腐汤
	清蒸鱼		海鲜汤
	烧鸡	面/饭:	米饭
	家常豆腐		蛋炒饭
	麻婆豆腐		素炒面
	青菜		素饺子

菜单

Individual Activity: Xiang'an's favorite dish is fried rice (炒饭: chǎofàn). Using the pictures and select the terms from the word bank below, write down each step for making this dish.

> 蛋 猪肉 葱 米饭 油 盐 酱油
> 切丁 拌匀 炒熟 克 匙 锅

练习 6.4: 介绍一道菜

Paired Activity: Working with your partner, share an interesting dish that you have recently eaten, including the ingredients the dish contained and how it tasted.

Example: 最近我吃了一道很好吃的中国菜，叫"麻婆豆腐"。这道菜的材料有豆腐、猪肉、辣椒、油、盐、糖、酱油和葱。麻婆豆腐又香又辣，实在太好吃了！

练习 6.5: 学做菜

Group Activity: Pick a dish that you know how to make. Describe the ingredients and steps required to make it.

	Radical	Stroke Order
谱	讠(言) yán speech	丶 讠 讠 讱 讱 讱 讱 讱 讱 讱 讱 谱 谱
克	一 yī one	一 十 十 古 古 卢 克
米	米 mǐ rice	丶 丷 丷 半 米 米
油	氵(水) shuǐ water	丶 氵 氵 沪 沪 油 油
盐	皿 mǐn utensil	一 十 土 扑 扑 盐 盐 盐
糖	米 mǐ rice	丶 丷 丷 半 半 米 米 粁 粃 粁 糖 糖 糖 糖
粉	米 mǐ rice	丶 丷 丷 半 半 米 米 粉 粉 粉
酒	氵(水) shuǐ water	丶 氵 氵 汇 汇 沉 沉 洒 酒
切	刀 dāo knife	一 十 切 切
锅	钅(金) jīn metal	丿 广 广 钅 钅 钷 钷 钷 锅 锅 锅
炒	火 huǒ fire	丶 丷 少 火 灶 炒 炒 炒
熟	灬(火) huǒ fire	丶 亠 六 六 亨 亨 享 享 孰 孰 孰 孰 熟 熟
盛	皿 mǐn utensil	一 厂 厂 成 成 成 成 盛 盛 盛
将	寸 cùn inch	丶 丬 丬 丬 丬 丬 将 将
葱	艹 cǎo grass	一 十 艹 艹 芴 芴 苅 苅 葱 葱 葱

练习 6.7: 线上聊天

Online chat: Working with a classmate, discuss if you prefer cooking at home or eating out at a restaurant. Provide reasons to support your preference.

练习 6.8: 阅读理解

> 为了准备参加中国美食比赛，小美请大家来家里吃饭，她要用玛丽给她的食谱做宫保鸡丁。宫保鸡丁很快就做好了，看起来让人很有胃口。可是祥安尝了尝，说鸡肉不辣。小美想起来她忘了放辣椒。不过大家都说没关系，说吃得太辣不健康。小美不好意思地说："因为我太粗心了，只好让你们吃这道不辣的宫保鸡丁了！"大家都笑了，而且吃得津津有味。

Read the passage and answer the following questions.
1. How did Xiaomei's Kung Pao Chicken turn out and why?
2. What opinion did everyone have regarding food that is too spicy?
3. How would you make Xiaomei feel better after she realized her mistake?

练习 6.9: 阅读理解

> 今天，我要教大家做一道菜，叫"辣椒炒肉"。
>
> 这道菜的材料有辣椒、猪肉、油、盐、糖、酱油、料酒和淀粉。
>
> 首先，我们要把猪肉切片，加入适量的酱油、料酒和淀粉，拌匀之后腌半个小时。猪肉腌好了以后，就可以开始做菜了：先在锅里放少许油，然后放入腌好的肉，用大火炒。肉片变色以后，加入切好的辣椒继续炒。这道辣椒炒肉就做好了。
>
> 喜欢吃辣的朋友可以多放一些辣椒。不喜欢吃猪肉的朋友可以用鸡肉来做这道菜，一样好吃！

Notes:
猪肉 (zhūròu): *n.* pork
切片 (qiēpiàn): *vo.* to cut into slices, to slice
腌 (yān): *v.* to marinate
变色 (biànsè): *vo.* to change color

Read the passage and answer the following questions.
1. Summarize the steps in numerical order for making this dish.
2. What variations can you make to this dish?
3. If you were making this dish for your family, what changes would you make to the recipe?

Ingredients in Chinese Cooking

There are 23 provinces across China, each known for its own unique way of cooking and a seemingly endless variety of dishes. As Chinese cuisine varies widely, each kitchen may carry a number of different basic items, including garlic, ginger, soy sauce, peanut oil, dried black mushrooms, scallions, rice, chili paste, oyster sauce, rice vinegar, and sesame oil. Despite regional differences, however, many Chinese households carry basic ingredients (材料: cáiliào) considered to be kitchen staples.

Garlic (蒜: suàn)

Garlic is an integral ingredient in Chinese cooking. Garlic has been used in cooking and in medicine for thousands of years. It is featured in dishes all over China, particularly in Sichuan cuisine. Another way of using garlic is in Traditional Chinese Medicine (TCM): it is believed to remove poisons from the body and ward off plagues.

Ginger (姜: jiāng)

Like garlic, ginger has been used in both Chinese dishes and in TCM. Ginger is a frequent ingredient in Cantonese cuisine, and in TCM, has been employed for over two thousand years to treat illnesses such as stomachaches, diarrhea, indigestion, and nausea.

Soy Sauce (酱油: jiàngyóu)

Known as an indispensable Chinese seasoning, soy sauce has been in use for over three thousand years. It is made from a mixture of soybean, flour, salt, and water that is either fermented or brewed. Soy sauce comes in a variety of types, from light to dark, thick to thin, mushroom flavored to shrimp flavored. Soy sauce eventually spread to other surrounding countries, and over time, many regions developed their own varieties. As in the past, soy sauce is widely used today as a substitute for salt.

Oil (油: yóu)

Depending on what cooking technique is employed, a variety of oils can be used. Peanut oil is the traditional choice because of its nutty flavor and because it can be cooked at high temperatures. This oil is used in many different cooking methods, from stir-frying to braising.

The Palace Guardian's Chicken

One dish that is well-known in China and North America is Gong Bao chicken (宫保鸡丁: Gōngbǎojīdīng), also known as Kung Pao Chicken. The etymology of this dish came from the late Qing Dynasty (1644 - 1912 AD) official and governor of Sichuan Ding Baozhen, whose official title "gongbao" means palace guardian. Ding's love for Gong Bao chicken popularized the dish in China during the 19th century. It later traveled outside of China as immigrants created their own versions, becoming a staple of Chinese restaurants everywhere.

Pinyin

Qīn'ài de Xiǎoměi:

Gōngxǐ nǐmen shēnqǐng dào le jiǎngxuéjīn! Nǐ xiǎng hǎo xiàzhōu de Zhōngguó měishí bǐsài zuò shénme cài le ma? Nǐ kěyǐ shìshi zuò Gōngbǎojīdīng. Wǒ yìzhí yǐwéi zhè dào cài huì hěn nán zuò, shàngxīngqī hé Zhōu Xìn yìqǐ zuòle Gōngbǎojīdīng zhīhòu, cái zhīdào qíshí zuòfǎ hěn jiǎndān. Zhè shì wǒmen de shípǔ:

Cáiliào: jīròu 400 kè, cōng 15 kè, làjiāo 20 kè, huāshēngmǐ 50 kè, yóu 500 kè, yán 1 xiǎo chí, táng 1 xiǎo chí, diànfěn 25 kè, liàojiǔ 1 dà chí, jiàngyóu 1/2 dà chí

Dì-yī, bǎ jīròu, cōng hé làjiāo qiē dīng.

Dì-èr, jīdīng lǐ fàngrù yán, liàojiǔ hé diànfěn hòu bànyún.

Dì-sān, bǎ jī dīng hé yóu fàng jìn guō lǐ; jī dīng chǎoshú hòu chéng chūlai.

Dì-sì, xiān jiāng cōng hé làjiāo dīng dàhuǒ chǎo yìhuǐr, ránhòu fàngrù chǎohǎo de jīdīng hé jiàngyóu, táng, yán; zuìhòu jiārù huāshēngmǐ chǎo yìhuǐr, zhè dào jiācháng cài jiù zuòhǎo le! Wúlùn zài nǎlǐ, Gōngbǎo Jīdīng dōu shífēn shòu huānyíng.

English

Dear Xiaomei,

Congratulations to all of you for being scholarship recipients! Have you decided on what you will prepare for next week's Chinese Cooking Competition? You could try making Kung Pao Chicken. I always thought this was a difficult dish to prepare, but after making it with Zhou Xin last week, I realized that making Kung Pao Chicken is actually quite simple. Here is the recipe:

Ingredients: chicken 400 grams, green onions 15 grams, chili peppers 20 grams, shelled peanuts 50 grams, oil 500 grams, salt 1 teaspoon, sugar 1 teaspoon, starch 25 grams, cooking wine 1 tablespoon, soy sauce 1/2 tablespoon

1. Dice the chicken, green onions, and chili peppers.
2. Add salt, cooking wine, and starch to the diced chicken, then mix evenly.
3. Add oil to the wok, then stir-fry and scoop out the cooked, cubed chicken.
4. Pour the diced green onions and chili peppers into the wok, stir-fry briefly at high heat, then add the diced chicken, soy sauce, sugar, and salt. Finally, add the shelled peanuts and stir-fry briefly to finish.

Duìle, nǐ kàndao Ānnà fāgěi wǒmen de yóujiàn le ma? Tā shuō míngnián chūntiān huì gēn Éluósī wǔdǎotuán lái Běijīng biǎoyǎn, wǒ yǐjīng shōudàole tā jìlái de piào. Ānnà dǎsuan biǎoyǎn jiéshù zhīhòu liú zài Běijīng hé wǒmen yìqǐ niànshū, shízài shì tài hǎo le! Hěn gāoxìng nǐmen xià xuéqī dōu néng lái Zhōngguó liúxué, wǒ hěn xiǎngniàn dàjiā!

Mǎlì

No matter where you are, Kung Pao Chicken is an extremely popular dish. By the way, have you seen the e-mail that Anna sent us? She said that she will be coming to Beijing to perform with the Russian dance troupe next spring. I've already received the tickets she mailed. Anna plans to remain in Beijing after the final performance to join us in our studies. This is so great! I'm so happy you will all be studying abroad here in China next semester. I miss everyone very much!

Mali

What Can You Do?

INTERPRETIVE
- I can interpret the level of difficulty of making a dish in terms of time, ingredients, and steps after reading a recipe.
- I can recognize cooking terms after reviewing a recipe.

INTERPERSONAL
- I can exchange opinions about how easy it is to make a dish.
- I can discuss the steps in a recipe.

PRESENTATIONAL
- I can describe how to make a dish.
- I can present how much of each ingredient is needed to make a dish.

逛超市
Going to the Supermarket

大东和朋友们打算在中国美食比赛做一些有特色(tè sè)的菜，于是(yú shì)他们一起去超市(chāo shì)买菜。正好超市(chāo shì)有很多食物和烹饪(pēng rèn)材料在减价(jiǎn jià)，买一送一，还有免费试吃(shì chī)。

大东，做宫保鸡丁的材料都买好了吗？

我买了辣椒、葱和蒜(suàn)，还差(chà)鸡肉。我看了一下鸡肉，觉得不够新鲜(gòu xīn xiān)，有的还快过期(guò qī)了。我们去另一家超市(chāo shì)看看吧。

这里的麻婆豆腐（má pó dòu fu）可以试吃（shì chī），看得我口水（kǒu shuǐ）都要流出来了！

哇！尝（cháng）起来几乎（jī hū）跟小美妈妈做的一样，又香（xiāng）又辣，让人很有胃口（wèi kǒu）！

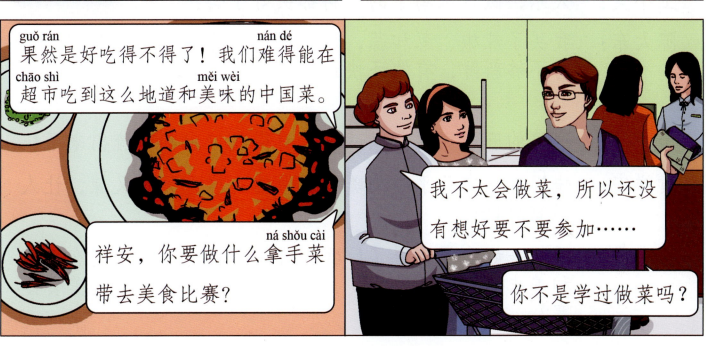

果然（guǒ rán）是好吃得不得了！我们难得（nán dé）能在超市（chāo shì）吃到这么地道和美味（měi wèi）的中国菜。

祥安，你要做什么拿手菜（ná shǒu cài）带去美食比赛？

我不太会做菜，所以还没有想好要不要参加……

你不是学过做菜吗？

是啊，可是怎么也做不好，为了大家的肚子着想（zhuó xiǎng），我还是不参加了。

哈哈，原来是这样！我会做家常（jiā cháng）豆腐（dòu fu），我们一起做吧，我教你。

LESSON TEXT 6.2

Going to the Supermarket 逛超市

It's time for the Chinese Cooking Competition. Dadong, Xiaomei, Zhongping, and Xiang'an are at the supermarket buying ingredients in preparation for the competition.

大东和朋友们打算在中国美食比赛做一些有特色的菜，于是他们一起去超市买菜。正好超市有很多食物和烹饪材料在减价，买一送一，还有免费试吃。

王小美： 大东，做宫保鸡丁的材料都买好了吗？

陈大东： 我买了辣椒、葱和蒜，还差鸡肉。我看了一下鸡肉，觉得不够新鲜，有的还快过期了。我们去另一家超市看看吧。

李中平： 这里的麻婆豆腐可以试吃，看得我口水都要流出来了！

黄祥安： 哇！尝起来几乎跟小美妈妈做的一样，又香又辣，让人很有胃口！

李中平： 果然是好吃得不得了！我们难得能在超市吃到这么地道和美味的中国菜。祥安，你要做什么拿手菜带去美食比赛？

黄祥安： 我不太会做菜，所以还没有想好要不要参加……

李中平： 你不是学过做菜吗？

黄祥安： 是啊，可是怎么也做不好，为了大家的肚子着想，我还是不参加了。

李中平： 哈哈，原来是这样！我会做家常豆腐，我们一起做吧，我教你。

Language Tip

 够 (gòu)

In the Lesson Text, Dadong uses 够, meaning "enough," to say that the chicken is not fresh enough. In English, the location of "enough" changes depending on how it is used in the sentence. For example, "I don't have enough money," versus "I am not rich enough." In Chinese, the position of 够 is the reverse of the English patterns. When 够 is used as an adjective, it follows the noun, as in "我的钱不够." When 够 is used as an adverb, it precedes what it modifies, as in "我不够有钱." For this reason, it may be helpful to think of 够 as meaning "sufficient" or "sufficiently," as in "My funds are not sufficient."

Example: 你的卧室够大吗？
Is your bedroom large enough?

字词 VOCABULARY

LESSON VOCABULARY 6.2

	SIMPLIFIED	TRADITIONAL	PINYIN	WORD CATEGORY	DEFINITION
1.	特色		tèsè	n	distinguishing feature or quality
2.	于是	於是	yúshì	cj	so; hence; as a result
3.	超市		chāoshì	n	supermarket
4.	烹饪	烹飪	pēngrèn	n	cooking
5.	减价	減價	jiǎnjià	vo	to reduce the price, to be discounted
6.	试吃	試吃	shìchī	v	to sample
7.	蒜		suàn	n	garlic
8.	差		chà	v	to be short of, to be missing
9.	够	夠	gòu	adj	enough
10.	新鲜	新鮮	xīnxiān	adj	fresh
11.	过期	過期	guòqī	vo	to expire
12.	口水		kǒushuǐ	n	saliva, drool, dribble
13.	尝	嘗	cháng	v	to taste
14.	几乎	幾乎	jīhū	adv	almost, nearly
15.	香		xiāng	adj	savory, appetizing
16.	胃口		wèikǒu	n	appetite
17.	果然		guǒrán	adv	indeed; as expected; sure enough
18.	难得	難得	nándé	adj	rare; hard to come by
19.	美味		měiwèi	adj, n	flavorful, delicious; delicacy
20.	拿手菜		náshǒucài	n	specialty dish, signature dish, a chef's best dish
	拿手		náshǒu	adj	be good at
21.	着想		zhuóxiǎng	v	to consider

PROPER NOUN

22.	麻婆豆腐		Mápódòufu	n	Mapo Tofu

REQUIRED VOCABULARY 6.2

SIMPLIFIED	TRADITIONAL	PINYIN	WORD CATEGORY	DEFINITION
23. 海鲜	海鮮	hǎixiān	*n*	seafood
24. 猪肉	豬肉	zhūròu	*n*	pork
25. 牛肉		niúròu	*n*	beef
26. 蔬菜		shūcài	*n*	vegetables
27. 调味料	調味料	tiáowèiliào	*n*	seasoning
28. 种类	種類	zhǒnglèi	*n*	type
类	類	lèi	*n*	kind

ONLINE RESOURCES

Visit *http://college.betterchinese.com* for more names of Chinese dishes.

Idiomatic Expression

wǔ huā bā mén
五花八门

五花八门 is used to mean "a wide range or variety (of something)" or "multifarious."

This expression appears in describing ancient military tactics, one called "five-row array" and another called "eight-door lock array." These tactics were used to change the soldiers' formations, depending on the enemy's position and strengths. Later, the expression evolved to connote all kinds of different jobs and today is used generally to mean "wide-ranging and diverse".

Example:
超市的烹饪材料种类很多，五花八门。
The supermarket has all kinds of cooking ingredients.

Writing an E-mail

The format and components of writing an e-mail in Chinese are very similar to that of a letter. When writing a letter in Chinese, here is some helpful advice:

1. Depending on your relationship to the recipient, you may begin the letter in several ways:
   a. 亲爱(的) (qīn'ài(de): dear) - usually used for family and close friends.
   b. 敬爱(的) (jìng'ài(de): dear) and 尊敬(的) (zūnjìng (de): respected) - more formal, emphasizes that the addressee is respected, but they are not used for close relationships.
   c. The name of the addressee: this is standard for acquaintances.
   d. Using the surname or the complete name with 先生 (xiānsheng) or 女士 (nǚshì) such as 陈先生 or 张玛丽女士 for formal and business correspondence.
2. Always indent two spaces before beginning a new paragraph.
3. Expressing good wishes: 祝好! Note that there are two spaces before the character 好. 好 can be replaced with any wishes, such as 身体健康 and 幸福 (xìngfú: happiness).
4. The name of the sender and the date are placed at the end of the letter.

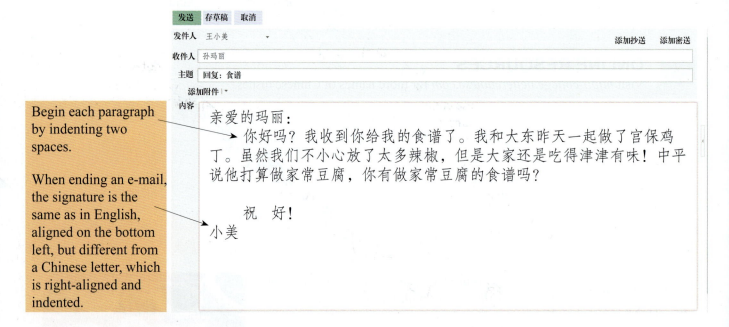

Begin each paragraph by indenting two spaces.

When ending an e-mail, the signature is the same as in English, aligned on the bottom left, but different from a Chinese letter, which is right-aligned and indented.

Below are some key terms one might frequently encounter:

Chinese	Pinyin	Meaning
发送	fāsòng	to send
存草稿	cún cǎogǎo	to save as a draft
发件人	fājiànrén	sender
收件人	shōujiànrén	recipient
抄送	chāosòng	Cc (carbon copy)
密送	mìsòng	Bcc (blind carbon copy)
主题	zhǔtí	title
添加附件	tiānjiā fùjiàn	to attach a file
内容	nèiróng	content
回复	huífù	to reply

STRUCTURE NOTE 6.5

Use 于是 to say "hence" or "thus"

于是 (yúshì) *is a conjunction most often seen in formal writing. Its meaning is similar to* 所以, *meaning "so," but it is more precisely equivalent to "and thus."* 于是 *introduces an event that is explained or caused by the conditions in the previous clause.*

> Condition clause + 于是 + Result clause

From the Lesson Text:

于是他们一起去超市买菜。
Yúshì tāmen yìqǐ qù chāoshì mǎicài.
So they all go the supermarket to buy ingredients.

Other examples:

她一直对中国文化很有兴趣，于是她打算去中国留学。
Tā yìzhí duì Zhōngguó wénhuà hěn yǒu xìngqù, yúshì tā dǎsuàn qù Zhōngguó liúxué.
She has always been very interested in Chinese culture, and thus she plans to study abroad in China.

那时有很多事不能跟别人说，于是我就开始写日记了。
Nàshí yǒu hěn duō shì bù néng gēn biérén shuō, yúshì wǒ jiù kāishǐ xiě rìjì le .
At that time, I had a lot of things I couldn't talk to anyone else about. Therefore, I began keeping a diary.

Practice: Expand the sentences using 于是 and the information provided.

Example:
我和安娜都饿了……
→于是我们找了一家饭馆吃饭。

1. 玛丽很喜欢音乐……

   _____

2. 离电影开始还有两个多小时……

   _____

3. 我的房东要收回房子……

   _____

4. 老师建议我去中国留学……

   _____

5. 我对这个社团很感兴趣……

   _____

STRUCTURE NOTE 6.6
Use 几乎 *to say "nearly"*

几乎 *(jīhū) is an adverb meaning "almost" or "nearly." It can be used to express "nearly did something" or "nearly some amount." In the Lesson Text,* 几乎 *appears in the pattern* 几乎跟······一样, *meaning "almost the same as . . ."* 几乎 *and* 大概 *are very similar. While* 大概 *means "approximately" or "probably,"* 几乎 *implies that the actual number is lower.*

几乎 + Verb / Noun / Adjective Phrase

From the Lesson Text:

尝起来几乎跟小美妈妈做的一样。
Cháng qǐlai jīhū gēn Xiǎoměi māma zuò de yíyàng.
This tastes almost exactly like how Xiaomei's mom makes it.

Other examples:

山猫队赢了，他高兴得几乎跳起来。
Shānmāo duì yíngle, tā gāoxìng de jīhū tiào qǐlai.
When the Mountain Lions won, he was so happy he almost jumped up.

他们几乎每个人都有自己的电脑。
Tāmen jīhū měi ge rén dōu yǒu zìjǐ de diànnǎo.
Almost everyone one of them has his or her own computer.

Practice: Insert 几乎 or 大概 to complete the question/sentences.

1. 这台电脑多少钱？

   _____

2. 明天就要去中国了，他高兴得睡不着。

   _____

3. 这个学校每个人都认识她。

   _____

4. 我下星期一去北京。

   _____

5. 玛丽今年十九岁。

   _____

STRUCTURE NOTE 6.7

Use 果然 *to indicate that something happened as expected*

果然 *(guǒrán) is an adverb expressing the sense "indeed" or "as I thought," implying that a situation is consistent with what the speaker expected to happen.* 果然 *can introduce a sentence, or occur before a verb or an adjective phrase.*

果然 + Sentence

Subject + 果然 + Adjective / Verb Phrase

From the Lesson Text:

果然是好吃得不得了！
Guǒrán shì hǎochī de bùdeliǎo!
It is indeed very delicious!

Other examples:

在这家商店买电器果然
比较划算。
Zài zhè jiā shāngdiàn mǎi diànqì
guǒrán bǐjiao huásuàn.
The electronics in this store are really
more cost-effective.

李教授果然是中国文化的
专家。
Lǐ jiàoshòu guǒrán shì Zhōngguó wén-
huà de zhuānjiā.
As I thought, Professor Li is an expert on
Chinese culture.

Practice: Create complete sentences using 果然 and appropriate outcomes for the given scenarios.

Example:　小美妈妈做的菜……
→小美妈妈做的菜果然好吃得让我们停不了嘴。

1. 这套公寓……
   _____

2. 他太粗心了！这个月……
   _____

3. 住宿舍……
   _____

4. 这里的天气真好！昆明的天气……
   _____

5. 在网上购物……
   _____

STRUCTURE NOTE 6.8
Use 难得 *to describe rare situations and opportunities*

难得 *(nándé), literally meaning "hard to come by," can be used as an adjective meaning "rare," or as an adverb meaning "rarely." This phrase is most often used to describe a rare opportunity or positive attribute, rather than a negative situation. When the subject is omitted, the implication is that the speaker believes this is a rare situation in general.*

> (Subject +) 难得 + Verb Phrase

From the Lesson Text:

我们难得能在超市吃到这么地道和美味的中国菜。
Wǒmen nándé néng zài chāoshì chīdao zhème dìdào hé měiwèi de Zhōngguó cài.
It's rare for us to eat such authentic and flavorful Chinese food at a supermarket!

Other examples:

这家商店难得会让客人免费试用产品。
Zhè jiā shāngdiàn nándé huì ràng kèrén miǎnfèi shìyòng chǎnpǐn.
It's rare for this store to let customers sample the merchandise.

我们难得见面，你多坐一会儿吧。
Wǒmen nándé jiànmiàn, nǐ duō zuò yìhuǐr ba.
We rarely get together, please do stay awhile.

Practice: Create complete sentences using 难得 and the information provided below.

Example: 去看／一场篮球赛／我
→ 我难得去看一场篮球赛。

1. 她／社团的活动／去参加

_____

2. 我们／一次／见面

_____

3. 这个周末／可以去爬山／我们

_____

4. 冬天／这里的／会下雪

_____

5. 春节／这个／大家／一起／过年

_____

💬 **练习 6.10: 课文理解**

Paired Activity: Discuss the following questions based on the Lesson Text. Be prepared to share your thoughts with the class.

> 1. 大东为什么没有在超市买鸡肉？
>
> 2. 祥安最后打算做什么菜去参加中国美食比赛？
>
> 3. 如果参加中国美食比赛，你会做什么菜？

💬 **练习 6.11 (上): 最喜欢的中国菜**

Group Activity: You are attending the Chinese Food Competition next week and some of your classmates will be judges. Survey three classmates for their favorite dishes and have them explain why they like these dishes.

姓名	中国菜名	理由
Example: 黄祥安	宫保鸡丁、 麻婆豆腐	因为他喜欢吃辣。辣的菜会让他很有胃口。

💬 练习 6.12 (中)：超市购物乐

Paired Activity: You need to buy ingredients for the dish you have decided to make. Using the supermarket ad below, discuss with a classmate what you need and how much you expect to spend. Research and present the price of items not available at this supermarket.

Notes:

斤 (jīn): *mw.* unit of weight equals to 500 grams   包 (bāo): *mw.* a bag of

✏️ 练习 6.13 (下)：参加中国美食比赛

Individual Activity: Your dish has made it to the Chinese Food Competition finals! Select a few words from the word bank below, then describe your dish to the judge.

特色　新鲜　尝　胃口　口水　地道　美味　拿手菜　香　辣

菜名	材料	做法	味道

💬 练习 6.14：评评这道菜

Group Activity: Working with your group, select a restaurant that you are all familiar with. Discuss the dishes available at the restaurant and create a review of the restaurant. Talk about food preferences, prices, customer service, and overall experience.

	Radical	Stroke Order
牛	牛 niú cow	丿 ╯ 二 牛
蒜	艹 cǎo grass	一 十 卝 艹 艾 芋 芽 萨 蒜 蒜 蒜
超	走 zǒu walk	一 十 土 丰 走 起 起 起 超 超
减	冫(冰) bīng ice	丶 冫 汇 汇 沤 沂 沶 减 减 减
猪	犭 quǎn dog	丿 犭 犭 犭 猪 猪 猪 猪 猪 猪
够	夕 xī evening	丿 勹 勹 句 句 句 够 够 够 够
鲜	鱼 yú fish	丿 ⺈ 夕 各 各 角 鱼 鱼 鱼 鲜 鲜 鲜 鲜
豆	一 yī one	一 ⼆ 戸 戸 豆 豆 豆
腐	广 yǎn shelter	丶 广 广 广 庐 府 府 府 腐 腐 腐 腐
水	水 shuǐ water	亅 水 水 水
尝	小 xiǎo little	丨 ⺌ 尚 尚 尚 尝 尝 尝 尝
乎	丿 piě slash	丿 ⺈ ⺈ 平 乎
香	禾 hé grain	一 二 千 禾 禾 禾 香 香 香
胃	月(肉) ròu meat	丨 口 口 田 田 甲 胃 胃 胃

练习 6.16: 线上聊天

Online chat: Working with a classmate, discuss whether or not you like the food on campus. Provide examples to support your opinion.

练习 6.17: 阅读理解

小美的妈妈很会做菜，她做的中国菜非常地道。于是祥安到小美家，想跟小美妈妈学做菜。小美的妈妈告诉祥安，做菜不难，只要学会一些烹饪方法，就能做出好吃的菜。中国菜五花八门，但祥安最喜欢吃麻婆豆腐，所以小美妈妈就教他做这个菜。做麻婆豆腐的材料很简单，只需要豆腐、辣椒、葱和蒜。祥安没想到做麻婆豆腐这么简单，他很快就学会做这个菜了，而且做得又香又辣，好吃极了！

Read the passage and answer the following questions.
1. Provide two reason why Xiang'an wants to go to Xiaomei's house?
2. What did Xiaomei's mom teach Xiang'an to make and what ingredients does he need?
3. What dish can you teach others to make? Provide the ingredients and procedure.

练习 6.18: 阅读理解

超市会员服务中心

怎样申请会员卡？
- 单次购物超过500元就可以申请会员卡
- 申请会员卡时要出示收据

会员有什么优惠？
- 全部食品有九折优惠
- 日用品、电子产品有会员价优惠
- 购物超过2000元可以免费送货
- 免费退换货

会员卡有年费吗？
- 没有，只要您单次购物超过500元就可以申请

Additional Vocabulary:
服务中心 (fúwù zhōngxīn): n. service center
会员卡 (huìyuánkǎ): n. membership card
单次 (dāncì): adj. single time
出示 (chūshì): v. to show
年费 (niánfèi): n. annual fee

Read the promotion and answer the following questions.
1. Mali has two receipts from this supermarket; one receipt is for ¥300, and the other is for ¥350. Can she apply for a membership card? Why?
2. What promotions do members receive?
3. What kind of membership cards do you have or would like to have? Explain the costs and benefits of this membership.

Street Food

Chinese street food can range from the strange to the mundane, from insects to dumplings. A couple of the most well-known items include chuanr (串儿: chuànr) and jianbing (煎饼: jiānbǐng).

Chuanr

Chuanr is a skewer of small pieces of meat. Popular in and around Beijing, Tianjin, and Jilin, these kebabs come from Xinjiang in the northwest, where mutton is the most commonly found meat. Although traditionally roasted and made of lamb, the kebabs can be made with many types of meat, vegetable, or bread. A variety of spices and sauces provide additional flavor.

Chuanr can be found at street stalls, carts, and restaurants, often advertised with the distinctive character 串 (chuàn) in bright neon. In many cities, people can be found gathered around a streetside cart or stall, eating one of these chuanrs to end an evening out.

Jianbing

Jianbing originated in the northeast, where the climate is more favorable for grains. Jianbing, a thin pancake fried with egg and folded around a fried crepe with green onions or cilantro covered with a mild chili sauce, usually eaten for breakfast. The ingredients in jianbing do vary widely from region to region. One of the most popular street foods in China, it can be found in indoor and outdoor stalls, street carts, and sometimes in major supermarkets.

An interesting story lies behind this popular street food. During the Warring States period, the famous strategist Zhuge Liang (诸葛亮: Zhūgě Liàng) was in Shandong with a large number of soldiers to feed and no woks available for cooking. He told the cooks to combine water and wheat flour evenly and cook it on a griddle over the fire, and the result was jianbing. Once fed, the troops bested the enemy in battle.

Chengdu Teahouse Culture

The city of Chengdu (成都: Chéngdū), the capital of Sichuan Province (四川省: Sìchuān Shěng), is famous for its teahouse (茶馆: cháguǎn) culture. While teahouses were once widespread across China, Sichuan is one of the places where teahouses continue to have a major role in community life. The people of Chengdu are known for their laid-back, slow-paced style of living, which is deeply tied to the atmosphere in the city's teahouses.

Teahouses have existed at least as far back as the Tang Dynasty (618 - 907 AD) but proliferated in the early twentieth century. In Chengdu, there are records of 454 teahouses in 1909 and 599 in 1939, reaching a ratio of nearly one teahouse for every street.

While they are less central than they used to be, traditional teahouses still play an important part in the daily life of many residents. Many people go not only to drink tea and chat, but also to read newspapers, discuss politics, play games, gamble, make business deals, or even get massages. Some teahouses will also provide entertainment, such as stand-up comic or acrobatic performances.

Teahouses face new competition with coffeehouses vying for customers. However, teahouses are also evolving: a modern version of teahouse culture may now include bubble tea (tea with chewy tapioca bubbles), a treat first invented in Taiwan and now widely popular with young people in Chinese communities around the world. Just like traditional teahouses, bubble tea cafes serve as meeting places for people to share snacks, read comic books, and socialize with friends.

Pinyin

Dàdōng hé péngyoumen dǎsuan zài Zhōngguó měishí bǐsài zuò yìxiē yǒu tèsè de cài, yúshì tāmen yìqǐ qù chāoshì mǎicài. Zhènghǎo chāoshì yǒu hěn duō shíwù hé pēngrèn cáiliào zài jiǎnjià, mǎi yī sòng yī, háiyǒu miǎnfèi shìchī.

Wáng Xiǎoměi: Dàdōng, zuò Gōngbǎo Jīdīng de cáiliào dōu mǎi hǎo le ma?

Chén Dàdōng: Wǒ mǎile làjiāo, cōng hé suàn, hái chà jīròu. Wǒ kànle yíxià jīròu, juéde bú gòu xīnxiān, yǒude hái kuài guòqī le. Wǒmen qù lìng yì jiā chāoshì kànkan ba.

Lǐ Zhōngpíng: Zhèlǐ de Mápódòufu kěyǐ shìchī, kàn de wǒ kǒushuǐ dōu yào liú chūlai le!

Huáng Xiáng'ān: Wā! Cháng qǐlai jīhū gēn Xiǎoměi māma zuò de yíyàng, yòu xiāng yòu là, ràng rén hěn yǒu wèikǒu!

Lǐ Zhōngpíng: Guǒrán shì hǎochī de bùdeliǎo! Wǒmen nándé néng zài chāoshì chīdào zhème dìdào hé měiwèi de Zhōngguó cài. Xiáng'ān, nǐ yào zuò shénme náshǒucài dài qù měishí bǐsài?

English

Dadong and his friends are planning to make some special dishes for the Chinese Cooking Competition, so they all go to the supermarket to buy ingredients. As it happened, a number of items were being discounted, buy one get one free, and in addition they were giving out free samples.

Dadong, did you buy all the ingredients to make Kung Pao Chicken?

I got the chili peppers, green onions, and garlic but am still missing the chicken. I just checked the chicken, but I don't think they're fresh enough as some of them are expiring soon. Let's go have a look at another supermarket.

You can try a sample of the Mapo Tofu here. Seeing it is making me drool!

Wow! This tastes almost exactly like how Xiaomei's mom makes it. It's both fragrant and spicy — it really builds up your appetite!

It is indeed, very delicious! It's rare for us to eat such authentic and flavorful Chinese food at a supermarket! Xiang'an, what specialty dish will you make for the cooking competition?

Huáng Xiáng'ān:	Wǒ bú tài huì zuòcài, suǒyǐ hái méiyǒu xiǎnghǎo yàobuyào cānjiā	I'm not very good at cooking, so I haven't really decided whether or not to join the competition . . .
Lǐ Zhōngpíng:	Nǐ bú shì xuéguo zuò cài ma?	Haven't you taken cooking classes before?
Huáng Xiáng'ān:	Shì a, kěshì zěnme yě zuò bu hǎo, wèile dàjiā de dùzi zhuóxiǎng, wǒ háishì bù cānjiā le.	Yes, but no matter what I did, the food did not turn out well. I think it's in the best interest of everyone's stomach if I don't participate in the competition.
Lǐ Zhōngpíng:	Hāha, yuánlái shì zhèyàng! Wǒ huì zuò Jiāchángdòufu, wǒmen yìqǐ zuò ba, wǒ jiāo nǐ.	Haha, that explains things! I'm going to prepare a home-style tofu. We can make it together and I can teach you.

What Can You Do?

INTERPRETIVE
- I can state impressions regarding a dish after hearing others review it.
- I can recognize promotions at a supermarket.

INTERPERSONAL
- I can exchange opinions on how a particular dish tastes.
- I can discuss the experience of shopping at a supermarket.

PRESENTATIONAL
- I can summarize what has been purchased at a supermarket and what is still needed.
- I can present the pros and cons of shopping at different supermarkets.

单元复习 UNIT REVIEW

ACT IT OUT

Working in groups, compose an original two-minute skit that utilizes the vocabulary and structures introduced in Unit 6. Each of you should assume a role and have a roughly equal number of lines in the skit. Be prepared to perform your skit in class. You can either come up with your own story or choose from one of the following situations:

A) You and a few other customers at a supermarket are sampling some of the food the shop clerks are offering. Discuss with the customers what you are eating, what you think of the taste, and whether you like it or not.

B) You go to a supermarket to buy ingredients to make Kung Pao chicken. Ask a shop clerk were to find each ingredient in the store.

C) You and your family are at a restaurant, trying to decide what to order. Ask the waiter what he recommends and why.

CHECK WHAT YOU CAN DO

RECOGNIZE

Adjectives
- 适量
- 少许
- 新鲜
- 香
- 难得
- 美味

Adverbs
- 实在
- 够
- 几乎
- 果然

Conjunctions
- 无论……都

- 于是

Idiomatic Expression
- 拿手菜

Measure Word
- 道

Nouns
- 做法
- 宫保鸡丁
- 做法
- 食谱
- 材料
- 鸡肉
- 克
- 葱

- 辣椒
- 花生米
- 油
- 盐
- 匙
- 糖
- 淀粉
- 料酒
- 酱油
- 锅
- 大火
- 家常菜
- 特色
- 超市
- 烹饪
- 蒜

- 麻婆豆腐
- 口水
- 胃口
- 海鲜
- 猪肉
- 牛肉
- 蔬菜
- 调味料
- 种类

Prepositions
- 将

Verbs
- 以为
- 切丁

- 拌匀
- 炒熟
- 盛
- 试吃
- 差
- 尝
- 着想

Verb-Object Compounds
- 减价
- 过期

WRITE
- 谱
- 克
- 米
- 油
- 盐
- 糖
- 粉
- 酒
- 切
- 锅
- 炒
- 熟
- 盛
- 将
- 葱

- 牛
- 蒜
- 超
- 减
- 猪
- 够
- 鲜
- 豆
- 腐
- 水
- 尝
- 乎
- 香
- 烹
- 胃

USE
- Use 以为 to express mistaken belief.
- Use 将 to indicate an action performed on a specific object in formal contexts.
- Use 无论…都… to express "no matter what" something is always the case.
- Use 实在 to mean "really" and "honestly."
- Use 于是 to say "hence" or "thus."
- Use 几乎 to say "nearly."
- Use 果然 to indicate that something happened as expected.
- Use 难得 to describe rare situations and opportunities.

228 第六单元 ▪ 第二课 ▪ 逛超市

祸

Emergencies

第七单元
UNIT 7

Communication Goals

Lesson 1: 交通意外 **A Traffic Accident**
- Report a traffic accident to the police.
- Talk about traffic violations.
- Talk about injuries and going to hospitals.
- Recognize common traffic and driving terms.

Lesson 2: 自然灾难 **Natural Disasters**
- Talk about common natural disasters.
- Talk about accidents.
- Discuss a disaster report about casualties and damages.
- Discuss preparations for a natural disaster.

交通意外
A Traffic Accident

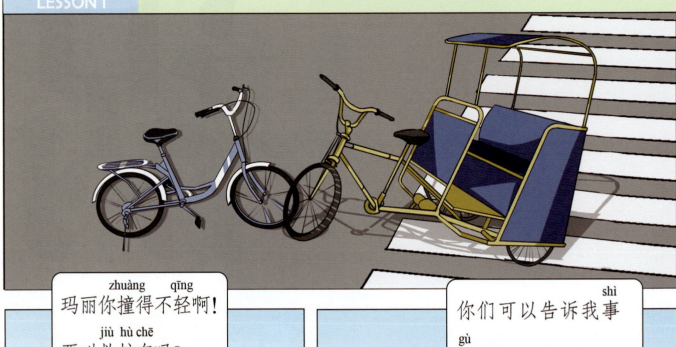

玛丽你撞(zhuàng)得不轻(qīng)啊！
要叫救护车(jiù hù chē)吗？

我还好，等一会儿去
诊所检查(zhěn suǒ jiǎn chá)一下就行。

你们可以告诉我事(shì)
故(gù)是怎么发生的吗？

我们过马路的时候，这辆(liàng)
三轮车突然撞(sān lún chē tū rán zhuàng)了过来。

师傅(shī fu)，请让我看看
你的身份证(shēn fèn zhèng)。

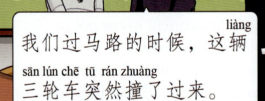

哎呀，我的身份证呢？
这个人常常丢三落四(diū sān là sì)的，
又忘了带身份证(shēn fèn zhèng)了……
再说这件事不能完全怪(wán quán guài)
我，是他们闯(chuǎng)了红灯。

不对，我们并
没有闯红灯！

shī fu
师傅，这条路禁止三轮
chē tōng xíng
车通行，你又没带身份
zhèng yīn cǐ
证，因此我要给你开一
fá dān
张罚单。

dǎo méi
哎，今天真倒霉！我以后再也不
zháo jí
这么着急了。对不起，我会负责
yī liáo
你的医疗费。

zhěn suǒ
玛丽，我现在就带你去诊所看看。

不好意思，麻烦你了！

LESSON TEXT 7.1

A Traffic Accident 交通意外

Zhou Xin and Mali were crossing the road when they were hit by a motorized pedicab. A police officer arrives at the scene of the accident, and Zhou Xin, Mali, and the pedicab driver recount what happened.

周信： 玛丽你撞得不轻啊！要叫救护车吗？

孙玛丽： 我还好，等一会儿去诊所检查一下就行。

交警： 你们可以告诉我事故是怎么发生的吗？

周信： 我们过马路的时候，这辆三轮车突然撞了过来。

交警： 师傅，请让我看看你的身份证。

师傅： 哎呀，我的身份证呢？我这个人常常丢三落四的，又忘带身份证了……再说这件事不能完全怪我，是他们闯了红灯。

周信： 不对，我们并没有闯红灯！

交警： 师傅，这条路禁止三轮车通行，你又没带身份证，因此我要给你开一张罚单。

师傅： 哎，今天真倒霉！我以后再也不这么着急了。对不起，我会负责你的医疗费。

周信： 玛丽，我现在就带你去诊所看看。

孙玛丽： 不好意思，麻烦你了！

Language Tip

开 (kāi)

In the Lesson Text, the police officer uses 开 to express that he is going to give a ticket to the driver. 开 literally means "open." It is also used to mean "write . . . out" in the context of handing out, for example, tickets, prescriptions (开药), or receipts (开收据), or writing a check (开支票).

Example:
买了电视以后不要忘了让店员给你开收据。
Don't forget to ask the salesclerk for a receipt after you buy the television.

LESSON VOCABULARY 7.1

	SIMPLIFIED	TRADITIONAL	PINYIN	WORD CATEGORY	DEFINITION
1.	撞		zhuàng	*v*	to collide, to run into
2.	轻	輕	qīng	*adj*	(injury/illness) not serious; light
3.	救护车	救護車	jiùhùchē	*n*	ambulance
4.	诊所	診所	zhěnsuǒ	*n*	clinic
5.	检查	檢查	jiǎnchá	*v, n*	to examine, to check; examination
6.	警察		jǐngchá	*n*	policeman
7.	事故		shìgù	*n*	accident
8.	辆	輛	liàng	*mw*	(used for vehicles)
9.	三轮车	三輪車	sānlúnchē	*n*	pedicab
10.	突然		tūrán	*adv*	suddenly
11.	师傅	師傅	shīfu	*n*	sir (respectful formal address for a male elder)
12.	身份证	身份證	shēnfènzhèng	*n*	identity card
13.	丢三落四		diūsān làsì	*ie*	forgetful, always forgetful
	丢		diū	*v*	to lose
	落		là	*v*	to be missing, to leave behind, to forget to bring
14.	完全		wánquán	*adv, adj*	totally, completely; complete
15.	怪		guài	*v*	to blame
16.	闯	闖	chuǎng	*v*	to rush
17.	并	並	bìng	*adv*	actually; truly (intensifier before a negative)
18.	禁止		jìnzhǐ	*v*	to prohibit, to forbid
19.	通行		tōngxíng	*v*	to go through
20.	因此		yīncǐ	*conj*	therefore; consequently
21.	罚单	罰單	fádān	*n*	violation ticket
22.	倒霉		dǎoméi	*adj*	be out of luck, unlucky
23.	着急		zháojí	*adj*	hurried; worried; feel anxious

SIMPLIFIED	TRADITIONAL	PINYIN	WORD CATEGORY	DEFINITION
24. 医疗	醫療	yīliáo	*n*	medical treatment

REQUIRED VOCABULARY 7.1

SIMPLIFIED	TRADITIONAL	PINYIN	WORD CATEGORY	DEFINITION
25. 危险	危險	wēixiǎn	*adj*	dangerous
26. 受伤	受傷	shòushāng	*vo*	to be wounded, to be injured
伤	傷	shāng	*n*	wound, injury
27. 司机	司機	sījī	*n*	driver
28. 乘客		chéng kè	*n*	passenger
乘		chéng	*v*	to travel by
29. 车祸	車禍	chēhuò	*n*	traffic accident
30. 意外		yìwài	*n, adj*	accident; unexpected
31. 驾驶执照	駕駛執照	jiàshǐ zhízhào	*n*	driver's license
驾驶	駕駛	jiàshǐ	*v*	to drive
执照	執照	zhízhào	*n*	license

Idiomatic Expression

diū sān là sì

丢三落四

丢三落四 means to "drop three items and miss four things." It is used to describe people who are careless and forgetful.

The description appears in the Qing Dynasty (1644 – 1912 AD) novel *Dream of the Red Chamber* (《红楼梦》: *Hónglóu Mèng*). In the novel, a mother tells her son to focus on things needed to have a good standing in society: building up his business and finding someone to marry. If he remains such a careless person and misses his chance to gain both of these now, he will become a laughingstock of society.

Example:

她是个丢三落四的人，常常忘记把东西放在哪儿了。

She is so careless that she often forgets where she has left things.

Verbs and Directional Complements

Compound directional complements are used to indicate the direction of physical movements. In previous lessons, simple directional complements, 来 (see *Modern Chinese* Textbook Vol. 1A, Unit 7, Lesson 1) and 去 (see *Modern Chinese* Textbook Vol. 1B, Unit 11, Lesson 1), were used to add information about the direction of an action in relation to the speaker.

Examples:
他回家去了 indicates that the subject went home, away from the speaker.
他回家来 indicates that the subject came home towards the speaker.

To provide more information about an action, an additional directional complement can be placed between the main verb and 来 or 去, creating a compound directional complement. Just as 来 and 去 describe motion towards or away from the speaker, an additional directional complement can be supplemented to provide more details about movement.

Below lists some of the most common compound directional complements. Each can be followed by 来 or 去, except for 起, which can only be paired with 来.

Compound Directional Complements	Type of Motion
上 + 来 / 去	Upward
下 + 来 / 去	Downward
过 + 来 / 去	Crossing over
进 + 来 / 去	Entering
出 + 来 / 去	Exiting
回 + 来 / 去	Returning
起 + 来	Rising

If the verb takes an object, it must appear after the entire directional complement.

Verb + 上/下/过/进/出/回/起 + Location + 来 / 去

Example:
他走进屋子来了 indicates that the subject walked into the room.

The possible combinations of verbs and compound directional complements can be daunting, so rather than memorize all the permutations, simply think about the directional movement to determine valid pairings.

For example, the verb 掉 (diào: falling or dropping), can be associated with downward motions such as:
掉下来 / 去 (to fall down)
掉过来 / 去 (to fall over)
掉进来 / 去 (to fall into something)
掉出来 / 去 (to fall out of something)
掉回来 / 去 (to fall back down)

ONLINE RESOURCES
Visit *http://college.betterchinese.com* for more examples of verb and directional complements.

STRUCTURE NOTE 7.1
Use 完全 *to say "completely"*

完全 *(wánquán) is an adverb meaning "completely," "totally," or "entirely." As in English, the placement of the negative* 不 *before or after* 完全 *affects its meaning:* 完全不 *means "entirely not," and* 不完全 *means "not entirely."*

完全 + Adjective / Verb Phrase

From the Lesson Text:

再说这件事不能完全怪我。
Zàishuō zhè jiàn shì bù néng wánquán guài wǒ.
Besides, this accident is not totally my fault.

Other examples:

这两个人的性格完全不一样。
Zhè liǎng ge rén de xìnggé wánquán bù yíyàng.
The personalities of these two people are totally different.

他紧张得完全睡不着。
Tā jǐnzhāng de wánquán shuì bu zháo.
He is so nervous and can't fall asleep at all.

Practice: Use 完全 to rewrite the following sentences.

Example: 他的书我一点也看不懂。
→他的书我完全看不懂。

1. 这次比赛输了不都是你的问题。

   _____

2. 他做的宫保鸡丁和我做的一样。

   _____

3. 音乐剧和戏剧是非常不同的。

   _____

4. 他说的中文我们一点儿都听不懂。

   _____

5. 我什么中国菜都不会做。

   _____

STRUCTURE NOTE 7.2
Use 并 to emphasize a negative contrast

并 *(bìng) has been previously introduced as a shorter way of saying* 并且, *"and," in formal contexts.* 并 *can also be used as a particle with a sense of "however," indicating that something has happened contrary to expectation.* 并 *is only used in negative constructions, as in* 并不是.

> Subject + 并 + Verb Phrase

From the Lesson Text:

我们并没有闯红灯！
Wǒmen bìng méiyǒu chuǎng hóngdēng!
That's not true. We didn't run any lights!

Other examples:

其实，我不太喜欢吃蛋糕，但我并没跟他们说。
Qíshí, wǒ bú tài xǐhuan chī dàngāo, dàn wǒ bìng méi gēn tāmen shuō.
Actually, I don't really like cake, but I didn't tell them that.

中国的礼节并不复杂，你只要多练习就能学会。
Zhōngguó de lǐjié bìng bú fùzá, nǐ zhǐyào duō liànxí jiù néng xuéhuì.
Chinese etiquette isn't very complicated at all; as long as you practice more, you will be able to master it.

Practice: Create complete sentences including 并 and the provided information.

Example: 下星期有一个很重要的考试/我不紧张。
→下星期有一个很重要的考试，但我并不紧张。

1. 我感冒了/没有告诉我的朋友

   _____

2. 我会打篮球/不喜欢打篮球

   _____

3. 小美喜欢吃中餐/不常常吃中餐

   _____

4. 他的性格很开朗/不喜欢参加派对

   _____

5. 这个队的实力很强，配合得也很好/没有赢这场比赛。

   _____

STRUCTURE NOTE 7.3
Use 因此 to say "therefore"

In 因此 *(yīncǐ)*, 因 means 因为, and 此 means 这个, so 因此 *literally meaning "because of this," is a more formal way of stating* 所以, *"so" or "therefore."*

因此 + Sentence

From the Lesson Text: 因此我要给你开一张罚单。
Yīncǐ wǒ yào gěi nǐ kāi yì zhāng fádān.
Therefore, I must issue you a ticket.

Other examples: 玛丽迷上了中国文化，因此她决定继续留在北京念书。
Mǎlì míshangle Zhōngguó wénhuà, yīncǐ tā juédìng jìxù liúzài Běijīng niànshū.
Mali has fallen in love with Chinese culture. Because of this, she has decided to continue studying in Beijing.

这道菜很好吃，而且做法非常简单，因此十分受欢迎。
Zhè dào cài hěn hǎochī, érqiě zuòfǎ fēicháng jiǎndān, yīncǐ shífēn shòu huānyíng.
This dish is very tasty, and also the method for making it is very easy. Because of this, the dish is extremely popular.

Practice: Complete the sentences using 因此 and the information provided.

Example: 对她非常了解 / 我认识她很多年
→我认识她很多年，因此对她非常了解。

1. 加入保护环境的社团 / 他想要让地球变得更美好
   _____

2. 昆明有山有水，很漂亮 / 我们一直想去那里旅游
   _____

3. 主修中国文化课 / 我迷上了中国历史小说
   _____

4. 想要搬出去 / 她觉得住宿舍一点隐私都没有
   _____

5. 球队的队员不重视团队精神 / 最后输了比赛
   _____

STRUCTURE NOTE 7.4

Use 再也 (不 / 没) to emphatically state "never ever again"

再, *meaning "again," is ordinarily negated with a preceding* 不. *The phrase* 不再敢, *for example, means "won't dare again." To make this expression more emphatic,* 也不/没 *may be placed following the* 再, *implying that no matter what, this won't happen again.*

Subject + 再也不 / 没 + Verb Phrase

From the Lesson Text:　　　我以后开车再也不这么着急了。
Wǒ yǐhòu kāichē zài yě bú zhème zháojí le.
I will never be in such a rush when driving in the future.

Other examples:　　　我们再也没见过那个人。　　　我再也不相信他了。
Wǒmen zài yě méi jiànguo nà ge rén.　　　Wǒ zài yě bù xiāngxìn tā le.
We never saw that person again.　　　I'll never believe him again.

Practice: Create complete sentences using 再也不 / 没 and information provided.

Example:　　　我 / 在网上买东西
　　　→我再也不在网上买东西了。

1. 我以后约会 / 来晚

　　　_____

2. 我以后 / 相信广告

　　　_____

3. 小张 / 吃辣椒

　　　_____

4. 这个赛季山猫队 / 输给飞鼠队

　　　_____

5. 这次比赛以后，那个乐队 / 获得冠军

　　　_____

练习 7.1: 课文理解

Paired Activity: Discuss the following questions based on the Lesson Text. Be prepared to share your thoughts with the class.

1. 事故发生的经过是什么？

2. 事故为什么会发生？

3. 你觉得怎么样可以减少事故发生？

练习 7.2（上）: 交通标志

Individual Activity: You encounter some unfamiliar signs on the road. Next to each sign, write down what you think each one means.

Example: 禁止三轮车通行

练习 7.3（中）：问路

Paired Activity: Your friend is new to the community and would like to know how to get to various destinations in the area. With your partner, take turns giving each other driving directions using the map below and be sure to mention the various signs he or she will see.

Example:

A: 开车从公寓到超市要怎么走？

B: 从公寓出来先到大华北街，然后一直往西走。超市就在大学宿舍的对面。穿过大同路的时候要注意汽车禁止左转。

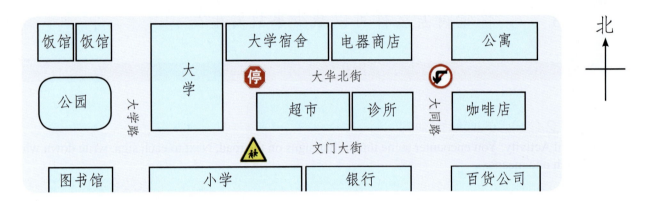

练习 7.4（下）：交通事故

Paired Activity: While returning from the park on the bus, the bus gets into an accident with a taxi. As a witness, explain what happened to the police officer that arrives on the scene.

交通事故　辆　禁止　通行　突然　撞　危险　受伤

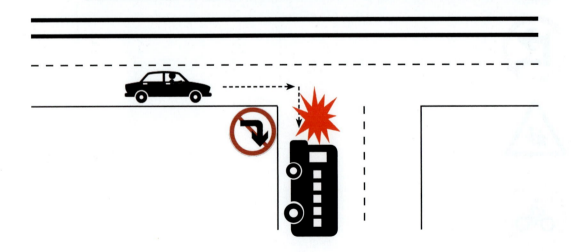

练习 7.5：认识中国的交通标志

Group Activity: You and your classmates would like to know more about street signs in China. Find images of Chinese street signs and research what they mean.

	Radical	Stroke Order
救	攵(攴) pū knock	一 十 寸 寸 求 求 求 求 求 救
警	言 yán speech	一 一 艹 艹 芍 芍 苟 苟 苟 敬 敬 敬 敬 警 警 警 警 警
察	宀 mián roof	丶 宀 宀 宀 宀 宀 宀 宓 宓 宓 宓 宓 察 察
故	攵(攴) pū knock	一 十 古 古 古 古 故 故
突	穴 xuè cave	丶 宀 宀 宀 宀 空 空 突 突
丢	厶 sī self	一 二 千 壬 丢 丢
落	艹(草) cǎo grass	一 十 艹 艹 艹 艹 艹 茓 落 落 落
全	人 rén person	丿 人 人 今 仝 全
撞	扌(手) shǒu hand	一 十 扌 扩 扩 扩 护 护 搏 搏 搏 撞 撞 撞
危	刀 dāo knife	丿 丿 ㄅ 产 产 危
险	阝 fù hill	了 阝 阝 队 阶 险 险 险
禁	示 shì spirit	一 十 才 木 木 村 村 林 林 梵 禁 禁 禁
止	止 zhǐ stop	丨 卜 止 止
倒	亻(人) rén person	丿 亻 亻 亻 仾 伄 侄 倒 倒 倒

练习 7.7: 线上聊天
Online chat: Working with a classmate, discuss emergencies you have experienced or seen and explain what happened.

练习 7.8: 阅读理解

> 玛丽你好点了吗？请你一定要去医院做一下检查，不要担心医疗费。那天我着急回家吃饭，过马路的时候忘了看红绿灯，也没有注意那条路禁止三轮车通行。事故之后我紧张得很，还跟警察说是因为你们闯红灯，真的很对不起！回到家之后我的女儿也怪我太不小心。我的女儿跟你一样大，我相信你受伤以后你的父母一定会非常担心。希望你好好休息，早日康复！

Read part of the letter that the pedicab driver wrote to Mali and answer the following questions.
1. Why did the driver write to Mali?
2. Why did the driver blame Mali and Zhou Xin on the day of the accident?
3. Assume that you are Mali and write a response back to the driver.

练习 7.9: 阅读理解

违法停车罚单

车牌号：京Z·M1996
车身颜色：红
违法停车时间：7月26日14时38分
违法停车地点：北京市花园路
罚款：200元

Notes:
违法 (wéifǎ): *adj.* illegal
车牌号 (chēpáihào): *n.* license number
公安局 (gōng'ānjú): *n.* public security bureau
罚款 (fákuǎn): *n.* fine

这条路禁止停车，请您在十天以内到公安局或银行交罚款。如果有问题，请打电话：88776---。

Read the ticket and answer the following questions.
1. Why did this car get a ticket?
2. After receiving the ticket, what should the car owner do?
3. Explain what other types of violations will cause you to get a traffic ticket?

Major Natural Disasters in China's History

Tangshan (唐山: Tángshān) Earthquake of 1976

On June 28th, 1976 at 3:42am in China, 93% of all residential and 78% of all industrial buildings collapsed, over 240,000 people died, over 164,000 people were seriously injured, and 4,204 children became orphans all within a mere 23 seconds. What took place when most of the citizens were still asleep was a catastrophic 7.8 magnitude earthquake that obliterated Tangshan city. With the energy that equaled 400 atomic bombs, even Beijing (about 93 miles away) and Tianjin (about 65 miles away) clearly felt the seismic waves: the pillars at the Tiananmen gate tower in Beijing trembled convulsively, and the noise of collapsing buildings woke up the former Australian prime minister who was visiting Tianjin.

Although much of Tangshan collapsed into ruins in less than half a minute, the reconstruction of the city took 10 years during which people lived in makeshift houses. Foreign aid was quite rare due to the political environment at that time. Meanwhile the local government also stressed "self-reliance" (自力更生) despite the disastrous conditions. For example, 60-year-old women had to forge iron together with young people. Despite relying on the citizens' own strength and taking twice as long as expected to renovate the city, the people of Tangshan are proud of their spirit of self-reliance, and the Tangshan government even won the United Nations Habitat Scroll of Honour Award for its efforts in improving living conditions.

Wenchuan (汶川: Wènchuān) Earthquake of 2008

On May 12, 2008 at 2:28 p.m., the 7.9 magnitude Wenchuan earthquake, also known as the Sichuan (四川: Sìchuān) earthquake, struck Wenchuan county. It became the deadliest quake in China since 1976, killing over 69,000 people, leaving another 17,921 people missing but presumed dead, and injuring over 370,000 others. The destruction to the buildings and infrastructure was equally devastating, collapsing an estimated more than five million buildings, creating landslides and barrier lakes, cracking roads and pipelines, and leaving millions homeless.

Despite some negativity toward the government in part due to buildings that collapsed because of inadequate engineering, society as a whole came together to help and support their fellow citizens. Billions of dollars were donated from people all over the world. Ordinary Chinese citizens came in droves to lend help in whatever way they could. They brought food, water, clothes, and other supplies; comforted people who lost loved ones and homes; and donated blood. Tens of thousands of young people heeded the text messages and TV advertisements the Communist Youth League sent out calling for volunteers. Mountaineers and people trained in emergency medical response hiked their way to places inaccessible by car to provide aid to people that rescue workers had yet to reach. Banners posted everywhere in China appealed to people to "Fight the earthquake!" expressing the overall sentiment of unity among the Chinese people.

For the people of Tangshan, the 1976 catastrophe undoubtedly left a deep scar in the hearts of many. So when the Wenchuan earthquake happened, it evoked painful memories of the Tangshan earthquake, causing numerous older citizens to suffer heart attacks and high blood pressure. However, understanding the pain better than many others, the people of Tangshan came together again, this time giving aid to others. Tangshan's first aid and rescue crew were the first to arrive after the Wenchuan earthquake happened, and it was also the first to send a group of psychological consultant volunteers to take care of the victims.

To rebuild the worst hit areas, the Chinese government set in place a restoration and reconstruction plan not long after the earthquake hit Sichuan Province. Almost four years later in February of 2012, the government reached a major milestone, announcing that 99 percent of all the rebuilding projects had been successfully completed.

Pinyin

Zhōu Xìn: Mǎlì nǐ zhuàng de bù qīng a! Yào jiào jiùhùchē ma?

Sūn Mǎlì: Wǒ hái hǎo, děng yìhuǐr qù zhěnsuǒ jiǎnchá yíxià jiù xíng.

Jiāojǐng: Nǐmen kěyǐ gàosù wǒ shìgù shì zěnme fāshēng de ma?

Zhōu Xìn: Wǒmen guò mǎlù de shíhou, zhè liàng sānlúnchē tūrán zhuàngle guòlai.

Jiāojǐng: Shīfu, qǐng ràng wǒ kànkan nǐ de shēnfènzhèng.

Shīfù: Āiyā, wǒ de shēnfènzhèng ne? Wǒ zhège rén chángchang diūsān làsì de, yòu wàng dài shēnfènzhèng le… zàishuō zhè jiàn shì bù néng wánquán guài wǒ, shì tāmen chuǎngle hóngdēng.

Zhōu Xìn: Bú duì, wǒmen bìng méiyǒu chuǎng hóngdēng!

Jiāojǐng: Shīfu, zhè tiáo lù jìnzhǐ sānlúnchē tōngxíng, nǐ yòu méi dài shēnfènzhèng, yīncǐ wǒ yào gěi nǐ kāi yì zhāng fádān.

Shīfù: Ài, jīntiān zhēn dǎoméi! Wǒ yǐhòu kāichē zài yě bú zhème zháojí le. Duìbùqǐ, wǒ huì fùzé nǐ de yīliáofèi.

English

Mali, your injury looks serious! Should we call the ambulance?

I'm all right. It'll be fine if we just go to the clinic in a bit.

Can you tell me how the accident happened?

We were just crossing the street when this pedicab suddenly hit us!

Sir, I'd like to see your ID.

Oh, my goodness! Where is my ID? I am a forgetful person . . . I forgot to bring my ID again. Besides, this accident is not totally my fault. They ran a red light.

That's not true. We didn't run any red lights!

Sir, pedicabs are prohibited on this street and you also forgot your ID. Therefore, I must issue you a ticket.

Oh, what an unlucky day! I will never be in such a rush when driving in the future. I'm sorry. I'll pay for your medical bill.

| Zhōu Xìn: | Mǎlì, wǒ xiànzài jiù dài nǐ qù zhěnsuǒ kànkan. | Mali, I'm going to take you to the hospital to get a checkup now. |
| Sūn Mǎlì: | Bùhǎoyìsi, máfan nǐ le! | Thank you and sorry to trouble you. |

What Can You Do?

INTERPRETIVE
- I can recognize terms related to driving in traffic tickets.
- I can explain the meanings of street signs related to driving after seeing the signs.

INTERPERSONAL
- I can discuss how a traffic accident occurred.
- I can exchange information about an injury.

PRESENTATIONAL
- I can present what is permitted and not permitted on the road.
- I can summarize the consequences of a traffic accident.

自然灾难
Natural Disasters

不知道玛丽现在怎么样，没想到她会遇到(yù dao)意外！

玛丽说她的伤快好了，我表哥在照顾她。

啊？周信能把玛丽照顾好吗？

你不用太担心玛丽，她很快就能康复(kāng fù)了。

我们去北京也要注意安全。我在网上看到了一个关于(guān yú)北京自然灾害(zì rán zāi hài)的报告，你们都来看看。

北京自然灾害报告

在北京，最常见的自然灾害是沙尘暴和暴雨，也有可能发生地震。沙尘暴多出现在春天。沙尘天气需要外出时，要戴上口罩和眼镜。暴雨多出现在夏天。发生暴雨时要减少外出，必须外出时不要走积水严重的地方。暴雨天气时遇到雷电，不要在室外用手机，在家里最好把电器关掉。地震的时候要远离大型的物品，找安全的地方蹲下。此外，要多关注自然灾害的预报，以减少意外发生。

图片一：北京沙尘暴以后，去急诊室的人多了很多。

图片二：北京出现暴雨天气，多个航班延误。这是今年以来最大的一场暴雨。

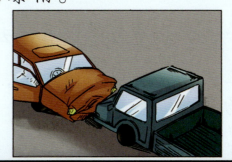

图片三：地震导致多起车祸，幸运的是没有人严重受伤。

LESSON TEXT 7.2

Natural Disasters 自然灾难

Dadong, Xiaomei, Xiang'an, and Zhongping are in Dadong and Xiang'an's dorm. While surfing the web, Dadong comes across a report on Beijing's natural disasters.

陈大东： 不知道玛丽现在怎么样，没想到她会遇到意外！

王小美： 玛丽说她的伤快好了，我的表哥在照顾她。

李中平： 啊？周信能把玛丽照顾好吗？

黄祥安： 你不用太担心玛丽，她很快就能康复了。

陈大东： 我们去北京也要注意安全。我在网上看到了一个关于北京自然灾害的报告，你们都来看看。

————

北京自然灾害报告

在北京，最常见的自然灾害是沙尘暴和暴雨，也有可能发生地震。沙尘暴多出现在春天。沙尘天气需要外出时，要戴上口罩和眼镜。暴雨多出现在夏天。发生暴雨时要减少外出，必须外出时不要走积水严重的地方。暴雨天气时遇到雷电，不要在室外用手机，在家里最好把电器关掉。地震的时候要远离大型的物品，找安全的地方蹲下。此外，要多关注自然灾害的预报，以减少意外发生。

图片一：北京沙尘暴以后，去急诊室的人多了很多。

图片二：北京出现暴雨天气，多个航班延误。这是今年以来最大的一场暴雨。

图片三：地震导致多起车祸，幸运的是没有人严重受伤。

Language Tips

场 (cháng / chǎng)

场 has two tones: cháng and chǎng. It is pronounced as cháng when used to mean a flat open area, like 打谷场 (dǎgǔcháng: threshing ground), as a measure word for short duration, as in "一场暴雨," or as a measure word for accidents, as in "几场车祸." It is pronounced as chǎng when use to mean a "stage" or "scene," like 出场 (enter the stage; come on the scene), or as a measure word for recreational events, such as games and performances, as in "这场比赛" and "一场中国民乐演奏."

Examples:

这场(cháng)暴雨导致多个航班延误。
This rainstorm led to a lot of flight delays.

这场(chǎng)古筝演奏令人十分难忘。
This guzheng performance was very memorable.

掉 (diào)

In the "Report on Natural Disasters in Beijing," 关掉 is used to indicate that electronic devices indoors should be turned off during thunderstorms. The word 掉 is a resultative complement (see *Modern Chinese* Textbook Vol. 1A, Unit 5, Lesson 2, Structure Note 5.8) with a number of possible meanings. In 关掉 it means "off" as in "to turn off." When Xiang'an said "飞鱼会被山猫吃掉" in the Lesson Text from *Modern Chinese* Textbook Vol. 2A, Unit 5, Lesson 1, he used 吃掉 in a joking manner to mean that the Flying Fish would be eaten up or wiped out by the Mountain Lions.

Example:

她把过期的优惠券丢掉了。
She threw away the expired coupon.

LESSON VOCABULARY 7.2

	SIMPLIFIED	TRADITIONAL	PINYIN	WORD CATEGORY	DEFINITION
1.	遇到		yùdao	rv	to come across; to encounter
2.	康复	康復	kāngfù	v, n	to recover; to restore to health
3.	关于	關於	guānyú	prep	regarding; about
4.	自然灾害	自然災害	zìrán zāihài	n	natural disaster
	自然		zìrán	adj, n, adv	natural; nature; naturally
	灾害	災害	zāihài	n	disaster
5.	常见	常見	chángjiàn	adj	frequently encountered; commonly seen
6.	暴雨		bàoyǔ	n	rainstorm
7.	沙尘暴	沙塵暴	shāchénbào	n	sandstorm
8.	地震		dìzhèn	n	earthquake
9.	出现	出現	chūxiàn	v	to occur; to appear
10.	外出		wàichū	v	to go out
11.	口罩		kǒuzhào	n	surgical mask
12.	雷电	雷電	léidiàn	n	thunder and lighting
13.	减少	減少	jiǎnshǎo	v	to reduce
14.	积水	積水	jīshuǐ	n, v	flood, accumulated water; to flood
15.	关	關	guān	v	to close, to turn off
16.	远离	遠離	yuǎnlí	v	to be away from
17.	大型		dàxíng	adj	large-scale
18.	物品		wùpǐn	n	goods
19.	蹲下		dūnxia	rv	to crouch, to hunker
20.	此外		cǐwài	cj	in addition
21.	关注	關注	guānzhù	v	to pay more or close attention to
22.	以		yǐ	prep	in order to
23.	图片	圖片	túpiàn	n	image, picture

SIMPLIFIED	TRADITIONAL	PINYIN	WORD CATEGORY	DEFINITION
24. 急诊室	急診室	jízhěnshì	*n*	emergency room
25. 航班		hángbān	*n*	scheduled flight
班		bān	*n, mw*	class, shift; (used for a trip by bus, plane, etc.)
26. 延误	延誤	yánwù	*v*	to delay
27. 以来	以來	yǐlái	*prep*	since
28. 场	場	cháng	*mw*	(used for non-recreational events)
29. 导致	導致	dǎozhì	*v*	to result in; to lead to; to cause
30. 起		qǐ	*mw*	a case or a batch

REQUIRED VOCABULARY 7.2

31. 增加		zēngjiā	*v*	to increase
增		zēng	*v*	to increase, to add

ONLINE RESOURCES

Visit *http://college.betterchinese.com* for a list of other types of natural disasters.

Idiomatic Expression

fēi lái hèng huò
飞来横祸

飞来横祸 means "unexpected disasters descend." 横祸 means "unexpected disasters."

The expression appears in *Astonished Slaps Upon the Desktop Vol. 2* (《二刻拍案惊奇》: *Èr Kè Pāi'àn Jīngqí*), a collection of short stories written during the Ming Dynasty (1368 – 1644 AD). The author wrote, "Who would have thought such an unexpected disaster would befall upon me; if not for his help, I might have died already." It is used to describe a situation in which an unpleasant incident unexpectedly occurs.

Example:

昨天的暴雨导致了多起车祸，真是一场飞来横祸！
The storm yesterday caused many car accidents. It was such an unexpected disaster!

Weather Warning Signals

In China, the Central Weather Bureau sends out warning signs on television using a color system to indicate imminent or current severe weather. Rainstorms are one example of a major weather phenomena that the bureau will alert people of and below are the warning signals viewers will see.

The scale consists of four color-coded signals, from blue being the mildest warning to red being the most severe. They are each dependent on the amount of rainfall expected within a specific amount of time or the current rainfall levels.

In addition to the weather conditions introduced in the Lesson Text, below is a list of other common types of weather in China, which the Central Weather Bureau will provide warning signals for:

Chinese	Pinyin	Meaning
沙尘暴	shāchénbào	sandstorm
台风	táifēng	typhoon
高温	gāowēn	high temperature
寒潮	háncháo	cold wave
大雾	dàwù	dense fog
雷雨	léiyǔ	thunderstorm
大风	dàfēng	strong wind, gale
冰雹	bīngbáo	hail
雪灾	xuězāi	snow disaster
道路结冰	dàolù jiébīng	icy road

Terms Found in News Articles

The following are words commonly found in news articles:

Sections of a Newspaper:

Chinese	Pinyin	Meaning	Chinese	Pinyin	Meaning
国际新闻	guójì xīnwén	international news	体育	tǐyù	sports
国内新闻	guónèi xīnwén	domestic news	健康	jiànkāng	health
特别报道	tèbié bàodào	special report	生活	shēnghuó	lifestyle
财经	cáijīng	finance and economics	娱乐	yúlè	entertainment
科技	kējì	science and technology	分类广告	fēnlèi guǎnggào	classified ads

People:

Chinese	Pinyin	Meaning	Chinese	Pinyin	Meaning
编辑	biānjí	editor	专栏作家	zhuānlán zuòjiā	columnist
记者	jìzhě	reporter	投稿人	tóugǎorén	contributor

STRUCTURE NOTE 7.5
Use 关于 *to say "with regard to" a topic*

Unlike in English, modifying clauses in Chinese precede the noun, as in 我昨天买的书, *"the book that I bought yesterday." To explain that a noun is about a particular topic,* 关于 *(guānyú), meaning "regarding," is added to the beginning of the modifying clause. For example,* 关于中文语法的书, *"a book about Chinese grammar."*

> 关于 + Topic + 的 + Noun

From the Lesson Text:

我在网上找到了一个关于北京自然灾害的报告。
Wǒ zài wǎngshang zhǎodàole yí ge guānyú Běijīng zìrán zāihài de bàogào.
I found an online report regarding Beijing's natural disasters.

Other examples:

我刚看到了一个关于社团招募的通知。
Wǒ gāng kàndaole yí ge guānyú shètuán zhāomù de tōngzhī.
I just saw a notification regarding club recruitment.

你知道有什么关于中国历史的电影吗?
Nǐ zhīdào yǒu shénme guānyū Zhōngguó lìshǐ de diànyǐng ma?
Do you know of any movies about Chinese history?

Practice: Translate the following sentences into Chinese and use 关于 in your translations.

Example: I found a blog about Chinese cuisine, which is very interesting.
→ 我找到一个关于中国美食的博客,很有意思。

1. This book has a lot of resources on Chinese culture.

   _____

2. I have found a book about Chinese history.

   _____

3. I have finished writing a report about English literature.

   _____

4. There are many fun stories about him.

   _____

5. I have a different opinion on this report.

   _____

STRUCTURE NOTE 7.6
Use 此外 *to introduce additional points*

Formal written Chinese often uses shorter versions of expressions that occur in spoken Mandarin. 此外 *(cǐwài) is an abbreviated form of* 除了这个以外, *meaning "other than this" (*此 *is a formal term for "this" used primarily in written Chinese). This phrase can be used like the English "in addition" to introduce new ideas.*

此外 + Sentence

From the Lesson Text:

此外，要多关注自然灾害的预报。
Cǐwài, yào duō guānzhù zìrán zāihài de yùbào.
In addition, pay more attention to natural disaster reports.

Other examples:

想学好一门语言一定要多听录音，此外要多练习口语。
Xiǎng xué hǎo yì mén yǔyán yídìng yào duō tīng lùyīn, cǐwài yào duō liànxí kǒuyǔ.
To master a language, you must listen to a lot of recordings. In addition, you must frequently practice your speaking skills.

他的英语和法语都说得很好，此外他还会一点儿中文。
Tā de Yīngyǔ hé Fǎyǔ dōu shuō de hěn hǎo, cǐwài tā hái huì yìdiǎnr Zhōngwén.
He can speak English and French well. In addition, he can speak a little bit of Chinese.

Practice: Complete the following sentences using 此外.

Example:

篮球比赛如果想赢就一定要有团队精神，此外……
→篮球比赛如果想赢就一定要有团队精神，此外还需要一点运气。

1. 在网上买东西要注意比较价格……

   _____

2. 租房时要先问清楚有什么家电……

   _____

3. 想了解中国文化要多看书……

   _____

4. 申请中国的大学要参加中文考试……

   _____

5. 参加大学的社团可以认识很多新朋友……

   _____

STRUCTURE NOTE 7.7
Use 以 to indicate the purpose of an action
In formal contexts, 以 (yǐ) may function as a preposition meaning "for" or "in order to," introducing the purpose or reason behind doing something.

> Subject + Action + 以 + Purpose

From the Lesson Text:

要多关注自然灾害的预报，以减少意外发生。
Yào duō guānzhù zìrán zāihài de yùbào, yǐ jiǎnshǎo yìwài fāshēng.
Pay more attention to natural disaster reports in order to minimize accidents.

Other examples:

老师建议我们多去图书馆看书，以增加知识。
Lǎoshī jiànyì wǒmen duō qù túshūguǎn kàn shū, yǐ zēngjiā zhīshi.
Our teacher suggested that we go to the library more often in order to increase our knowledge.

长辈给你东西的时候要用双手接受，以表示尊敬。
Zhǎngbèi gěi nǐ dōngxi de shíhou yào yòng shuāngshǒu jiēshòu, yǐ biǎoshì zūnjìng.
When your elders give you something, you have to receive it with both hands to express respect.

Practice: Connect sentences in the left column with the phrases in the right column using the 以 structure.

1. 我们要多学习自然灾害的知识   更好地了解中国文化
2. 一定要写清楚你的联系方式   减少退换货时的麻烦
3. 买东西要留好收据   保证我们可以联系到你
4. 他建议我去中国上大学   减少意外的发生

STRUCTURE NOTE 7.8

Use (从)……以来 to indicate "ever since" a certain time in the past

The pattern 从 *+ Time +* 以后 *means, "from after (time)" and expresses that something has been (or will continue to be) the case, following a particular point in time in the past, present, or future. The pattern* (从) *+ Time +* 以来 *(yǐlái) has a more limited use, and means that something has continued to be the case from a point in the past up until the present day. In this sense, it is similar to the English term "since," which can only be used to indicate a time period starting in the past and continuing up to the present.*

> (从 +) Time + 以来, + Clause

> Subject + (从 +) Time + 以来 + Verb Phrase

From the Lesson Text:
这是今年以来最大的一场暴雨。
Zhè shì jīnnián yǐlái zuì dà de yì cháng bàoyǔ.
This is the biggest rainstorm of the year.

Other examples:

这两个月以来，我都很忙。
Zhè liǎng ge yuè yǐlái, wǒ dōu hěn máng.
For the past two months, I've been very busy.

他从上高中以来一直对中国文学有兴趣。
Tā cóng shàng gāozhōng yǐlái yìzhí duì Zhōngguó wénxué yǒu xìngqù.
Ever since he was in high school, he has always been interested in Chinese literature.

Practice: Complete the sentences using 以来 and the information provided.

Example: 三个月 / 他都吃素
→ 这三个月以来，他都吃素。

1. 上大学 / 他一直在校外租公寓住

   _____

2. 十年 / 最大的一场暴雪

   _____

3. 这学期 / 最重要的一次考试

   _____

4. 今年 / 最棒的一场音乐会

   _____

5. 上高中 / 我都自己打工挣钱

   _____

练习 7.10: 课文理解

Paired Activity: Discuss the following questions based on the Lesson Text. Be prepared to share your thoughts with the class.

> 1. 北京有哪些最常见的自然灾害?
>
> 2. 发生沙尘暴的时候你要怎么做?
>
> 3. 你还知道哪些关于自然灾害的知识?

练习 7.11: 中国各地的自然灾害

Paired Activity: Below is a map indicating major natural threats. Choose two cities and describe the common natural hazards for each area and its impact.

Notes:

西安 (Xī'ān): *n.* Xi'an   杭州 (Hángzhōu): *n.* Hangzhou

武汉 (Wǔhàn): *n.* Wuhan   成都 (Chéngdū): *n.* Chengdu

广州 (Guǎngzhōu): *n.* Guangzhou   洪水 (hóngshuǐ): *n.* flood

Examples:

A: 在北京，最常见的自然灾害是什么?
B: 北京的夏天常常发生暴雨。
A: 暴雨会导致什么样的事情发生?
B: 暴雨会导致航班延误。

✏️ Paired Activity: Survey three classmates on their experiences with natural disasters and what precautions they would take for each.

Example: A: 遇到暴雨时，应该怎么做？

B: 发生暴雨时应减少外出。此外，开车的时候要注意积水严重的地方。

自然灾害	应该怎么做？

✏️ 练习 7.13 (下): 自然灾害报告

Individual Activity: Write a short report below about a natural disaster common to your area. Discuss its impact and what precautions you would take.

常见　出现　发生　遇到　减少　意外
严重　受伤　此外　以　以来　导致

Example: 这里最常见的自然灾害是……

💻 练习 7.14: 中国与自然灾害

Group Activity: Working in groups, research a recent natural disaster that occurred in China and its impact.

	Radical	Stroke Order
遇	辶 chuò walk	丶 口 日 日 昌 禺 禺 禺 遇 遇 遇
康	广 yǎn shelter	丶 亠 广 庀 庐 庐 序 序 康 康
灾	宀 mián roof	丶 丷 宀 宀 灾 灾 灾
害	宀 mián roof	丶 丷 宀 宀 宀 宝 宝 害 害
雷	雨 yǔ rain	一 广 广 冊 而 雨 雨 雨 雪 雪 雷 雷
暴	日 rì sun	丨 口 日 日 旦 旦 昗 昗 昜 暴 暴 暴 暴 暴
尘	土 tǔ earth	丨 丄 小 小 尘 尘
罩	罒 (网) wǎng web	丨 口 口 四 四 甲 甲 甲 罒 罩 罩 罩
积	禾 hé grain	一 二 千 千 禾 禾 和 和 积
此	止 zhǐ stop	丨 卜 卜 止 此 此
注	氵 (水) shuǐ water	丶 丶 氵 氵 汁 汁 注 注
图	囗 wéi enclosure	丨 冂 门 冈 冈 图 图 图
延	廴 yǐn go	丿 彳 千 正 延 延
导	寸 cùn inch	丨 口 巳 旦 早 导
致	攵 (攴) pū knock	一 工 丞 丞 至 至 至 致 致 致

Online chat: Working with a classmate, discuss what kind of natural disasters you have in your area and what kind of preparations are needed before it occurs, such as buying extra food supplies.

练习 **7.17**: 阅读理解

To:	孙玛丽
From:	王小美
Subject:	注意安全！

玛丽：

听中平说你在中国出了意外，这真是飞来横祸！我们都很担心你。你现在还好吗？伤得重吗？希望你能快一点好起来。

今天，大东在网上找到了一个关于北京常见自然灾害的报告。我把这个报告发给你看看，教你如何保护自己。现在是北京的雨季，有时候会下暴雨，你外出的时候一定要注意安全。还有，你这段时间不要太累，要注意休息！我们都很想念你，你要多保重！

小美

Read Xiaomei's e-mail and answer the following questions.
1. Why did Xiaomei write an e-mail to Mali?
2. What information did Xiaomei send in her e-mail to Mali?
3. Assume that you are Mali and reply to Xiaomei's e-mail.

练习 **7.18**: 阅读理解

暴雨警告

明天白天会有大暴雨，请大家尽量减少外出。如果外出，请带好雨伞或雨衣。雨天路滑，开车的朋友要注意安全。开车时遇到暴雨，请保持冷静，最好先找一个安全的地方把车停下来，等雨小一些再开车。如果发生交通意外，请马上打110报警。

Notes:
尽量 (jǐnliàng): *adv.* do all one can
路滑 (lùhuá): *adj.* slippery roads
保持 (bǎochí): *v.* to maintain
停 (tíng): *vo.* to park
报警 (bàojǐng): *v.* to report to the police

Read the report and answer the following questions.
1. What will the weather and temperature be like tomorrow?
2. If a rainstorm begins while you are driving, what should you do?
3. What other precautions do you think you should take during the natural disaster mentioned in the report?

Predicting Natural Disasters

From earthquakes to floods to typhoons, China has experienced more than its fair share of natural disasters; in fact, half of the top ten deadliest natural disasters in recorded history have occurred in China. Given the threat that natural disasters posed to trade, civil life, and government, the ancient Chinese found it imperative to devise ways of predicting natural disasters. Two vastly different methods of prediction were developed: the oracle bones and the first seismometer.

Oracle Bones (甲骨: jiǎgǔ)

Known primarily for their role in the origins of Chinese script, oracle bones were also used by the ancient emperors as far back as the Shang Dynasty emperors (1600 – 1046 BC) to predict the future. Questions were carved on cattle bones and tortoise shells to ask revered ancestors and gods about natural disasters, military expeditions, weather, and harvests. Afterwards, the oracle bone was heated in fire until it cracked, and a priest would interpret the natural symmetry of the bone and cracks for the answers. Thousands of oracle bones have been uncovered with questions prosaic and profound, ranging from which ancestor was causing a toothache to whether or not misfortune would occur over the next ten days.

The First Seismometer (测震仪: cèzhènyí)

The seismometer was a large bronze machine that resembled a sturdy vase, with a swinging pendulum inside and eight dragons around its rim. The first seismometer was invented by the imperial official Zhang Heng in 132 AD. According to ancient records, it was used to predict earthquakes and allow villagers in the areas affected to prepare and evacuate. Because the ancient Chinese believed that earthquakes were caused by an imbalance in the earth's yin and yang — which were then expressed as disturbances in the air — the seismometer measured both the movements of the earth and the winds. When a tectonic disturbance was detected, the dragon that most accurately represented the direction of the earthquake would release the ball placed in its mouth, alerting palace officials to which area was affected.

Da Yu Introduces Flood Control

In ancient China about 4,000 years ago, frequent floods along the Yellow River Basin washed away homes and covered up landmasses, forcing people to move up into the mountains. The man who finally developed a system of flood controls and allowed people to live and flourish along the rivers was Yu (禹: Yǔ). As an expression of deep gratitude and respect toward Yu, people referred to him as "Yu the Great" (大禹: Dà Yǔ) and his work in managing the floods became renowned as "Da Yu controls the great flood" (大禹治水: Dà Yǔ zhìshuǐ).

Originally, King Yao (尧: Yáo), the leader of the Yan-Huang tribal alliances, appointed Gun (鲧: Gǔn) to regulate the waterways and prevent floods. Gun spent nine years building levees wherever there might be floods. But the water was too strong and it ended up smashing through the levees, leading to Gun's failure.

Emperor Yao's successor, Shun (舜: Shùn), appointed Gun's son Yu to continue his father's work. Yu discovered that some of the valleys were too narrow for floods to rush through and some rivers were heavily silted. Thus, he adopted the methods of dredging and creating irrigation canals to relieve flood waters rather than using levees. He broadened estuaries and dredged river ways, connecting main streams, tributaries, lakes, and at last guiding the water into sea.

After 13 years of hard work, Yu succeeded in controlling the floodwaters. He was so devoted that during that time it was said that he passed by his house three times but never stepped in, not even when his wife gave birth to their child. In large part due to Yu's achievement as well as his ability and integrity, Shun selected Yu as his successor. Under his rule, Yu founded the Xia Dynasty (夏朝: Xià Cháo), the first hereditary dynasty in Chinese history.

Pinyin

Li Zhōngpíng: Bù zhīdào Mǎlì xiànzài zěnmeyàng, méi xiǎngdào tā huì yùdào yìwài!

Wáng Xiǎoměi: Mǎlì shuō tā de shāng kuài hǎo le, wǒ de biǎogē zài zhàogù tā.

Li Zhōngpíng: Á? Zhōu Xìn néng bǎ Mǎlì zhàogù hǎo ma?

Huáng Xiáng' ān: Nǐ búyòng tài dānxīn Mǎlì, tā hěn kuài jiù néng kāngfù le.

Chén Dàdōng: Wǒmen qù Běijīng yě yào zhùyì ānquán. Wǒ zài wǎngshang kàndaole yí ge guānyú Běijīng zìrán zāihài de bàogào, nǐmen dōu lái kànkan.

Běijīng Zìrán Zāihài Bàogào

Zài Běijīng, zuì chángjiàn de zìrán zāihài shì shāchénbào hé bàoyǔ, yě yǒu kěnéng fāshēng dìzhèn. Shāchénbào duō chūxiàn zài chūntiān. Shāchén tiānqì xūyào wàichū shí, yào dàishang kǒuzhào hé yǎnjìng. Bàoyǔ duō chūxiàn zài xiàtiān. Fāshēng bàoyǔ shí yào jiǎnshǎo wàichū, bìxū wàichū shí búyào zǒu jīshuǐ yánzhòng de dìfang. Bàoyǔ tiānqì shí yùdào léidiàn, bú yào zài shìwài yòng shǒujī, zài jiā li zuìhǎo bǎ diànqì guāndiao.

English

I wonder how Mali is doing now. I never thought she would be involved in an accident.

Mali said she's just about recovered from her injuries and my cousin is taking care of her.

Really? Zhou Xin can take care of Mali?

Don't be too worried about Mali, she will recover in no time.

We must also be careful when we go to Beijing. I saw an online report about natural disasters in Beijing. Come take a look.

A Report of Natural Disasters in Beijing

In Beijing, the most frequently encountered natural disasters are sandstorms and rainstorms; earthquakes might also occur. Sandstorms occur during summertime. When venturing outdoors during sandstorms, one must bring surgical masks and glasses. Rainstorms tend to occur in the summer. During rainstorms, try to refrain from going outdoors. If you absolutely must go outside, avoid flooded areas. During thunderstorms, avoid using mobile phones outdoors, and turn off electric devices indoors.

Dìzhèn de shíhou yào yuǎnlí dàxíng de wùpǐn, zhǎo ānquán de dìfang dūnxia. Cǐwài, yào duō guānzhù zìrán zāihài de yùbào, yǐ jiǎnshǎo yìwài fāshēng.

During earthquakes, keep away from large objects and find a safe place to crouch under. In addition, pay more attention to natural disaster reports in order to minimize accidents.

Túpiàn yī: Běijīng shāchénbào yǐhòu, qù jízhěnshì de rén duō le hěn duō.

Túpiàn èr: Běijīng chūxiàn bàoyǔ tiānqì, duō ge hángbān yánwù. Zhè shì jīnnián yǐlái zuì dà de yì cháng bàoyǔ.

Túpiàn sān: Dìzhèn dǎozhì duō qǐ chēhuò, xìngyùn de shì méiyǒu rén yánzhòng shòushāng.

Image 1: After Beijing's sandstorm, there was a huge increase in the number of people going to the hospital.

Image 2: Rainstorms in Beijing, many scheduled flights were delayed. This is the biggest rainstorm of the year.

Image 3: The earthquake caused a lot of car accidents. Fortunately, no one was seriously injured.

What Can You Do?

INTERPRETIVE
- I can identify different natural disasters and their impact after reading about them in written text.
- I can recognize terms related to natural disasters in oral text.

INTERPERSONAL
- I can discuss natural disasters.
- I can compare with others how to prepare for different natural disasters.

PRESENTATIONAL
- I can present information about natural disasters and their consequences.
- I can describe precautions to take during natural disasters.

ACT IT OUT

Working in groups, compose an original two-minute skit that utilizes the vocabulary and structures introduced in Unit 7. Each of you should assume a role and have a roughly equal number of lines in the skit. Be prepared to perform your skit in class. You can either come up with your own story or choose from one of the following situations:

A) You are watching the evening news with your roommates. Discuss the natural disaster that is being reported on TV.

B) You and your family decide to prepare for a common natural phenomenon that occurs in your area. Talk about how you are going to prepare and create a plan.

C) You witness a car accident in which the driver hits a bicyclist. Explain to the police officer what you saw. The driver, however, has a different story.

CHECK WHAT YOU CAN DO

RECOGNIZE

Adjectives
- □ 轻
- □ 倒霉
- □ 着急
- □ 危险
- □ 常见
- □ 大型
- □ 自然

Adverbs
- □ 突然
- □ 并
- □ 完全

Conjunctions
- □ 此外
- □ 因此

Idiomatic Expression
- □ 丢三落四

Measure Words
- □ 辆
- □ 场
- □ 起

Nouns
- □ 救护车
- □ 诊所
- □ 警察
- □ 事故
- □ 三轮车
- □ 师傅
- □ 身份证
- □ 罚单
- □ 医疗

- □ 司机
- □ 乘客
- □ 车祸
- □ 驾驶执照
- □ 自然灾害
- □ 暴雨
- □ 沙尘暴
- □ 地震
- □ 口罩
- □ 雷电
- □ 室外
- □ 物品
- □ 图片
- □ 急诊室
- □ 航班
- □ 意外
- □ 积水

Prepositions
- □ 关于
- □ 以
- □ 以来

Resultative Verbs
- □ 遇到
- □ 蹲下

Verbs
- □ 撞
- □ 怪
- □ 闯
- □ 禁止
- □ 通行
- □ 出现
- □ 外出

- □ 减少
- □ 远离
- □ 关注
- □ 延误
- □ 导致
- □ 增加
- □ 检查
- □ 康复

Verb-Object Compound
- □ 受伤

WRITE

- □ 救
- □ 警察
- □ 故
- □ 突
- □ 落
- □ 全
- □ 撞
- □ 危险
- □ 禁止
- □ 检
- □ 倒

- □ 遇
- □ 康
- □ 灾害
- □ 雷
- □ 暴
- □ 尘
- □ 罩
- □ 积
- □ 此
- □ 注
- □ 图
- □ 延
- □ 导致

USE

- □ Use 完全 to say "completely."
- □ Use 并 to emphasize a negative contrast.
- □ Use 因此 to say "therefore."
- □ Use 再也(不/没) to emphatically state "never ever again."

- □ Use 关于 to say "with regard to" a topic.
- □ Use 此外 to introduce additional points.
- □ Use 以 to indicate the purpose of an action.
- □ Use (从)……以来 to indicate "ever since" a certain time in the past.

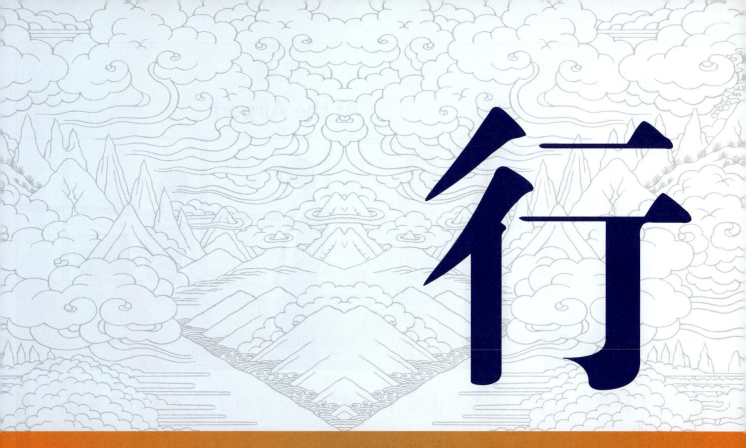

行

Travel

第八单元
UNIT 8

Communication Goals

Lesson 1: 在机场 **At the Airport**
- Talk about the steps involved in checking in at the airport.
- Talk about encountering problems at the airport.
- Talk about making changes in one's reservations.

Lesson 2: 中国游 **Traveling in China**
- Explain the various ways to keep a record of one's travels.
- Talk about local dishes while traveling.
- Discuss one's impressions of a trip.

在机场
At the Airport

中平和他的朋友们将去中国留学。他们都申请到了奖学金，办签证
和订机票也都很顺利，可是在出发的那一天，却遇到了一些麻烦。

先生，您的行李超重了。

只超重两磅也不行吗？

对不起，这是航空公司的规定。除非您付超重费，要不然我们不能托运这些行李。

中平，你放一些东西到我的箱子里吧。你给玛丽带的礼物太多了吧！

先生，这是您的登机牌，座位靠窗户。

不好意思，座位可以换成靠走道的吗？

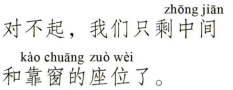
对不起，我们只剩中间
zhōng jiān

kào chuāng zuò wèi
和靠窗的座位了。

祥安，我跟你换座位吧，我的座位靠
zuò wèi   zuò wèi kào
走道。我有一点儿头疼，想坐窗边。
zǒu dào   chuāng

糟糕，要登机了，
祥安在哪儿？

大东，我们去找他吧！

祥安你跑到哪里去了？
给你打电话你也不接。
快走吧，要不然就赶
gǎn
不上飞机了！
shang

小美，这是给你的药，
希望你的头疼能好一些。

不好意思，
我看错了
登机时间。

原来你刚才是去给
gāng cái
我买药啊！谢谢你！

LESSON TEXT 8.1

At the Airport 在机场

The group is heading to China! Zhongping, Xiaomei, Dadong, and Xiang'an are at the airport. Before they board the plane, they encounter a few minor problems.

中平和他的朋友们将去中国留学。他们都申请到了奖学金，办签证和订机票也都很顺利，可是在出发的那一天，却遇到了一些麻烦。

工作人员：　先生，您的行李超重了。

李中平：　　只超重两磅也不行吗？

工作人员：　对不起，这是航空公司的规定。除非您付超重费，要不然我们不能托运这些行李。

陈大东：　　中平，你放一些东西到我的箱子里吧。你给玛丽带的礼物太多了吧！

工作人员：　先生，这是您的登机牌，座位靠窗户。

黄祥安：　　不好意思，座位可以换成靠走道的吗？

工作人员：　对不起，我们只剩中间和靠窗的座位了。

王小美：　　祥安，我跟你换座位吧，我的座位靠走道。我有一点儿头疼，想坐窗边。

―――――――――――

陈大东：　　糟糕，要登机了，祥安在哪儿？

王小美：　　大东，我们去找他吧！

陈大东： 祥安你跑到哪里去了？给你打电话你也不接。快走吧，要不然就赶不上飞机了！

黄祥安： 不好意思，我看错了登机时间。小美，这是给你的药，希望你的头疼能好一些。

王小美： 原来你刚才是去给我买药啊！谢谢你！

Language Tip

糟糕 (zāogāo)

In the Lesson Text, Dadong uses 糟糕 to express his surprise and concern that Xiang'an seems to be missing when it is almost time to board the airplane. The expression can be used as both an interjection and an adjective. In the former usage, 糟糕 conveys surprise in bad situations. When using the phrase as an adjective, it means a situation is very bad.

Examples:

糟糕，我找不到我的护照！
Oh no, I can't find my passport!

我看的那个公寓太糟糕了，又旧又脏。
The apartment I saw is terrible; it is old and dirty.

字词 VOCABULARY

LESSON VOCABULARY 8.1

	SIMPLIFIED	TRADITIONAL	PINYIN	WORD CATEGORY	DEFINITION
1.	将	將	jiāng	adv	will, about to
2.	办签证	辦簽證	bàn qiānzhèng	vo	to obtain a visa, to apply for a visa
	办	辦	bàn	v	to handle
3.	订	訂	dìng	v	to book
4.	顺利	順利	shùnlì	adj	smooth, without a hitch
5.	却	卻	què	cj	however, but
6.	人员	人員	rényuán	n	personnel, staff
7.	行李		xíngli	n	luggage
8.	超重		chāozhòng	adj, n	overweight
	超		chāo	v	to exceed
	重		zhòng	n, adj	weight; heavy
9.	磅		bàng	mw	pound
10.	航空公司		hángkōng gōngsī	n	airline, airline company
	航空		hángkōng	v	aviation
11.	规定	規定	guīdìng	n	rule
12.	除非……要不然		chúfēi...... yàoburán	cj	unless, only if . . . or else, otherwise
13.	托运	托運	tuōyùn	v	to consign or check for shipment
14.	登机牌	登機牌	dēngjīpái	n	boarding pass
	登	登	dēng	v	to board; to climb
	牌		pái	n	card
15.	座位		zuòwèi	n	seat
16.	靠窗户		kào chuānghu	vo	by the window
	靠		kào	adj, v	near; to depend
	窗户		chuānghu	n	window

LESSON VOCABULARY 8.1 (continued)

	SIMPLIFIED	TRADITION-AL	PINYIN	WORD CATEGORY	DEFINITION
17.	走道		zǒudào	*n*	aisle
18.	中间	中間	zhōngjiān	*n*	middle, center
19.	赶上	趕上	gǎnshang	*rv*	to catch up with; to be in time for, to be able to make something
20.	刚才	剛才	gāngcái	*adv*	just now; a moment ago

REQUIRED VOCABULARY 8.1

21.	起飞	起飛	qǐfēi	*v*	to take off
22.	地铁	地鐵	dìtiě	*n*	subway
23.	船		chuán	*n*	boat, ship
24.	目的地		mùdìdì	*n*	destination
	目的		mùdì	*n*	aim; destination
25.	公斤		gōngjīn	*mw*	kilogram

Idiomatic Expression

yì bō sān zhé
一波三折

一波三折 means "twists and turns" or "ups and downs."

This appears in the Jin Dynasty (265 – 420 AD) and was used by calligrapher Wang Xizhi (王羲之: Wáng Xīzhī) to describe his style of calligraphy. He wrote, "to write the Chinese stroke na (捺: nà) beautifully, one needs to twist the brush three times." Today, it is used to indicate unexpected obstacles.

Example:
这次旅游真是一波三折，我们遇到了很多麻烦。
There were so many twists and turns during this trip. We met with many unpleasant situations.

At the Airport

There are many specialized terms related to air travel. Below is an example of some of the key terms and locations that one might encounter when travelling through an airport in China.

出租车乘车点 (chūzūchē chéngchē diǎn: taxi pick-up point)

问询处 (wènxúnchù: inquiry desk)

行李领取处 (xíngli lǐngqǔ chù: luggage claim)

1/F

乘机手续 (chéngjī shǒuxù: check-in)

海关 (hǎiguān: customs)

2/F

自动电梯 (zìdòng diàntī: escalator)

银行 (yínháng: bank)

餐厅 (cāntīng: restaurant)

3/F

免税店 (miǎnshuìdiàn: duty-free shop)

洗手间 (xǐshǒujiān: restroom)

候机室 (hòujīshì: airport lounge)

Chinese	Pinyin	English
Arrival and Departure		
进港	jìngǎng	arrival
出港	chūgǎng	departure
入境	rùjìng	to enter (a country)
出境	chūjìng	to leave (a country)
抵达	dǐdá	arrival
转机	zhuǎnjī	to make a transfer
Flight Information		
航空	hángkōng	airline
准时	zhǔnshí	on time
误点	wùdiǎn	delayed
取消	qǔxiāo	canceled
国际	guójì	international
国内	guónèi	domestic
班机	bānjī	scheduled flight

ONLINE RESOURCES
Visit *http://college.betterchinese.com* for more terms related to the airport and flight information.

STRUCTURE NOTE 8.1
Use 将 (要 / 会) to describe future events in formal contexts

In Modern Chinese Textbook Vol. 1A, Unit 3, Lesson 1, Structure Notes 3.1 and Modern Chinese Textbook Vol. 1A, Unit 5, Lesson 1, Structure Notes 5.4, 会 and 要 were introduced respectively as ways to indicate that an event will happen in the future. In formal situations, particularly in writing, 将 (jiāng) can be used in the same way as these other terms to mark the future. 将 can also be combined with 会 and 要, resulting in 将会 and 将要. As in the uses of 会 and 要 on their own, these combined expressions are mostly equivalent, but 将要 implies a bit more certainty than 将会.

> Subject + 将 (+ 要 / 会) + Verb Phrase

From the Lesson Text:

中平和他的朋友们将去中国留学。
Zhōngpíng hé tā de péngyoumen jiāng qù Zhōngguó liúxué.
Zhongping and his friends are off to study abroad in China.

Other examples:

他明天将会送女儿一个礼物。
Tā míngtiān jiāng huì sòng nǚ'ér yí ge lǐwù.
Tomorrow, he will give his daughter a present.

中平将会跟我们一起去中国。
Zhōngpíng jiāng huì gēn wǒmen yìqǐ qù Zhōngguó.
Zhongping is going to China with us.

Practice: Create complete sentences using 将 and the information provided.

Example: 下个月 / 我 / 去中国留学
→ 下个月我将去中国留学。

1. 明年 / 他 / 申请去一个公司实习

   _____

2. 大东 / 送我们去机场 / 明天

   _____

3. 我的信用卡 / 下个月 / 到期

   _____

4. 绿色地球社 / 举办社团招募活动

   _____

5. 给你开一张罚单 / 警察

   _____

STRUCTURE NOTE 8.2
Use 却 *to indicate a reversal or contrast*

Similarly to the particle 并, 却 (què) is used in a sentence to emphasize that the situation being described is contrary to what was expected or to what had been happening previously. 却 is placed before the verb in the sentence, and often appears in conjunction with "but" term such as 可是 at the beginning of the clause. Unlike 并, however, 却 can appear in affirmative sentences, not only negative ones.

> Subject + 却 + Verb Phrase

From the Lesson Text:

可是在出发的那一天，却遇到了一些麻烦。
Kěshì zài chūfā de nà yì tiān, què yùdaole yìxiē máfan.
However, on the day of their departure, they ran into some difficulties.

Other examples:

我的爸爸妈妈希望我当医生，但是我却不想当。
Wǒ de bàba māma xīwàng wǒ dāng yīsheng, dànshì wǒ què bù xiǎng dāng.
My parents hope that I'll become a doctor, but I actually don't want to.

为什么别的学校都有健身房，我们学校却没有呢？
Wèishénme biéde xuéxiào dōu yǒu jiànshēnfáng, wǒmen xuéxiào què méiyǒu ne?
Why do other schools all have gyms, and yet our school doesn't?

Practice: Create complete sentences using 却 and the information provided.

Example:　大家都觉得我们能赢/我们输了
→ 大家都觉得我们能赢，但是我们却输了。

1. 别的超市都有优惠/这家没有

　　_____

2. 大家都想去中国旅游/我没有兴趣

　　_____

3. 我们觉得这次考试很难/小美觉得很简单

　　_____

4. 玛丽很喜欢这套公寓/中平觉得太贵了

　　_____

5. 现在年轻人都喜欢过情人节/小王觉得没意思

　　_____

STRUCTURE NOTE 8.3

Use 除非… 要不然… to make "unless" statements

In the English sentence pattern "unless A happens, B will happen," the A condition is preceded by "unless," while the B result clause is not marked with any special expression. In Chinese, the A condition is preceded by 除非 (chúfēi), meaning "unless," and the B result clause is often preceded by some phrase that means "otherwise," such as 要不然.

除非 + Condition, + 要不然 + Result

From the Lesson Text:

除非您付超重费，要不然我们不能托运这些行李。
Chúfēi nín fù chāozhòng fèi, yàoburán wǒmen bù néng tuōyùn zhèxiē xíngli.
Unless you pay an overweight baggage fee, we can't check your luggage through.

Other examples:

除非你早到，要不然在
图书馆找不到座位。
Chúfēi nǐ zǎo dào, yàoburán zài
túshūguǎn zhǎo bu dào zuòwèi.
Unless you come early, you won't be
able to find a seat in the library.

除非天气不好，要不然我
明天一定要去爬山。
Chúfēi tiānqì bù hǎo, yàoburán wǒ
míngtiān yídìng yào qù pá shān.
Unless the weather is bad, I'll definitely
go mountain climbing tomorrow.

Practice: Create complete sentences using 除非…要不然… pattern and the information provided.

Example:
你的中文很好 / 你看不懂这部电影。
→ 除非你的中文很好，要不然你看不懂这部电影。

1. 你不怕冷 / 明天不要出去玩

_____

2. 你想和他分手 / 不要问他这个问题

_____

3. 你很爱吃辣 / 不要点这道菜

_____

4. 明天下雨 / 我一定要去打网球

_____

5. 明天你不发烧 / 你一定要去看医生

_____

STRUCTURE NOTE 8.4
Use 刚才 *to talk about events or situations that have just occurred*

Previous lessons have introduced 刚 *and* 刚刚 *to mark an event that has just occurred.* 刚才 *(gāngcái) has a similar use, but it can also function as a noun and adjective, equivalent to "just a moment ago." As a result, it can be used in certain cases where* 刚 *cannot appear, such as* 刚才的消息 *("the latest news"). Also,* 刚刚, *"just," "just now," or "exactly," is generally used to describe events, while* 刚才 *is used more often to describe states.*

> Subject + 刚才 + Verb Phrase

> 刚才 + Subject + Verb Phrase

> 刚才 + 的 + Noun

From the Lesson Text: 原来你刚才是去给我买药啊！
Yuánlái nǐ gāngcái shì qù gěi wǒ mǎiyào a!
I didn't realize you had gone to buy medicine for me!

Other examples: 对不起，刚才我太忙了。   刚才的那个人是谁？
Duìbuqǐ, gāngcái wǒ tài máng le.   Gāngcái de nàge rén shì shéi?
Sorry, just now I was too busy.   Who was that just now?

Practice: Choose 刚 or 刚才 to fill in the blanks.

1. _____老师说了什么？
2. 我_____回家就收到了他的电子邮件。
3. 我的中文不太好，因为我_____学中文半年。
4. 他_____给我打电话了，但是我没有接到。
5. 她把_____的事忘了。

练习 8.1: 课文理解

Paired Activity: Discuss the following questions based on the Lesson Text. Be prepared to share your thoughts with the class.

1. 如果行李超重怎么办？

2. 祥安去了哪里？为什么？

3. 如果飞机误点了五个小时，你会在机场做什么？

练习 8.2（上）：出国前的准备

Individual Activity: You and your friend are preparing to study abroad. In the space below, write down the things you would advise that your friend do in preparation before he or she leaves.

Example: 你要先把机票订好，要不然可能订不到座位。

Paired Activity: Below is a seating map that indicates which seats are vacant for the flight. Choose an open seat and discuss with your partner why you want that particular seat.

Example: A: 你会选哪个座位？

B: 我会选座位30A。

A: 为什么？

B: 因为我坐飞机的时候想自己安静地看书，所以我想坐后面一点靠窗户的座位。

练习 8.4（下）：航空公司规定

Paired Activity: Your friend has brought a lot of luggage with her. Using the information below, explain to your friend the airline's policies regarding luggage.

Example: A: 我的行李只不过超过1公斤而已，可以免费托运吗？

B: 这是航空公司规定，除非你付超重费，要不然他们不能帮你托运这些行李。

航空公司规定

1. 每位乘客可以免费托运两件行李
2. 每位乘客只能带一件手提行李登机
3. 每件托运行李不得超过20公斤
4. 手提行李不得超过7公斤
5. 行李超重费是每公斤8美元

Notes:

乘客 (chéngkè): n. passenger

手提行李 (shǒutí xíngli): n. hand baggage; carry-on luggage

不得 (bùdé): n. may not

练习 8.5：机场交通

Group Activity: You are now in Beijing. Research online how your group can get to Wudaokou, Beijing's university district, from the airport. Create a plan describing your options and what decision your group makes.

	Radical	Stroke Order
铁	钅 jīn gold	丿 丿 钅 钅 钅 钅 钅 铁 铁
订	讠(言) yán hand	丶 讠 讠 订
利	刂(刀) dāo knife	一 二 千 禾 禾 利 利
却	卩 jié seal	一 十 土 去 去 去 却
李	木 mù wood	一 十 才 木 本 李 李
斤	斤 jīn half a kilogram	丿 厂 斤 斤
航	舟 zhōu boat	丿 丿 丿 舟 舟 舟 舟 舟 航
定	宀 mián roof	丶 丷 宀 宀 宁 宁 定 定
托	扌(手) shǒu hand	一 十 扌 扌 托 托
座	广 yǎn shelter	丶 一 广 广 广 广 座 座 座
靠	非 fēi opposition	丿 丿 土 生 告 告 告 告 告 靠 靠 靠 靠 靠
窗	穴 xué cave	丶 丷 宀 宀 空 空 窗 窗 窗 窗
户	户 hù household	丶 丷 立 户
间	门 mén door	丶 门 门 间 间 间
船	舟 zhōu boat	丿 丿 丿 舟 舟 舟 舟 舟 船 船

Online chat: Working with a classmate, describe a place that you would like to visit and what you would like to do there. Provide reasons to support your preferences.

练习 8.8: 阅读理解

亲爱的中平：

　　明天你们就要来北京了。一想到快要见到你，我就很高兴！知道你们这次出国前的准备都做得很顺利，我就放心了。记得当时我来北京留学之前，办签证和订机票的时候一波三折，不但护照过期，而且机票也订错了。

　　当时我也跟你一样，出国前还是很紧张，不知道我在中国学习的时候会遇到什么问题，我的中文够好吗？上课的时候会不会有听不懂的地方？但是来了以后，发现老师和同学都很热情，常常帮我。所以你不用担心，你一定会喜欢在中国的留学生活。

玛丽

Read Mali's letter and answer the following questions.
1. What happened to Mali when she was preparing to go abroad?
2. Why was Mali nervous before she left for China?
3. Describe one of your experiences while preparing to travel on a trip and how you felt.

练习 8.9: 阅读理解

机场广播

（上午 11:20）

　　飞往北京的乘客请注意，由于暴雨，CA1188 航班的起飞时间将会延迟一个小时。对飞机延误给您带来的不便，我们非常抱歉！

（中午 12:20）

　　尊敬的 CA1188 航班的乘客，我们的航班开始登机了。请您出示登机牌，在十九号登机口登机。谢谢！

Notes:
延迟 (yánchí): *v.* to delay
不便 (búbiàn): *n.* inconvenience
登机口 (dēngjīkǒu): *n.* gate

Read the announcements and answer the following questions.
1. Why was the flight delayed?
2. What do you need to board this flight? Where should you go to board?
3. Discuss a flight delay you have experienced or seen, including why the flight was delayed.

Chinese Exploration

One of the most important pioneers in Chinese exploration is fleet admiral and mariner Zheng He (郑和: Zhèng Hé), who embarked on a series of naval missions commissioned by the Yongle Emperor during the fifteenth century. Decades before European explorers set sail, Zheng conducted seven naval voyages that showed the might of the Ming Dynasty (1368 – 1644 AD). The fleets were large (the largest consisted of 317 ships) and they carried with them the treasures of the empire: gold, silver, embroidered silks, porcelains, and a great variety of literature on topics such as navigation, science, and medicine.

Zheng's naval expeditions were intended to expand China's influence beyond its borders, develop imperial trade, and extend the Ming Empire's tributary system around the Indian Ocean. Not only did the expeditions improve Chinese understanding of the world outside, they also brought back spices and exotic animals that were presented as tribute to the emperor.

Zheng He's expeditions were temporarily halted when the Yongle Emperor died in 1424, and his successor, the Hongxi Emperor, decided to end foreign expeditions. The Hongxi Emperor's reign lasted only a couple of years. His heir, the Xuande Emperor, ordered what would become Zheng's last mission to improve weakened relations with countries in the Indian Ocean.

In his time, Zheng established important cross cultural and mercantile exchanges. Today, Zheng's legacy lives on in Southeast Asia and in China, where there are temples and museums dedicated to his memory. Books and television shows have also examined his journeys—most controversially, one scholar claimed Zheng He discovered North America before Christopher Columbus. China also designates July 11th as Maritime Day, commemorating Zheng He's first voyage.

Marco Polo's Journey to China

While Chinese explorers set out to explore the world, Western travelers also came to China. Marco Polo (马可•波罗: Mǎkě Bōluó) is one of the most famous and influential travelers in history, known primarily for his experiences in China.

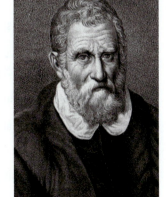

Marco Polo was among the first to make a significant journey east along the Silk Road to China. When Marco was 6 years old, his father and uncle, Nicolo and Maffeo Polo, embarked on an unprecedented expedition that spanned Central and East Asia. The two elder Polos eventually returned to Venice to meet Marco, who was now 17 years old. In 1271, the three men set off on an expedition from Venice. They went through Armenia, Persia, and Afghanistan, and then along the Silk Road to China.

The Polos lived in China for many years, eventually making their way to the court of Kublai Khan, the founder of the Yuan Dynasty (1206 - 1368 AD). While in China, the family was closely associated with the imperial court, and Marco Polo may have even become an imperial official. Returning after 24 years abroad, Marco Polo dictated a detailed account of his travels, *The Travels of Marco Polo*, which was widely read in Europe and served as a reference for future travelers.

A well-known book even in its time, *The Travels of Marco Polo* continues to provide inspiration for others to explore new places. His narratives have since inspired books, poems, television shows, operas, and even video games.

Pinyin

English

Zhōngpíng hé tā de péngyoumen jiāng qù Zhōngguó liúxué. Tāmen dōu shēnqǐng dào le jiǎngxuéjīn, bàn qiānzhèng hé dìng jīpiào yě dōu hěn shùnlì, kěshì zài chūfā de nà yì tiān, què yùdàole yìxiē máfan.

Zhongping and his friends are off to study abroad in China. They were all successful in their scholarship applications. Obtaining visas and booking plane tickets also went very smoothly. However, on the day of their departure, they ran into some difficulties.

Gōngzuò rényuán: Xiānsheng, nín de xínglǐ chāozhòng le.

Sir, your luggage is overweight.

Li Zhōngpíng: Zhǐ chāozhòng liǎng bàng yě bù xíng ma?

It's only overweight by two pounds, isn't it ok?

Gōngzuò rényuán: Duìbuqǐ, zhè shì hángkōng gōngsī de guīdìng. Chúfēi nín fù chāozhòngfèi, yàoburán wǒmen bù néng tuōyùn zhèxiē xínglǐ.

I'm sorry, but this is the airline's regulation. Unless you pay an overweight baggage fee, we can't check your luggage through.

Chén Dàdōng: Zhōngpíng, nǐ fàng yìdiǎn dōngxi dào wǒ de xiāngzi li ba. Nǐ gěi Mǎlì dài de lǐwù tài duō le ba!

Zhongping, why don't you put some stuff into my suitcase? Aren't you bringing a little too much stuff for Mali?

Gōngzuò rényuán: Xiānsheng, zhè shì nín de dēngjī pái, zuòwèi kào chuānghu.

Sir, here is your boarding pass. You have a window seat.

Huáng Xiáng'ān: Bùhǎoyìsi, zuòwèi kěyǐ huàn chéng kào zǒudào de ma?

Excuse me, would it be possible to switch to an aisle seat?

Gōngzuò rényuán: Duìbùqǐ, wǒmen zhǐ shèng kào zhōngjiān hé kào chuāng de zuòwèi le.

I'm sorry, we only have window and middle seats left.

Wáng Xiǎoměi: Xiáng'ān, wǒ de zuòwèi kào zǒudào, wǒ gēn nǐ huàn zuòwèi ba. Wǒ yǒu yìdiǎnr tóuténg, xiǎng zuò chuāng biān.

Xiang'an, my seat is an aisle seat, let's switch seats. I have a bit of a headache, so I'd prefer a window seat.

Chén Dàdōng:	Zāogāo, yào dēngjī le, Xiáng'ān zài nǎr?	Oh no! It's almost boarding time. Where's Xiang'an?
Wáng Xiǎoměi:	Dàdōng, wǒmen qù zhǎo tā ba!	Dadong, let's go look for him!
Chén Dàdōng:	Xiáng'ān nǐ pǎo dào nǎlǐ qù le? Gěi nǐ dǎ diànhuà nǐ yě bù jiē. Kuài zǒu ba, yàoburán jiù gǎn bú shàng fēijī le!	Xiang'an, where did you go? You didn't even pick up the phone when I called. Let's go or else we'll miss the flight!
Huáng Xiáng'ān:	Bùhǎoyìsi, wǒ kàn cuò le dēngjī shíjiān. Xiǎoměi, zhè shì gěi nǐ de yào, xīwàng nǐ de tóuténg néng hǎo yìxiē.	Sorry, I misread the boarding time. Xiaomei, here's some medicine for you, hope it will help with your headache.
Wáng Xiǎoměi:	Yuánlái nǐ gāngcái shì qù gěi wǒ mǎi yào a! Xièxie nǐ!	I didn't realize you had gone to buy medicine for me! Thank you!

What Can You Do?

INTERPRETIVE
- I can identify travel-related terms while in an airport.
- I can recognize travel issues at the check-in counter while in an airport.

INTERPERSONAL
- I can exchange information documents needed to travel abroad.
- I can discuss reasons for a flight delay.

PRESENTATIONAL
- I can talk about travel-related preparations needed before traveling abroad.
- I can describe the check-in and boarding processes while in the airport.

中国游
Traveling in China

（李中平的日记）

　　我们的中国游今天上路了！旅游路线是从北京坐火车到上海，然后去苏州。今天我买票的时候太紧张，把票买错了。之后周信换了票，但我觉得其实他不是为了帮我，而是为了得到大家的好感……虽然玛丽说我做得还不错，能自己去买票，但实际上我的中文不够好，还需要多练习。

（黄祥安的博客）

洋熊猫游中国：美食在上海
_{shàng hǎi}

来上海玩的游客非常多，人山人海。我们趁这次旅游的
_{shàng hǎi} _{yóu kè} _{rén shān rén hǎi} _{chèn}

机会，尝了各种好吃的特色小吃，难怪上海的饮食文化这么有
_{xiǎo chī} _{shàng hǎi}

名！看看我们都吃了些什么：

_{xiǎo lóng bāo}

小笼包真是好吃得不得了！不过我吃的时候太着急了，

嘴被烫了一下，人们常说"心急吃不了热豆腐"，其实应该是
_{tàng} _{xīn jí}

"心急吃不了小笼包"……
_{xīn jí} _{xiǎo lóng bāo}

（陈大东的游记）
_{yóu jì}

我们在苏州报名参加了旅游团。导游
_{sū zhōu bào míng} _{dǎo yóu}

带我们游园林，还介绍了苏州的历史。这趟
_{yuán lín} _{sū zhōu}

旅游给我最大的感受是"百闻不如一见"，
_{gǎn shòu} _{bǎi wén bù rú yí jiàn}

只有亲自到中国来，才能更深地体会中国的
_{qīn zì} _{shēn tǐ huì}

文化和风俗。到中国以后，小美开朗了很多
_{fēng sú}

。从机场那一天起，小美就跟祥安成了好朋
_{cóng} _{qǐ}

友。不知道这次留学会给大家带来什么样的

改变……
_{gǎi biàn}

LESSON TEXT 8.2

Traveling in China 中国游

Before the semester begins, the group decides to take a trip from Beijing to Shanghai and Suzhou.

李中平的日记

我们的中国游今天上路了！旅游路线是从北京坐火车到上海，然后去苏州。今天我买票的时候太紧张，把票买错了。之后周信换了票，但我觉得其实他不是为了帮我，而是为了得到大家的好感……虽然玛丽说我做得还不错，能自己去买票，但实际上我的中文不够好，还需要多练习。

———————————

黄祥安的博客

洋熊猫游中国：美食在上海

来上海玩的游客非常多，人山人海。我们趁这次旅游的机会，尝了各种好吃的特色小吃，难怪上海的饮食文化这么有名！看看我们都吃了些什么：

小笼包：小笼包真是好吃得不得了！不过我吃的时候太着急，嘴被烫了一下。人们常说"心急吃不了热豆腐"，其实应该是"心急吃不了小笼包"……

陈大东的游记

　　我们在苏州报名参加了旅游团。导游带我们游园林，还介绍了苏州的历史。这趟旅游给我最大的感受是"百闻不如一见"，只有亲自到中国来，才能更深地体会中国的文化和风俗。到中国以后，小美开朗了很多。从机场那一天起，小美就跟祥安变成了好朋友。不知道这次留学会给大家带来什么样的改变……

Language Tip

烫 (tàng)

In the Lesson Text Xiang'an uses 烫 to express that he burned his tongue when he ate steamed dumplings. 烫 means "very hot" as an adjective and "to burn" or "to scald" as a verb. When 烫 is an adjective, it is primarily used to describe hot liquid; it cannot be used to describe the weather. When it is used as a verb, it means to be burned by fire or hot liquid, to iron, or to burn.

Examples:　　　　这碗酸辣汤很烫。　　　　　　　　　我的手被火烫伤了。
　　　　　　　　This bowl of hot and sour soup is very hot.　　My hand was scalded by fire.

LESSON VOCABULARY 8.2

	SIMPLIFIED	TRADITIONAL	PINYIN	WORD CATEGORY	DEFINITION
1.	上路		shànglù	*vo*	to set out on a journey
2.	路线	路綫	lùxiàn	*n*	route, itinerary
3.	好感		hǎogǎn	*n*	favorable impression
4.	实际上	實際上	shíjìshang	*adv*	in reality; as a matter of fact
5.	游客	遊客	yóukè	*n*	tourist
6.	人山人海		rénshān rénhǎi	*ie*	a sea of people, huge crowds of people
7.	趁		chèn	*prep*	take advantage of; to avail oneself of
8.	小吃		xiǎochī	*n*	dish; snack; refreshments
9.	烫	燙	tàng	*v, adj*	to burn, to scald; very hot
10.	心急		xīnjí	*adj*	impatient, short-tempered
11.	游记	遊記	yóujì	*n*	travel journal
12.	报名	報名	bàomíng	*vo*	to sign up
13.	导游	導遊	dǎoyóu	*n*	tour guide
14.	园林	園林	yuánlín	*n*	garden
15.	感受		gǎnshòu	*n, v*	impression; to feel
16.	百闻不如一见	百聞不如一見	bǎiwén bùrú yíjiàn	*ie*	seeing is believing
17.	亲自	親自	qīnzì	*adv*	firsthand, personally
18.	深		shēn	*adj*	deep; profound
19.	体会	體會	tǐhuì	*v*	to acquire; to learn from experience
20.	风俗	風俗	fēngsú	*n*	custom
21.	从……起	從……起	cóng……qǐ	*cj*	ever since; from . . . on
22.	改变	改變	gǎibiàn	*n, v*	change; to change

PROPER NOUN

23.	上海		Shànghǎi	*n*	Shanghai

LESSON VOCABULARY 8.2 (continued)

	Simplified	Traditional	Pinyin	Word Category	Definition
24.	苏州	蘇州	Sūzhōu	*n*	Suzhou
25.	小笼包	小籠包	Xiǎolóngbāo	*n*	small steamed meat-filled buns with soup

REQUIRED VOCABULARY 8.2

	Simplified	Traditional	Pinyin	Word Category	Definition
26.	门票	門票	ménpiào	*n*	entrance ticket, admission ticket
27.	行程		xíngchéng	*n*	itinerary
28.	旅馆	旅館	lǚguǎn	*n*	inn, hotel

Idiomatic Expressions

rén shān rén hǎi
人山人海

人山人海 literally means "people mountain and people sea."

This expression appears in a description about an illustration depicting prosperity of Hangzhou during the Song Dynasty (960 – 1279 AD). In the picture, throngs of people crowd the streets. Today, it is used to indicate a huge crowd of people.

Example:
这是今年最重要的篮球比赛，体育馆里人山人海。
This is the most important basketball match this year. The stadium is filled with spectators.

bǎi wén bù rú yī jiàn
百闻不如一见

百闻不如一见 means "hearing something a hundred times is not as good as seeing it once."

The expression appears in *The History of the Former Han Dynasty* (《汉书》: *Hàn Shū*), written during the Eastern Han Dynasty (206 BC – 25 AD). In the book, a general advised the emperor that the best way to know their opponent's situation is to inspect from the front lines. The expression is now normally used in a positive manner to describe things that are better than one's expectations when experienced in person. It is often used in a similar way equivalent to the English phrase "seeing is believing."

Example:
故宫比我想象的还要漂亮，真是百闻不如一见！
The Forbidden City is more beautiful than I imagined. Seeing really is believing!

Options for Train Travel

As Zhongping discovered in this lesson, buying train tickets can be complicated. There are many details to consider when purchasing train tickets, which come in a variety of classes, berths, and seats. In most cities, there are two kinds of trains: the regular 火车 and high-speed rail (和谐号: héxiéhào). In Shanghai, there is third type of train known as the maglev train, which links the airport to the city.

Tickets for high-speed trains are more expensive than regular trains, and come in two classes: first and second. When traveling by regular rail, riders may opt for a sleeper berth (a bunk bed within a compartment) rather than an upright seat. Both berths and seats come in two classes: soft (more luxurious class) and hard (regular class). More specifically, private compartments come with four soft sleepers that you can fold away during the day, making the price higher than other types of seats. Compartments without doors contain six fixed hard sleepers, which are less comfortable and tend to be more cramped than soft sleepers but are nonetheless more cost-effective.

Below is an example of a regular rail ticket:

Departure Station			Train Number
Departure Date & Time			Arrival Station
Price			Carriage Number & Seat Number
Valid Time			Seat Type
Passport Number			

京 A D 鲁
C062551　北 京　T271次　吉 林 西
Beijing　Jilinxi
2010年10月22日19:10 开　11车015号上铺
¥246.00元　新空调硬卧
限乘当日当次车 在3日内到有效
10001201691019 C062551

Chinese	Pinyin	Meaning
Train details		
号	hào	number
线	xiàn	line
站	zhàn	station
时刻表	shíkèbiǎo	timetable
车次	chēcì	train number
首班车	shǒubānchē	first bus/train
末班车	mòbānchē	last bus/train
Classes of Tickets (火车票类: Huǒchē piào lèi)		
卧铺	wòpù	sleeping berth
软卧	ruǎnwò	soft sleeper
硬卧	yìngwò	hard sleeper
坐票	zuòpiào	seating ticket
软座	ruǎnzuò	soft seat
硬座	yìngzuò	hard seat
无座/站票	wúzuò/zhànpiào	standing room only
一等座	yī děng zuò	first class seat
二等座	èr děng zuò	second class seat

Chinese	Pinyin	Meaning
Ticket Types (票类: piào lèi)		
成人票	chéngrén piào	adult ticket
儿童票	értóng piào	child ticket
老人票	lǎorén piào	senior ticket
学生票	xuésheng piào	student ticket
Seat Location (位置: wèizhi)		
上铺	shàngpù	top sleeping berth
中铺	zhōngpù	middle sleeping berth
下铺	xiàpù	lower sleeping berth
前排	qiánpái	front row
后排	hòupái	back row
过道座位	guòdào zuòwèi	aisle seat
中间座位	zhōngjiān zuòwèi	middle seat
靠窗座位	kào chuāng zuòwèi	window seat

STRUCTURE NOTE 8.5

Use 不是 A 而是 B to emphasize a contrast between A and B

而 *is a connecting term commonly used in formal writing that indicates a contrast similar to "rather" or "but." The pattern* 不是 A 而是 B *expresses that not only is A not the case, but actually B is the case.*

> Subject + 不是 + Noun Phrase / Verb Phrase + 而是 + Noun Phrase / Verb Phrase

> 不是 + Sentence + 而是 + Sentence

From the Lesson Text:

我觉得其实他不是为了帮我，而是为了得到大家的好感……

Wǒ juéde qíshí tā bú shì wèile bāng wǒ, érshì wèile dédào dàjiā de hǎogǎn……
I don't think he did it to help me. I think he did it to impress the group . . .

Other examples:

他能成功不是因为运气好，而是因为努力工作。

Tā néng chénggōng bú shì yīnwèi yùnqi hǎo, érshì yīnwèi nǔlì gōngzuò.
His success wasn't due to good luck, it was because he worked hard.

她去中国不是为了旅游，而是为了了解中国的文化。

Tā qù Zhōngguó búshì wèile lǚyóu, érshì wèile liǎojiě Zhōngguó de wénhuà.
She went to China, not because she wanted to travel, but because she wanted to understand Chinese culture.

Practice: Create complete sentences using 不是…而是… and the word pairs provided below.

Example: 我们赢得比赛/运气/团队精神
→ 我们赢得比赛靠的不是运气，而是团队精神。

1. 我不想去北京旅游/我没有空

_____

2. 他们最喜欢吃的中国菜/宫保鸡丁/麻婆豆腐

_____

3. 我不想租这套公寓/房租太贵了

_____

4. 他/想要靠走道的座位/想要靠窗户的座位

_____

5. 大家/想去中国旅游/想去中国留学

_____

STRUCTURE NOTE 8.6
Use 实际上 *to explain how things really are*

Adding 上 *to the word* 实际, *"reality," results in the expression "in reality," or "in fact."* 实际上 *(shíjìshang) can either introduce a sentence, or precede a verb or adjective phrase.*

> 实际上, + Sentence

> Subject + 实际上 + Verb / Adjective Phrase

From the Lesson Text:
实际上我的中文不够好，还需要多练习。
Shíjìshang wǒ de Zhōngwén bú gòu hǎo, hái xūyào duō liànxí.
I think in reality my Chinese is not good enough and requires more practice.

Other examples:

实际上，申请去中国留学并不是很难。
Shíjìshang, shēnqǐng qù Zhōngguó liúxué bìng bú shì hěn nán.
In reality, applying to study abroad in China isn't that hard.

队员们都以为比赛输了是因为运气不好，实际上是因为裁判不公平。
Duìyuánmen dōu yǐwéi bǐsài shūle shì yīnwèi yùnqi bù hǎo, shíjìshang shì yīnwèi cáipàn bù gōngpíng.
The players all thought that they lost the game because of bad luck; in reality, it was because the referee wasn't fair.

Practice: Change the following sentences into Chinese and use 实际上 within your sentences.

Example: Actually, it is not difficult to make Chinese food.
→ 实际上中国菜不难做。

1. Actually, he does not speak Chinese very well.

_____

2. Actually, he always likes her.

_____

3. Actually I don't like this house at all. It's too noisy.

_____

4. Actually, she doesn't shop online very often.

_____

5. The rent seems a little bit expensive, but actually it includes the utilities and net charge.

_____

STRUCTURE NOTE 8.7
Use 趁(着) *to take advantage of a situation*

趁 *(chèn) means to take advantage of a favorable opportunity or situation. In this pattern,* 趁 *introduces the favorable situation, which is then followed by the action taken.* 趁 *may be followed by* 着, *as in the Lesson Text, or it may appear on its own.*

Subject + 趁(着) + Noun Phrase + Verb Phrase

From the Lesson Text:	我们趁这次旅游的机会，尝了各种好吃的特色小吃。 Wǒmen chèn zhè cì lǚyóu de jīhuì, chángle gèzhǒng hǎochī de tèsè xiǎochī. We took advantage of this travel opportunity to try out all types of local dishes.

Other examples:

趁着年轻我们要多出去走走。 Chènzhe niánqīng wǒmen yào duō chūqu zǒuzou. Taking advantage of our youth, we are going to go out more.	希望趁这次活动，更多人能了解这个社团。 Xīwàng chèn zhè cì huódòng, gèng duō rén néng liǎojiě zhè ge shètuán. I hope that by taking advantage of this event, more people can understand this organization.

Practice: Match the clauses in the left column with the clauses in the right column to form a complete sentence.

Example: 趁着这次旅游的机会，我认识了很多新朋友。

1.	趁着你明天有空	你们最好快点去校外租房。
2.	趁着最近天气好	我们要买很多家电。
3.	趁着张教授有时间	我问了他几个问题。
4.	趁着现在房租不贵	我们去看音乐剧吧。
5.	趁着下星期商场打折	我们去爬山吧。

STRUCTURE NOTE 8.8
Use 只有…才… *to describe necessary conditions for a condition to occur*
The two-part pattern 只有 A, 才 B *expresses the meaning "only if A, then B," indicating that A is a necessary condition for B to happen.*

> 只有 + Condition Clause, (+ Subject) + 才 + Verb Phrase

> Subject + 只有 + Verb Phrase, + 才 + Verb Phrase

From the Lesson Text:

只有亲自到中国来，才能更深地体会中国的文化和风俗。

Zhǐyǒu qīnzì dào Zhōngguó lái, cái néng gèng shēn de tǐhuì Zhōngguó de wénhuà hé fēngsú.

One can only acquire a deep understanding of Chinese culture and customs by experiencing it firsthand.

Other examples:

教授告诉我，只有多说多练，我的中文水平才能提高。

Jiàoshòu gàosu wǒ, zhǐyǒu duō shuō duō liàn, wǒde Zhōngwén shuǐpíng cái néng tígāo.

The professor told me that only by speaking and practicing more can I raise my level of Chinese.

只有好好学习自然灾害的知识，才知道怎么保护自己和减少受伤。

Zhǐyǒu hǎohāo xuéxí zìrán zāihài de zhīshi, cái zhīdào zěnme bǎohù zìjǐ hé jiǎnshǎo shòushāng.

Only by learning about natural disasters can you know how to protect yourself and reduce injury.

Practice: Create complete sentences using 只有…才….

Example: 多听多说／能学好一门新的语言
→只有多听多说，才能学好一门新的语言。

1. 付了超重费／能托运这些行李

   _____

2. 工作经验多的人／能得到去那家公司实习的机会

   _____

3. 亲自来到中国／能更好地了解中国文化

   _____

4. 篮球比赛／配合得好／能赢

   _____

5. 烹饪材料新鲜／做出来的菜／好吃

   _____

练习 8.10: 课文理解

Paired Activity: Discuss the following questions based on the Lesson Text. Be prepared to share your thoughts with the class.

> 1. 中平为什么会觉得自己的中文不够好？
>
> 2. 大东最大的收获是什么？
>
> 3. 你最感兴趣的中国的小吃或景点是什么？为什么？

练习 8.11（上）: 你会选哪家饭馆？

Paired Activity: You and your classmate are now in Shanghai. Using the restaurant reviews below and taking into account your own preferences, choose between these two options for dinner and explain your choice.

大上海饭馆

上海菜

地点：上海市南京路5号　　　电话：021-86765588

消费：每人50元　信用卡✓　优惠券✓　无线上网✓　电视

价钱：★★　　　　食物：★★★★★
服务：★★★★　　环境：★★★　　　交通：★

上海迎客餐厅

上海菜

地点：上海市大华街37号　　　电话：021-84965---

消费：每人25元　信用卡✓　优惠券　无线上网✓　电视✓

价钱：★★★★★　食物：★★★
服务：★★　　　　环境：★　　　　交通：★★★★

✏️ 练习 8.12（下）：写旅游日记

Individual Activity: Write a diary entry about a trip that you have taken. Use the questions below as a guideline.

> 1. 今天你参观了哪个景点？跟谁一起去？
>
> 2. 你吃了什么有特色的菜或小吃？
>
> 3. 你喜欢那个地方吗？为什么？
>
> 4. 这次旅游给你最大的感受是什么？

Example: 我和朋友们今天到上海旅游。我们买了很多东西，还吃了小笼包。我很喜欢上海，因为上海有各种好吃的特色小吃。这次旅游给我最大的感受是想要了解一个地方，一定要亲自来看看！

💬 练习 8.13（上）：旅游与交通

✏️ Paired Activity: Survey your classmates on the places they want to visit, transportation preferences, and why. Record their responses below.

名字	地方	交通	你为什么想去这个地方？
Example: 大东	苏州	火车	因为我想多了解关于园林的历史。

🖥️ 练习 8.14（下）：计划一趟中国游

Group Activity: Working with your group, plan a one-week trip through China. Research different destinations and create an itinerary, including transportation options.

	Radical	**Stroke Order**
海	氵(水) shuǐ water	丶 氵 氵 氵 汇 汇 海 海 海 海
苏	艹(草) cǎo grass	一 十 艹 艻 苏 苏 苏
州	丶 diǎn dot	丶 丿 丬 州 州 州
际	阝 fù hill	阝 阝 阝 阡 阡 阡 际
趁	走 zǒu walk	一 十 土 丰 丰 走 走 走 赴 赴 趁 趁
笼	竹(竹) zhú bamboo	丿 广 广 广 广 广 竿 竿 笼 笼 笼
烫	火 huǒ fire	丶 氵 氵 汤 汤 汤 汤 烫 烫
急	心 xīn heart	丿 勹 刍 刍 刍 急 急 急
林	木 mù wood	一 十 才 木 木 村 材 林
闻	门 mén door	丶 门 门 门 门 闻 闻 闻
亲	亠 tóu head	丶 二 亠 立 立 辛 辛 亲
深	氵(水) shuǐ water	丶 氵 氵 汇 沪 沪 泙 泙 浑 深
俗	亻(人) rén person	丿 亻 亻 亻 俗 俗 俗 俗 俗
改	攵(攴) pū knock	乛 己 己 己 改 改 改
变	又 yòu again	丶 二 亠 亦 亦 变 变

练习 8.16: 线上聊天

Online chat: Working with a classmate, discuss a trip that you have taken. Describe where you went and what you enjoyed about the trip.

练习 8.17: 阅读理解

尊敬的刘老师:

您好！我们在中国玩得很开心。我们先到北京，然后去了上海和苏州。每个城市都很有特色。我们在北京逛了胡同和参观了故宫；上海是很现代化的大城市，我们逛了购物中心，还尝了上海最有名的小笼包；苏州有非常漂亮的园林，我们拍了很多照片。我们来到苏州之后才知道园林有多美，真是百闻不如一见！相信我们在中国不但能提高中文水平，而且能更深地了解中国文化。

祝您工作顺利，身体健康。

您的学生：陈大东

Read Dadong's letter and answer the following questions.
1. What did Dadong and his friends do in the cities they visited?
2. What are Dadong's impressions of his trip to China?
3. Would you choose to visit a big city or the countryside? Why?

练习 8.18: 阅读理解

中心旅行社苏杭三日游行程和价格
第一天　北京到苏州　(包晚餐)
　　　　中午12点45分从北京飞苏州。游览苏州园林。住苏州。
第二天　苏州到杭州　(包早午晚三餐)
　　　　白天游览苏州。下午3点半坐汽车到杭州。住杭州。
第三天　回北京　(包早餐)
　　　　早餐后，坐上午11点的飞机回北京。

价格：每人1499元　　发团时间：每周一、三、五
报名电话：010-818054634

Notes:
游览 (yóulǎn): v. to tour
杭州 (Hángzhōu): n. Hangzhou
发团 (fātuán): n. departure

Read the itinerary and answer the following questions.
1. What day will you go to Hangzhou? What will you do in Hangzhou?
2. What kind of transportation will you take during this trip?
3. Describe an itinerary of a trip you have taken, including transportation methods.

Journey to the West: The Real Story and Travels of Xuanzang

In Chinese literature, *Journey to the West* (西游记: Xīyóujì) is the most famous among the novels considered the most renowned works of fiction called the Four Great Classical Novels (四大名著: Sìdà Míngzhù). It was attributed to Wu Cheng'en and written in the sixteenth century during the Ming Dynasty. Also known as the *Monkey King*, this book is a fictionalized account of the actual travels of the Buddhist monk Xuanzang (玄奘: Xuán Zàng) and his journey from China to India and back again an attempt to obtain copies of the sacred Buddhist texts.

Although *Journey to the West* is a saga beloved by many, having been made into numerous movies, television dramas, cartoon series, comics, and games, the real story of Xuanzang is no less fantastical. Xuanzang was distressed by the fact that the Buddhist holy writings in China were incomplete, even contradictory, and could not answer his questions. He decided he had to journey to India, the birthplace of Buddhism, and bring back copies of the original scriptures. After much preparation, he began his 16-year pilgrimage in 629 AD.

At the start of his journey, Xuanzang met his first challenge: the Taizong Emperor had closed China's borders allowing no one to enter or leave. His chance finally came when crops around Chang'an — where Xuanzang lived — failed and the emperor ordered all monks to move to regions with more food. The monk took this opportunity to head to Gansu province, and from there, he decided to sneak out of China.

During the early part of his voyage, Xuanzang faced many hurdles. Relief eventually came when he stumbled upon Hami, an oasis town. Having heard of Xuanzang's arrival, the king of another oasis, Turfan, sent royal guards to invite the monk to his kingdom.

After the monk arrived, the king wanted Xuanzang to stay and teach. However, he refused. Taken aback, the king threatened him, and Xuangzang protested by refusing all sustenance. Feeling guilty, the king quickly repented and even equipped Xuanzang with travel supplies, including guards, official letters, and gifts for rulers he would encounter along the way.

The extra supplies slowed down Xuanzang's expedition, and he was forced to stop in another oasis kingdom for the winter. However, the monk was impatient to continue on. Against the advice of locals, he and his group braved the treacherous and cold Tian Shan mountains. Although Xuanzang made it out with his life, he suffered an agonizing loss of men and livestock due to an avalanche they caused.

The next leg of the journey was relatively easy in comparison. In 630 AD, they finally arrived in India. Xuanzang spent years exploring different parts of the country: visiting various Buddhist monasteries, studying, copying, and buying scriptures, commissioning and buying replicas of Buddha figures, and recording all that he had experienced.

Finally, after fourteen years in India, Xuanzang left for home. The king of northern India also generously furnished Xuanzang with supplies, letters to other rulers, and soldiers for protection. Xuanzang's return to China was triumphant and received with great honor. Emperor Taizong had two pagodas built to house the scriptures and a monastary built for Xuanzang to continue his work on interpreting and teaching the texts.

Many of the cities Xuanzang passed through still exist today. Chang'an is better known now as the city of Xi'an, the home of the terracotta warriors. Hami and Turfan are popular places to visit in Xinjiang Province.

Pinyin

Lǐ Zhōngpíng de rìjì

Wǒmen de Zhōngguó yóu jīntiān shànglù le! Lǚyóu de lùxiàn shì cóng Běijīng zuò huǒchē dào Shànghǎi, ránhòu qù Sūzhōu. Jīntiān wǒ mǎipiào de shíhou tài jǐnzhāng, bǎ piào mǎi cuò le. Zhīhòu Zhōu Xìn huànle piào, dàn wǒ juéde qíshí tā bú shì wèile bāng wǒ, érshì wèile dédào dàjiā de hǎogǎn……Suīrán Mǎlì shuō wǒ zuòde hái búcuò, néng zìjǐ qù mǎi piào, dàn shíjìshang wǒ de Zhōngwén búgòu hǎo, hái xūyào duō liànxí.

English

Li Zhongping's diary:

Our adventures in China begin today! The travel route begins in Beijing, where we take a train to Shanghai, and then on to Suzhou. When I went to buy tickets today, I got nervous and ended up buying the wrong tickets. Zhou Xin helped to exchange the tickets for us later on, but I don't think he did it to help me. I think he did it to impress the group . . . Even though Mali said I did a good job buying tickets on my own, in reality my Chinese is not good enough and requires more practice

---

Huáng Xiáng'ān de bókè

Yáng xióngmāo yóu Zhōngguó: Měishí Zài Shànghǎi

Lái Shànghǎi wán de yóukè fēicháng duō, rénshān rénhǎi. Wǒmen chèn zhècì lǚyóu de jīhuì, chángle gèzhǒng hǎochī de tèsè xiǎochī, nánguài Shànghǎi de yǐnshí wénhuà zhème yǒumíng! Kànkan wǒmen dōu chīle xiē shénme:

Xiǎolóngbāo: Xiǎolóngbāo zhēn shì hǎochī de bùdeliǎo! Búguò wǒ chī de shíhou tài zháojí, zuǐ bèi tàngle yíxià. Rénmen cháng shuō "xīn jí chī bu liǎo rè dòufu", qíshí yīnggāi shì "xīn jí chī bu liǎo Xiǎolóngbāo"......

Huang Xiang'an's blog:

Western Panda Touring China: Gourmet Food in Shanghai

So many tourists come to Shanghai — everywhere you go there's a sea of people. We took advantage of this trip to try out all kinds of local dishes. It's no wonder Shanghai's food culture is so famous! Take a look at what we've eaten:

Steamed Soup Dumplings: Steamed Soup Dumplings are so delicious! However, I was a bit too eager when I was eating and burned my mouth. People here often say "impatient people cannot eat hot tofu," but I think it's more appropriate to say "impatient people cannot eat steamed dumplings . . ."

Chén Dàdōng de yóujì

Wǒmen zài Sūzhōu bàomíng cānjiāle lǚyóutuán. Dǎoyóu dài wǒmen yóu yuánlín, hái jièshàole Sūzhōu de lìshǐ. Zhè tàng lǚyóu gěi wǒ zuì dà de gǎnshòu shì "bǎiwén bùrú yíjiàn", zhǐyǒu qīnzì dào Zhōngguó lái, cái néng gèng shēn de tǐhuì Zhōngguó de wénhuà hé fēngsú. Dào Zhōngguó yǐhòu, Xiǎoměi kāilǎngle hěnduō. Cóng jīchǎng nà yì tiān qǐ, Xiǎoměi jiù gēn Xiáng'ān biànchéngle hǎo péngyou. Bù zhīdào zhè cì liúxué huì gěi dàjiā dàilái shénmeyàng de gǎibiàn……

Chen Dadong's travel journal:

We signed up with a tour group in Suzhou. The tour guide took us to tour the gardens and also told us a bit about Suzhou's history. My impression after taking this trip is that "seeing is believing." You can only get a deep understanding of Chinese culture and customs by experiencing them firsthand. After arriving in China, Xiaomei seems much happier. Even since that day at the airport, Xiaomei and Xiang'an have become good friends. It'll be interesting to see how our time studying abroad changes everyone . . .

What Can You Do?

INTERPRETIVE
- I can list different impressions regarding local dishes after others have tasted them.
- I can recognize different kinds of travel narratives in written text.

INTERPERSONAL
- I can discuss feelings regarding a travel experience.
- I can exchange information about traveling.

PRESENTATIONAL
- I can describe the experience of going on a guided tour.
- I can summarize activities done while traveling.

ACT IT OUT

Working in groups, compose an original two-minute skit that utilizes the vocabulary and structures introduced in Unit 8. Each of you should assume a role and have a roughly equal number of lines in the skit. Be prepared to perform your skit in class. You can either come up with your own story or choose from one of the following situations:

A) It is almost time to board the plane! You and your friends run to your departure gate. When you arrive, you see that no one has boarded yet. Ask the station agent why there is a delay and when you will board.

B) You and your friends are at the terminal, waiting to board your flight. However, you can't find one of your friends. What happened to him or her? What do you do to find him or her?

C) You and your friend go to a travel agency to find out the price for different tours. Discuss with the travel agent the various package options.

CHECK WHAT YOU CAN DO

RECOGNIZE

Adjectives
- 顺利
- 心急
- 深
- 超重

Adverbs
- 将
- 实际上
- 亲自

Conjunctions
- 却
- 除非…要不然
- 从…起

Idiomatic Expressions
- 人山人海
- 百闻不如一见

Interjections
- 糟糕

Nouns
- 磅
- 公斤
- 人员
- 行李
- 航空公司
- 规定
- 登机牌
- 座位
- 走道
- 中间
- 刚才
- 地铁
- 船
- 目的地
- 路线

- 好感
- 游客
- 小吃
- 游记
- 导游
- 园林
- 风俗
- 上海
- 苏州
- 小笼包
- 门票
- 行程
- 旅馆
- 感受
- 改变

Preposition
- 趁

Resultative Verb
- 赶上

Verbs
- 订
- 托运
- 起飞
- 报名
- 体会
- 烫

Verb-Object Compounds
- 办签证
- 靠窗户
- 上路

WRITE

- 铁
- 订
- 利
- 却
- 李
- 斤
- 航
- 定
- 托
- 座
- 靠
- 窗
- 户
- 间
- 船

- 海
- 苏
- 州
- 际
- 趁
- 笼
- 烫
- 急
- 林
- 闻
- 亲
- 深
- 俗
- 改
- 变

USE

- Use 将(要/会) to describe future events in formal contexts.
- Use 却 to indicate a reversal or contrast.
- Use 除非…(否则/要不然)… to make "unless" statements.
- Use 刚才 to talk about events or situations that have just occurred.

- Use 不是A而是B to emphasize a contrast between A and B.
- Use 实际上 to explain how things really are.
- Use 趁(着) to take advantage of a situation.
- Use 只有…才… to describe necessary conditions for a condition to occur.

附录
APPENDIX

第一單元

第一課　天氣

中平剛旅遊回來，收到了朋友們寄來的明信片：

親愛的中平：

　　暑假過得好嗎？北京的夏天就跟小美的表哥周信說的一樣熱，氣溫一般在華氏八十多度，但是下雨以後會涼快一點兒。我迷上了中國的文化，打算繼續留在北京念書。天氣沒那麼熱的時候，希望你能來北京玩！

瑪麗
八月九日

中平，你好！

　　我們已經到倫敦了。倫敦的夏天很涼快，平均氣溫才七十度左右，可是常常下雨，難怪人們出門都帶着雨傘。小美很喜歡這樣的天氣，常常自己出去逛街。對了，說不定過幾天我們會去巴黎和別的地方旅遊。希望我們能遊遍歐洲的各個大城市！

大東
八月十六日

嗨，中平！

　　你玩得怎麼樣？南非現在是冬季，但是天氣很好，比較暖和。安娜有一個舞蹈團的面試，已經回俄羅斯了。等我下星期回去再跟你聊吧！

祥安
八月二十日

第二課　　旅遊和氣候

周信：　　　好久不見。暑假實習還好嗎？

孫瑪麗：　　好極了！實習結束以後，我去了中國各地旅遊。這是我從雲南給你帶回來的茶葉。

周信：　　　謝謝！你去了雲南的哪些地方旅遊？

孫瑪麗：　　我到了昆明，那裏的風景很漂亮，有山有水。

周信：　　　我聽說雲南的天氣"冬暖夏涼"，昆明一定很舒服吧？

孫瑪麗：　　昆明真是個好地方，氣候四季如春，夏天比北京氣溫低十度左右，涼快多了。

周信：　　　真羨慕你，北京這幾天特別悶熱。下次去旅遊一定要叫上我，我要當你的"驢友"！

孫瑪麗：　　甚麼？你要當我的女友？

周信：　　　是"驢友"，不是"女友"。"驢友"就是一起旅遊的朋友。

孫瑪麗：　　原來是這個意思啊！對了，這個周末我打算去爬山，你想和我一起去嗎？

周信：　　　好，讓我看看天氣預報……預報說周六早上是晴天，可是下午會颱風，還可能下雨。白天最高溫度二十九度，晚上會下降到十七度。我們要不要改天再去？或者去別的地方？

孫瑪麗：　　沒關係，我們帶着帽子和雨衣，早一點兒出發就行了。

第二單元

第一課　申請留學

陳大東：　中平，你選修的中國文化課怎麼樣？

李中平：　這門課很有意思，我們用中文討論和寫報告。你呢？這個學期選了甚麼課？

陳大東：　暑假的時候我迷上了中國歷史小説，所以這個學期我主修中國歷史課和中國文學課，教授要我們讀很多歷史書和中文小説。

李中平：　我覺得學習知識不見得只在書本上，特別是學習中國文化或歷史，最好的辦法就是去中國走一趟，學習一段時間。

王小美：　去中國學習聽起來挺有意思的！你想去中國哪個地方呢？

黃祥安：　中平當然想去北京！這樣他就可以去看瑪麗了，對吧？

李中平：　我只是想順便去看看瑪麗……我查了一下怎麼申請留學，只要準備必需的資料就可以了，我們還能申請獎學金。

陳大東：　沒想到這麼簡單。到中國留學能更好地了解和學習中國歷史，而且我一直都很想去參觀故宮和爬長城。

黃祥安：　那我也要去中國留學，這樣我就能吃到地道的餃子和北京烤鴨啦！

王小美：　哈哈，你去中國是爲了吃啊？不過我也很喜歡吃中國菜。這真是個好主意。如果你們都去中國留學，那麼我也去吧！

李中平：　太好了！那以後我們都能變成中國通了。我要把這個好消息告訴瑪麗！

第二課　加入社團

新學期開始了，我很高興能留在北京念書。今天下午我參加了大學社團的招募活動。這裏的社團多得不得了，有武術社、吉他社、文學社等等。

━━━━━━━━━━━━━━━━

當我正在煩惱不知道要加入哪一個社團的時候，碰見了周信。他給我介紹了楊冰冰，她是"綠色地球社"的負責人。由於社團準備在北京發展一個環境保護項目，所以在招募大學生志願者。我與冰冰一見如故！冰冰是巴西人，個子挺高的，超過一米七。她的性格很開朗，難怪周信説冰冰很受大家歡迎。

冰冰常常有機會在中國各地參加和舉辦很多的環保活動。我覺得她的工作很有意思！我決定加入這個社團，做一名志願者，希望和大家一起努力。

第一課　　住校與租房

王小美：　大東，想不到你們的宿舍這麼亂！你看床上都是衣服，桌上還有吃剩的東西。

陳大東：　這些都是祥安的，他常常亂放東西。

王小美：　那你為甚麼還要跟他住？

陳大東：　因為他很好相處，又會照顧人。上次安娜生病就是祥安帶她去看了醫生。再說，住宿舍也有很多好處。

王小美：　住宿舍的好處確實挺多，但是一點隱私都沒有，房租還很貴。

陳大東：　校內外的房租都不便宜，我平時也很忙，會忘了付水電費。住在宿舍費用全包，省心又省力。

王小美：　你只要找一個細心的室友就不用擔心啦！

陳大東：　不過我已經習慣和祥安一起住了。你去中國留學的時候想找甚麼樣的室友合租呢？

王小美：　到了北京以後，我想租一套三室一廳的公寓。我的室友一定要細心、愛乾淨、會做飯和做家務。這樣的室友很"理想"吧？

陳大東：　聽起來不錯，可是我恐怕沒有辦法做一個那麼"理想"的室友喔……

　　昨天，瑪麗收到了房東的通知，說合同到期之後不想再出租了，要收回公寓。瑪麗必須在一個月之內搬家，所以她急着找公寓。周信説他對北京的情況比較了解，要瑪麗看房的時候叫上他。瑪麗在報紙上看到了一個租房廣告，和周信一起去看了以後發現那套公寓又臟又舊，還沒有空調和洗衣機。然後他們去看了一套比較新的公寓，房租很便宜而且還有家具，但可惜離馬路很近，太吵了。

　　後來，他們在學校碰到了冰冰。冰冰告訴瑪麗她的室友剛搬走，有一個房間空了出來。公寓的家用電器包括電視和冰箱在內，而且在學校附近，環境非常好，也很安靜。瑪麗看了以後對這個公寓很滿意，也很高興能跟朋友做室友，覺得自己很幸運。

第四單元

第一課　網上購物

　　祥安一向很喜歡美食、攝影和寫博客。最近，他想用博客給朋友們介紹和分享中國美食，讓大家都有機會了解中國的飲食文化。

　　祥安打算買一個比較專業的數碼相機來拍照。大東建議祥安在網上買，因爲商店的價格常常不如網上的划算，並且網上有很多的打折活動。但中平提醒祥安注意網絡安全，他在報紙上常看到網絡購物的投訴。祥安找到了一個賣新款相機的網站，既打折又免費送貨，但不保修。他決定在網上購物之前，先去附近的商店比較一下。

　　中平陪祥安去了一家電器商店，那裏有很多打折的名牌數碼相機，產品有一年的保修期，還可以用優惠券在這家商店的網站上購物。後來，祥安看中了一款黑白色的相機，既便宜又好用。中平説相機的顏色和樣子讓他想起大熊貓。祥安覺得買這個相機真是最合適不過了，因爲這樣他的博客就可以叫"洋熊貓遊中國"！

第二課　　退貨

孫瑪麗：　不好意思，這台電暖器才用了兩次就用不了了，能退貨嗎？

店員：　　你是甚麼時候買的？有收據嗎？

孫瑪麗：　我是兩個星期前買的，這是收據。

店員：　　真的很抱歉，商品只能在一周之內退貨。

孫瑪麗：　甚麼？可是賣的時候你沒有告訴我啊。

店員：　　你看收據上寫得很清楚，不好意思。

周信：　　那麼確實是沒辦法退了。瑪麗，別不開心。我帶你去大商場買一台新的。

孫瑪麗：　可是大商場會比小商店的價錢貴吧？

周信：　　我認為像毛巾和牙膏這樣的日用品，在小商店買會比較划算，但是買電器還是在大商場更有保證。我家附近那家百貨公司就挺不錯的，還能在一個月之內退貨。

孫瑪麗：　好吧，我們去看看。其實不管買甚麼東西，我都應該先看退貨條件。

周信：　　你先看看退貨須知，有不懂的地方就問我吧。

退貨須知
一、商品可以在售後三十天之內退換。
二、退換時必須出示收據。
三、商品和包裝不能有損壞。

第五單元

第一課　籃球比賽

陳大東：　你們覺得這場比賽哪個隊會贏？山貓還是飛魚？

王小美：　當然是山貓！山貓隊的球員都像山貓一樣厲害，跑得快、跳得高，一定能贏！

黃祥安：　可是你別忘了飛魚隊除了隊長的實力非常強以外，另外還有兩個球員是籃球明星。這次飛魚贏定了！

王小美：　祥安，小心飛魚會被山貓吃掉喔！

陳大東：　小美，想不到你這麼迷山貓隊。比賽要開始了，我們看球吧。

────────────

山貓對飛魚最後的比分是99比101。

黃祥安：　哈哈！小美，沒想到飛魚比山貓厲害吧！

王小美：　這場比賽一點兒也不公平！有幾次飛魚犯規了，可是裁判都沒有吹哨！

黃祥安：　山貓隊不過輸了兩分而已。與其說裁判不公平，倒不如說山貓的運氣不好！

陳大東：　依我看，打籃球重視的就是團隊精神。這次飛魚隊配合得比山貓隊好。不過賽季才剛開始，誰是最後的冠軍還說不定呢！

第二課　採訪

校刊第81期：

中西音樂完美結合

　　上周，我校樂隊獲得了大學生才藝比賽的第一名。記者採訪了樂隊的隊長孫瑪麗，她是來自美國的留學生。

記者：　　恭喜你們贏得冠軍。你們的表演能受到評委和觀眾的喜愛，你認爲你們成功的原因是甚麼？

孫瑪麗：　我想是因爲我們用小提琴和古箏一起演奏，這種中西結合的音樂讓觀眾們覺得很特別。

記者：　　你們是怎麼想到這樣的表演形式呢？

孫瑪麗：　在美國的時候，我的好朋友小美帶我去聽過一場中國民樂演奏，裏面的古箏演奏令我十分難忘。來中國以後，我交了幾個玩民樂的朋友，所以就想試試一起演奏。

記者：　　你們樂隊以後有甚麼計劃嗎？

孫瑪麗：　希望我們能有機會去更多的地方表演，讓更多人欣賞這種中西結合的音樂。

記者：　　你現在最想感謝誰呢？

孫瑪麗：　我要感謝我的音樂伙伴們，是他們幫我實現了演奏中西音樂的理想。我也要謝謝我的好朋友小美，感謝她一直在音樂上支持我，希望我們以後能一起表演！

第一課　　學做中國菜

親愛的小美：

　　恭喜你們申請到了獎學金！你想好下周的中國美食比賽做甚麼菜了嗎？你可以試試做宮保雞丁。我一直以為這道菜會很難做，上星期和周信一起做了宮保雞丁之後，才知道其實做法很簡單。這是我們的食譜：

　　材料：雞肉400克，葱15克，辣椒20克，花生米50克，油500克，鹽1小匙，糖1小匙，澱粉25克，料酒1大匙，醬油1/2大匙

　　第一，把雞肉、葱和辣椒切丁。
　　第二，雞丁裏放入鹽、料酒和澱粉後拌勻。
　　第三，把雞丁和油放進鍋裏；雞丁炒熟後盛出來。
　　第四，先將葱和辣椒丁大火炒一會兒，然後放入炒好的雞丁和醬油、糖、鹽；最後加入花生米炒一會兒，這道家常菜就做好了！無論在哪裏，宮保雞丁都十分受歡迎。

　　對了，你看到安娜發給我們的郵件了嗎？她說明年春天會跟俄羅斯舞蹈團來北京表演，我已經收到了她寄來的票。安娜打算表演結束之後留在北京和我們一起念書，實在是太好了！很高興你們下學期都能來中國留學，我很想念大家！

瑪麗

第二課　逛超市

　　大東和朋友們打算在中國美食比賽做一些有特色的菜，於是他們一起去超市買菜。正好超市有很多食物和烹飪材料在減價，買一送一，還有免費試吃。

王小美：　大東，做宮保鷄丁的材料都買好了嗎？

陳大東：　我買了辣椒、葱和蒜，還差鷄肉。我看了一下鷄肉，覺得不夠新鮮，有的還快過期了。我們去另一家超市看看吧。

李中平：　這裏的麻婆豆腐可以試吃，看得我口水都要流出來了！

黃祥安：　哇！嘗起來幾乎跟小美媽媽做的一樣，又香又辣，讓人很有胃口！

李中平：　果然是好吃得不得了！我們難得能在超市吃到這麼地道和美味的中國菜。祥安，你要做甚麼拿手菜帶去美食比賽？

黃祥安：　我不太會做菜，所以還沒有想好要不要參加……

李中平：　你不是學過做菜嗎？

黃祥安：　是啊，可是怎麼也做不好，爲了大家的肚子着想，我還是不參加了。

李中平：　哈哈，原來是這樣！我會做家常豆腐，我們一起做吧，我教你。

第七單元

第一課　交通意外

周信：　　瑪麗你撞得不輕啊！要叫救護車嗎？

孫瑪麗：　我還好，等一會兒去診所檢查一下就行。

交警：　　你們可以告訴我事故是怎麼發生的嗎？

周信：　　我們過馬路的時候，這輛三輪車突然撞了過來。

交警：　　師傅，請讓我看看你的身份證。

師傅：　　哎呀，我的身份證呢？我這個人常常丟三落四的，又忘帶身份證了……再說這件事不能完全怪我，是他們闖了紅燈。

周信：　　不對，我們並沒有闖紅燈！

交警：　　師傅，這條路禁止電動三輪車通行，你又沒帶駕照，因此我要給你開一張罰單。

師傅：　　哎，今天真倒霉！我以後再也不這麼着急了。對不起，我會負責你的醫療費。

周信：　　瑪麗，我現在就帶你去診所看看。

孫瑪麗：　不好意思，麻煩你了！

陳大東：　不知道瑪麗現在怎麼樣，沒想到她會遇到意外！

王小美：　瑪麗說她的傷快好了，我的表哥在照顧她。

李中平：　啊？周信能把瑪麗照顧好嗎？

黃祥安：　你不用太擔心瑪麗，她很快就能康復了。

陳大東：　我們去北京也要注意安全。我在網上看到了一個關於北京自然災害的報告，你們都來看看。

北京自然災害報告

在北京，最常見的自然災害是沙塵暴和暴雨，也有可能發生地震。沙塵暴多出現在春天。沙塵天氣需要外出時，要戴上口罩和眼鏡。暴雨多出現在夏天。發生暴雨時要減少外出，必須外出時不要走積水嚴重的地方。暴雨天氣時遇到雷電，不要在室外用手機，在家裏最好把電器關掉。地震的時候要遠離大型的物品，找安全的地方蹲下。此外，要多關注自然災害的預報，以減少意外發生。

圖片一：北京沙塵暴以後，去急診室的人多了很多。

圖片二：北京出現暴雨天氣，多個航班延誤。這是今年以來最大的一場暴雨。

圖片三：地震導致多起車禍，幸運的是沒有人嚴重受傷。

第八單元

第一課　在機場

　　中平和他的朋友們將去中國留學。他們都申請到了獎學金，辦簽證和訂機票也都很順利，可是在出發的那一天，卻遇到了一些麻煩。

工作人員：　　先生，您的行李超重了。

李中平：　　　只超重兩磅也不行嗎？

工作人員：　　對不起，這是航空公司的規定。除非您付超重費，要不然我們不能托運這些行李。

陳大東：　　　中平，你放一些東西到我的箱子裏吧。你給瑪麗帶的禮物太多了吧！

工作人員：　　先生，這是您的登機牌，座位靠窗戶。

黃祥安：　　　不好意思，座位可以換成靠走道的嗎？

工作人員：　　對不起，我們只剩中間和靠窗的座位了。

王小美：　　　祥安，我跟你只座位吧，我的座位靠走道。我有一點兒頭疼，想坐窗邊。

陳大東：　　　糟糕，要登機了，祥安在哪兒？

王小美：　　　大東，我們去找他吧！

孫瑪麗：　　　好，等我到了北京以後，再麻煩你了！

陳大東：　　　祥安你跑到哪裏去了？給你打電話你也不接。快走吧，要不然就趕不上飛機了！

黃祥安：　　　不好意思，我看錯了登機時間。小美，這是給你的藥，希望你的頭疼能好一些。

王小美：　　　原來你剛才是去給我買藥啊！謝謝你！

李中平的日記

　　我們的中國遊今天上路了！旅遊路綫是從北京坐火車到上海，然後去蘇州。今天我去買票的時候太緊張，把票買錯了。之後周信換了票，但我覺得其實他不是爲了幫我，而是爲了得到大家的好感……雖然瑪麗説我做得還不錯，能自己去買票，但實際上我的中文不够好，還需要多練習。

黃祥安的博客

洋熊貓遊中國：美食在上海

　　來上海玩的遊客非常多，人山人海。我們趁這次旅遊的機會，嘗了各種好吃的特色小吃，難怪上海的飲食文化這麼有名！看看我們都吃了些甚麼：

　　小籠包：小籠包真是好吃得不得了！不過我吃的時候太着急，嘴被燙了一下。人們常説"心急吃不了熱豆腐"，其實應該是"心急吃不了小籠包"……

陳大東的遊記

　　我們在蘇州報名參加了旅遊團。導遊帶我們遊園林，還介紹了蘇州的歷史。這趟旅遊給我最大的感受是"百聞不如一見"，只有親自到中國來，才能更深地體會中國的文化和風俗。到中國以後，小美開朗了很多。從機場那一天起，小美就跟祥安變成了好朋友。不知道這次留學會給大家帶來甚麼樣的改變……

Vocabulary Index (Chinese-English)

The Chinese-English index is alphabetized according to pinyin. Required Vocabulary is shown in purple.

Characters	Pinyin	Word Category	Definition	Lesson
A				
爱好	àihào	n	hobby, interest	2.2
B				
巴黎	Bālí	n	Paris	1.1
巴西	Bāxī	n	Brazil	2.2
白天	báitiān	n	daytime	1.2
百货公司	bǎihuò gōngsī	n	department store	4.2
百闻不如一见	bǎiwén bùrú yíjiàn	ie	seeing is believing	8.2
搬	bān	v	to move	3.2
班	bān	n, mw	class, shift; (used for a trip by bus, plane, etc.)	7.2
搬家	bānjiā	vo	to move house	3.2
拌	bàn	v	to mix	6.1
办	bàn	v	to handle	8.1
办法	bànfǎ	n	method; means	2.1
办签证	bàn qiānzhèng	vo	to obtain a visa, to apply for a visa	8.1
拌匀	bànyún	v	to mix evenly	6.1
磅	bàng	mw	pound	8.1
包	bāo	v	to include, to contain	3.1
包括	bāokuò	v	to include	3.2
包装	bāozhuāng	n	packaging	4.2
保护	bǎohù	n, v	protection; to protect	2.2
保修期	bǎoxiū qī	n	guarantee period, warranty period	4.1
保证	bǎozhèng	n, v	guarantee, warranty; to guarantee, to warrant	4.2
报告	bàogào	n, v	report; to report	2.1
报名	bàomíng	v	to sign up	8.2
抱歉	bàoqiàn	v	to be sorry, to be apologetic	4.2
暴雨	bàoyǔ	n	rainstorm	7.2
报纸	bàozhǐ	n	newspaper	3.2

Characters	Pinyin	Word Category	Definition	Lesson
比	bǐ	n	ratio	5.1
比分	bǐfēn	n	score	5.1
必需	bìxū	adj	necessary; indispensable	2.1
必须	bìxū	av	must	3.2
遍	biàn	adv, mw	all over; (used for repetitive times and occurrences)	1.1
变成	biànchéng	rv	to become, to turn into	2.1
冰	bīng	n, v	ice; to be freezing	3.2
冰箱	bīngxiāng	n	refrigerator	3.2
并	bìng	adv	actually; truly (intensifier before a negative)	7.1
并且	bìngqiě	cj	and, besides, moreover	4.1
博客	bókè	n	blog	4.1
不过	búguò	cj	but; however	2.1
不过……而已	búguò……éryǐ	cj	only, merely, nothing more than	5.1
不见得	bújiàndé	adv	not necessarily	2.1
部分	bùfen	n	part	4.2
不管……都	bùguǎn……dōu	prep	no matter . . . all, regardless of . . . all	4.2
不如	bùrú	v	to be inferior to, not as good as	4.1

C

Characters	Pinyin	Word Category	Definition	Lesson
材料	cáiliào	n	material, ingredients	6.1
裁判	cáipàn	n	referee	5.1
才艺	cáiyì	n	talent and skill	5.2
采访	cǎifǎng	v	to cover, to interview	5.2
查	chá	v	to check; to investigate	2.1
差	chà	v	to be short of, to be missing	6.2
产品	chǎnpǐn	n	product	4.1
尝	cháng	v	to taste	6.2
场	cháng	mw	(used for non-recreational events)	7.2
常见	chángjiàn	adj	frequently encountered; commonly seen	7.2
场	chǎng	mw, n	(used for recreational or sports activities); field	5.1
超	chāo	v	to exceed	8.1
超过	chāoguò	rv	to exceed	2.2
超市	chāoshì	n	supermarket	6.2
超重	chāozhòng	adj, n	overweight	8.1
潮湿	cháoshī	adj	humid; damp	1.2

Characters	Pinyin	Word Category	Definition	Lesson
炒	chǎo	v	to stir-fry, to sauté	6.1
炒熟	chǎo shú	v	to stir-fry until the food is cooked	6.1
车祸	chēhuò	n	traffic accident	7.1
趁	chèn	prep	take advantage of; to avail oneself of	8.2
乘	chéng	v	to travel by	7.1
盛	chéng	v	to scoop out, to fill	6.1
乘客	chéng kè	n	passenger	7.1
成绩	chéngjì	n	result; grades	2.1
成员	chéngyuán	n	member	2.2
吃掉	chīdiào	rv	to eat up	5.1
匙	chí	n	spoon	6.1
出发	chūfā	v	to depart, to set out	1.2
出示	chūshì	v	to show	4.2
出现	chūxiàn	v	to occur; to appear	7.2
出租	chūzū	v	to rent, to let	3.2
除非……要不然	chúfēi……yàoburán	cj	unless, only if . . . or else, otherwise	8.1
船	chuán	n	boat, ship	8.1
窗户	chuānghu	n	window	8.1
闯	chuǎng	v	to rush	7.1
吹	chuī	v	to blow	5.1
吹哨	chuīshào	vo	to blow a whistle	5.1
此外	cǐwài	cj	in addition	7.2
葱	cōng	n	green onion, scallion	6.1
从……起	cóng……qǐ	cj	ever since; from . . . on	8.2
粗心	cūxīn	adj	careless	3.1

D

Characters	Pinyin	Word Category	Definition	Lesson
打折	dǎzhé	v	to discount	4.1
大火	dàhuǒ	n	high heat	6.1
大型	dàxíng	adj	large-scale	7.2
大熊猫	dàxióngmāo	n	giant panda	4.1
当	dāng	cj	when	2.2
倒霉	dǎoméi	adj	be out of luck, unlucky	7.1
导游	dǎoyóu	n	tour guide	8.2
导致	dǎozhì	v	to result in; to lead to; to cause	7.2
道	dào	mw	(used for a course of food)	6.1

Characters	Pinyin	Word Category	Definition	Lesson
到期	dàoqī	vo	to become due; to expire	3.2
得	dé	v	to get	5.2
登	dēng	v	to board; to climb	8.1
登机牌	dēngjīpái	n	boarding pass	8.1
低	dī	adj	low	1.2
地道	dìdao	adj	real, authentic	2.1
地点	dìdiǎn	n	place, site, locale	3.1
地球	dìqiú	n	earth	2.2
地铁	dìtiě	n	subway	8.1
地震	dìzhèn	n	earthquake	7.2
电	diàn	n	electricity	3.1
淀粉	diànfěn	n	starch	6.1
电暖器	diànnuǎnqì	n	heater	4.2
电器	diànqì	n	electrical appliance	3.2
丁	dīng	v	to dice (in cooking)	6.1
订	dìng	v	to book	8.1
丢	diū	v	to lose	7.1
丢三落四	diūsān làsì	ie	forgetful, always forgetful	7.1
冬季	dōngjì	n	winter	1.1
冬暖夏凉	dōngnuǎn xiàliáng	ie	warm in the winters and cool in the summers	1.2
度	dù	n, mw	degree; (used as a unit of measurement of temperature)	1.1
段	duàn	mw	a section; a part	2.1
队	duì	n	team	5.1
对	duì	v	versus	5.1
对了	duìle	interj	by the way; that's right	1.1
队长	duìzhǎng	n	captain	5.1
蹲下	dūnxia	rv	to crouch	7.2

F

发现	fāxiàn	v	to find, to discover	3.2
发展	fāzhǎn	v, n	to develop; development	2.2
罚单	fádān	n	violation ticket	7.1
烦恼	fánnǎo	adj, n	worried; worry, trouble	2.2
犯规	fànguī	vo	to foul, to break the rules	5.1

Characters	Pinyin	Word Category	Definition	Lesson
房东	fángdōng	n	landlord	3.2
房租	fángzū	n	rent	3.1
放弃	fàngqì	v	to give up, to let go	5.2
飞鱼	Fēiyú	n	Flying Fish	5.1
费	fèi	n	bill, cost, fee	3.1
费用	fèiyong	n	cost, expenses, charges	3.1
分享	fēnxiǎng	v	to share	4.1
风	fēng	n	wind	1.2
风景	fēngjǐng	n	scenery	1.2
风俗	fēngsú	n	custom	8.2
辅修	fǔxiū	v, n	to minor in; minor	2.1
附近	fùjìn	adv	nearby	3.2
付款	fù kuǎn	vo	to pay money	4.2
负责	fùzé	v, adj	to be in charge of; conscientious	2.2

G

Characters	Pinyin	Word Category	Definition	Lesson
改变	gǎibiàn	n, v	change; to change	8.2
改天	gǎitiān	n	another day, some other day	1.2
干燥	gānzào	adj	dry, arid	1.2
赶上	gǎnshang	rv	to catch up with; to be in time for, to be able to make something	8.1
感受	gǎnshòu	n, v	impression; to feel	8.2
感谢	gǎnxiè	v	to thank, to be grateful	5.2
刚才	gāngcái	n	just now; a moment ago	8.1
高	gāo	adj	high	1.2
各	gè	adj	each, every	1.1
个子	gèzi	n	height	2.2
宫保鸡丁	Gōngbǎojīdīng	n	Kung Pao Chicken (spicy fried diced chicken)	6.1
公斤	gōngjīn	mw	kilogram	8.1
公平	gōngpíng	adj	fair	5.1
够	gòu	adv	enough	6.2
购物	gòuwù	n, vo	shopping; to go shopping	4.1
古筝	gǔzhēng	n	stringed plucked instrument similar to the zither	5.2
顾客	gùkè	n	customer	4.2

Characters	Pinyin	Word Category	Definition	Lesson
刮	guā	v	to blow	1.2
刮风	guāfēng	v	to be windy	1.2
怪	guài	v	to blame	7.1
关于	guānyú	prep	regarding; about	7.2
观众	guānzhòng	n	audience	5.2
关注	guānzhù	v	to pay more or close attention to	7.2
冠军	guànjūn	n	champion	5.1
广告	guǎnggào	n	advertisement	3.2
规定	guīdìng	n	rule	8.1
锅	guō	n	wok	6.1
果然	guǒrán	adv	indeed; as expected; sure enough	6.2
过期	guòqī	vo	to expire	6.2

H

Characters	Pinyin	Word Category	Definition	Lesson
海鲜	hǎixiān	n	seafood	6.2
航班	hángbān	n	scheduled flight	7.2
航空	hángkōng	v	aviation	8.1
航空公司	hángkōng gōngsī	n	airline, airline company	8.1
好处	hǎochu	n	advantage, benefit	3.1
好感	hǎogǎn	n	favorable impression	8.2
好久不见	hǎojiǔ bújiàn	ie	long time no see	1.2
合同	hétong	n	contract	3.1
合租	hézū	v	to rent together	3.1
花生米	huāshēngmǐ	n	shelled peanut	6.1
华氏	huáshì	n	Fahrenheit (°F), °F = °C x 1.8 + 32	1.1
划算	huásuàn	adj	to be worth the price	4.1
坏	huài	adj	broken	4.2
坏处	huàichu	n	disadvantage	3.1
换	huàn	v	to exchange	4.2
火	huǒ	n	fire	6.1
伙伴	huǒbàn	n	partner, companion	5.2
货	huò	n	goods	4.1
获得	huòdé	v	to gain, to achieve	5.2

n

Characters	Pinyin	Word Category	Definition	Lesson
J				
几乎	jīhū	adv	almost, nearly	6.2
鸡肉	jīròu	n	chicken meat	6.1
积水	jīshuǐ	n, v	flood, accumulated water; to flood	7.2
急	jí	adj	anxious, worry	3.2
急诊室	jízhěnshì	n	emergency room	7.2
季	jì	n	season	1.2
季节	jìjié	n	season	1.1
继续	jìxù	v	to continue	1.1
既…又…	jì…yòu…	prep	both . . .and . . .	4.1
记者	jìzhě	n	journalist, reporter	5.2
家常	jiācháng	adj	family routine	6.1
家常菜	jiāchángcài	n	home cooking	6.1
家具	jiājù	n	furniture	3.2
加入	jiārù	v	to join; to add	2.2
家庭	jiātíng	n	family; household	3.2
家务	jiāwù	n	household chores, housefold duties	3.1
家用电器	jiāyòng diànqì	n	household electrical appliance	3.2
价格	jiàgé	n	price	4.1
驾驶	jiàshǐ	v	to drive	7.1
驾驶执照	jiàshǐ zhízhào	n	driver's license	7.1
检查	jiǎnchá	v, n	to examine, to check; examination	7.1
减价	jiǎnjià	vo	to reduce the price, to be discounted	6.2
减少	jiǎnshǎo	v	to reduce	7.2
将	jiāng	prep	(used to introduce the object before a verb)	6.1
将	jiāng	adv	will, about to	8.1
奖学金	jiǎngxuéjīn	n	scholarship	2.1
酱油	jiàngyóu	n	soy sauce	6.1
交通	jiāotōng	n	traffic	3.1
教练	jiàoliàn	n	coach	5.1
叫上	jiàoshang	v	to ask someone to go with	1.2
结合	jiéhé	n	combination, fusion	5.2
结束	jiéshù	v	to end, to finish	1.2
禁止	jìnzhǐ	v	to prohibit, to forbid	7.1
精神	jīngshén	n	spirit	5.1

Characters	Pinyin	Word Category	Definition	Lesson
警察	jǐngchá	n	policeman	7.1
久	jiǔ	adj	long time	1.2
旧	jiù	adj	old	3.2
救护车	jiùhùchē	n	ambulance	7.1
举办	jǔbàn	v	to hold	2.2
决定	juédìng	v, n	to decide; decision	2.2

K

Characters	Pinyin	Word Category	Definition	Lesson
开朗	kāilǎng	adj	optimistic	2.2
康复	kāngfù	v, n	to recover; to restore to health	7.2
靠	kào	adj, v	near; to depend	8.1
靠窗户	kào chuānghu	vo	by the window	8.1
可惜	kěxī	adj, adv	unfortunate; unfortunately	3.2
克	kè	n	gram	6.1
空	kōng, kòng	v, adj, n	to leave . . .empty; empty; spare time	3.2
空调	kōngtiáo	n	air-conditioner	3.2
恐怕	kǒngpà	v	to be afraid, to fear	3.1
口水	kǒushuǐ	n	saliva, drool, dribble	6.2
口罩	kǒuzhào	n	surgical mask	7.2
款	kuǎn	n	style, type	4.1
昆明	Kūnmíng	n	Kunming (city)	1.2

L

Characters	Pinyin	Word Category	Definition	Lesson
落	là	v	to be missing, to leave behind, to forget to bring	7.1
辣椒	làjiāo	n	hot pepper	6.1
来自	láizì	v	come from	5.2
篮球	lánqiú	n	basketball	5.1
篮球明星	lánqiú míngxīng	n	basketball star	5.1
雷电	léidiàn	n	thunder and lighting	7.2
类	lèi	n	kind	6.2
理想	lǐxiǎng	adj, n	ideal	3.1
力	lì	n	strength, power	3.1
厉害	lìhai	adj	fierce	5.1
凉快	liángkuai	adj	pleasantly cool	1.1
量	liàng	n	quantity	6.1

Characters	Pinyin	Word Category	Definition	Lesson
辆	liàng	mw	(used for vehicles)	7.1
料酒	liàojiǔ	n	cooking wine	6.1
零下	língxià	n	below zero	1.1
令	lìng	v	to make, to cause	5.2
另外	lìngwài	adv, adj	in addition; other	5.1
留	liú	v	to stay in a place, to remain	1.1
留学	liúxué	v	to study abroad	2.1
路线	lùxiàn	n	route, itinerary	8.2
驴友	lǚyǒu	n	traveling mates	1.2
旅馆	lǚguǎn	n	inn, hotel	8.2
旅游	lǚyóu	v, n	to tour; tourism	1.1
乱	luàn	adj	disorderly, messy	3.1
伦敦	Lúndūn	n	London	1.1

M

Characters	Pinyin	Word Category	Definition	Lesson
麻婆豆腐	Mápódòufu	n	Mapo Tofu	6.2
马路	mǎlù	n	road	3.2
满	mǎn	adj, adv	full; entirely	3.2
满意	mǎnyì	adj	satisfied	3.2
毛巾	máojīn	n	towel	4.2
美食	měishì	n	delicious food	4.1
美味	měiwèi	adj, n	flavorful, delicious; delicacy	6.2
闷热	mēnrè	adj	humid, muggy	1.2
门票	ménpiào	n	entrance ticket, admission ticket	8.2
梦	mèng	n, v	dream; to dream	5.2
梦想	mèngxiǎng	n	dream	5.2
迷	mí	v	to become enchanted with	1.1
迷上	míshàng	rv	to be fascinated by	1.1
米	mǐ	n	meter	2.2
免费	miǎnfèi	vo	free of charge, free, gratis	4.1
面试	miànshì	n, v	audition, interview; to have an interview or audition	1.1
民乐	mínyuè	n	folk instrumental music	5.2
名	míng	mw	(used for people or ranking)	2.2
名牌	míngpái	n	famous brand	4.1
明信片	míngxìnpiàn	n	postcard	1.1

Characters	Pinyin	Word Category	Definition	Lesson
明星	míngxīng	n	star	5.1
目的	mùdì	n	aim; destination	8.1
目的地	mùdìdì	n	destination	8.1

N

Characters	Pinyin	Word Category	Definition	Lesson
拿手	náshǒu	adj	to be good at	6.2
拿手菜	náshǒucài	ie	specialty dish, a chef's best dish	6.2
难得	nándé	adj	rare; hard to come by	6.2
难忘	nánwàng	adj	unforgettable, memorable	5.2
内外	nèiwài	n	inside and outside	3.1
牛肉	niúròu	n	beef	6.2
暖和	nuǎnhuo	adj	warm	1.1

P

Characters	Pinyin	Word Category	Definition	Lesson
爬	pá	v	to climb	1.2
爬山	páshān	vo	to hike; to climb a mountain	1.2
牌	pái	n	card	8.1
牌子	páizi	n	brand	4.2
配合	pèihé	v	to coordinate, to cooperate	5.1
烹饪	pēngrèn	n	cooking	6.2
碰	pèng	v	to bump into; to hit	2.2
碰见	pèngjian	rv	to meet unexpectedly, to run into	2.2
评	píng	v	to discuss, to judge	5.2
平均	píngjūn	adj, adv	average; on the average	1.1
平时	píngshí	adv	in ordinary, normal times	3.1
评委	píngwěi	n	judge, jury	5.2

Q

Characters	Pinyin	Word Category	Definition	Lesson
期	qī	n,mw	period of time; (used for an issue or term)	3.2
其实	qíshí	adv	as a matter of fact, actually	4.2
起	qǐ	mw	a case or a batch	7.2
起飞	qǐfēi	v	to take off	8.1
气候	qìhòu	n	climate	1.2
气温	qìwēn	n	temperature	1.1
签	qiān	v	to sign	3.1
签合同	qiān hétong	vo	to sign a contract	3.1

Characters	Pinyin	Word Category	Definition	Lesson
强	qiáng	adj	powerful	5.1
切	qiē	v	to cut	6.1
切丁	qiēdīng	v	to dice	6.1
亲爱的	qīn'àide	adj, n	dear; darling	1.1
亲自	qīnzì	adv	firsthand, personally	8.2
轻	qīng	adj	(injury/illness) not serious; light	7.1
清楚	qīngchu	adj	clear	4.2
晴天	qíngtiān	n	sunny day	1.2
球员	qiúyuán	n	ball-team member	5.1
券	quàn	n	ticket	4.1
却	què	cj	however, but	8.1
确实	quèshí	adv	really, definitely, indeed	3.1

R

Characters	Pinyin	Word Category	Definition	Lesson
人山人海	rénshān rénhǎi	ie	a sea of people, huge crowds of people	8.2
人员	rényuán	n	personnel, staff	8.1
认为	rènwéi	v	to think/believe that	4.2
日记	rìjì	n	diary	2.2
日用品	rìyòngpǐn	n	daily necessities	4.2
如	rú	adj	to be like	1.2
入	rù	v	to join; to enter	2.2

S

Characters	Pinyin	Word Category	Definition	Lesson
赛季	sàijì	n	sports competition season	5.1
三轮车	sānlúnchē	n	pedicab	7.1
沙尘暴	shāchénbào	n	sandstorm	7.2
山	shān	n	hill; mountain	1.2
山猫	Shānmāo	n	Mountain Lion	5.1
伤	shāng	n	wound	7.1
商场	shāngchǎng	n	market	4.2
商品	shāngpǐn	n	merchandise, goods, commodity	4.2
上海	Shànghǎi	n	Shanghai	8.2
上路	shànglù	vo	to set out on a journey	8.2
上升	shàngshēng	v	to rise, to go up	1.2
少许	shǎoxǔ	adj	a little	6.1
哨	shào	n	whistle	5.1

Characters	Pinyin	Word Category	Definition	Lesson
社	shè	n	organization; agency	2.2
摄氏	shèshì	n	Celsius (°C), °C = (°F - 32) / 1.8	1.1
摄影	shèyǐng	vo, n	to take a photograph; photography	4.1
深	shēn	adj	deep; profound	8.2
身份证	shēnfènzhèng	n	identity card	7.1
申请	shēnqǐng	v	to apply	2.1
省	shěng	v	to save	3.1
省心省力	shěngxīn shěnglì	vo	to avoid worry and save effort	3.1
剩	shèng	v, adj	to be left; surplus	3.1
师傅	shīfu	n	sir (respectful formal address for a male elder)	7.1
十分	shífēn	adv	very, fully, utterly	5.2
实际上	shíjìshang	adv	in reality; as a matter of fact	8.2
实力	shílì	n	strength	5.1
食谱	shípǔ	n	recipe, cookbook	6.1
实现	shíxiàn	v	to realize, to achieve	5.2
实在	shízai	adv	so; really; honestly	6.1
试吃	shìchī	v	to sample	6.2
事故	shìgù	n	accident	7.1
适量	shìliàng	adj	appropriate amount	6.1
收据	shōujù	n	receipt	4.2
受	shòu	v	to receive; to bear	2.2
售	shòu	v	to sell	4.2
受欢迎	shòu huānyíng	adj	be popular	2.2
受伤	shòushāng	vo	to be wounded, to be injured	7.1
输	shū	v	to lose	5.1
书本	shūběn	n	books	2.1
蔬菜	shūcài	n	vegetables	6.2
熟	shú	adj	cooked	6.1
数码	shùmǎ	n, adj	numeral; digital	4.1
数码相机	shùmǎ xiàngjī	n	digital camera	4.1
水电费	shuǐdiànfèi	n	water and electricity bills	3.1
税	shuì	n	tax	4.1
顺便	shùnbiàn	adv	conveniently; in passing	2.1
顺利	shùnlì	adj	smooth, without a hitch	8.1
说不定	shuōbudìng	adv	maybe, perhaps	1.1

Characters	Pinyin	Word Category	Definition	Lesson
司机	sījī	n	driver	7.1
四季如春	sìjì rúchūn	ie	like spring all year-round	1.2
送货	sònghuò	vo	to deliver goods	4.1
苏州	Sūzhōu	n	Suzhou	8.2
蒜	suàn	n	garlic	6.2
损坏	sǔnhuài	n, v	damage; to damage	4.2
所有	suǒyǒu	adj	all	4.2

T

Characters	Pinyin	Word Category	Definition	Lesson
台	tái	mw	(used for appliances, instruments, etc.)	4.2
糖	táng	n	sugar	6.1
烫	tàng	v, adj	to burn, to scald; very hot	8.2
趟	tàng	mw	(used to indicate a trip or trips made)	2.1
讨论	tǎolùn	v, n	to discuss; discussion	2.1
套	tào	mw	(used to indicate a series or sets of things)	3.1
特色	tèsè	n	distinguishing feature or quality	6.2
提醒	tíxǐng	v	to remind, to warn	4.1
体会	tǐhuì	v	to acquire; to learn from experience	8.2
天气预报	tiānqì yùbào	n	weather forecast	1.2
填表格	tián biǎogé	vo	to fill out the form	2.1
条件	tiáojiàn	n	policy, conditions	4.2
调味料	tiáowèiliào	n	seasoning	6.2
听说	tīngshuō	v	to be told; to hear of	1.2
挺	tǐng	adv	very, rather, quite	2.1
通	tōng	n	expert	2.1
通行	tōngxíng	v	to go through	7.1
通知	tōngzhī	n	notification	3.2
投诉	tóusù	n	complaint	4.1
突然	tūrán	adv	suddenly	7.1
图片	túpiàn	n	image, picture	7.2
团队	tuánduì	n	team, group	5.1
团	tuán	n	troupe, group	1.1
团队精神	tuánduì jīngshén	n	team spirit	5.1
退	tuì	v	to return	4.2
退货	tuìhuò	vo	to return merchandise/goods	4.2
托运	tuōyùn	v	to consign or check for shipment	8.1

Characters	Pinyin	Word Category	Definition	Lesson
W				
外出	wàichū	v	to go out	7.2
完美	wánměi	adj	perfect	5.2
完全	wánquán	adv, adj	totally, completely; complete	7.1
网站	wǎngzhàn	n	website	4.1
危险	wēixiǎn	adj	dangerous	7.1
胃口	wèikǒu	n	appetite	6.2
为了	wèile	prep	for the purpose of; for the sake of	2.1
温度	wēndù	n	temperature	1.2
无论……都	wúlùn……dōu	cj	no matter what . . . all; regardless of . . . all	6.1
舞蹈	wǔdǎo	n	dance	1.1
舞蹈团	wǔdǎotuán	n	dance troupe	1.1
物品	wùpǐn	n	goods	7.2
X				
洗	xǐ	v	to wash	3.2
喜爱	xǐ'ài	n	like, love	5.2
洗衣机	xǐyījī	n	washing machine	3.2
细心	xìxīn	adj	careful, attentive	3.1
下降到	xiàjiàngdào	v	to drop to; to fall to	1.2
箱	xiāng	n	box, chest	3.2
香	xiāng	adj	savory, appetizing	6.2
相处	xiāngchǔ	v	to get along with	3.1
相机	xiàngjī	n	camera	4.1
项目	xiàngmù	n	project; item	2.2
消息	xiāoxi	n	news	2.1
小吃	xiǎochī	n	dish; snack; refreshments	8.2
小笼包	Xiǎolóngbāo	n	small steamed meat-filled buns with soup	8.2
小说	xiǎoshuō	n	novel, fiction	2.1
校刊	xiàokān	n	school magazine	5.2
心急	xīnjí	adj	impatient, short-tempered	8.2
欣赏	xīnshǎng	v	to appreciate, to admire	5.2
新鲜	xīnxiān	adj	fresh	6.2
行程	xíngchéng	n	itinerary	8.2
行李	xíngli	n	luggage	8.1

Characters	Pinyin	Word Category	Definition	Lesson
形式	xíngshì	n	form, shape, format	5.2
性格	xìnggé	n	character	2.2
幸运	xìngyùn	adj, n	lucky; good luck	3.2
修	xiū	v	to repair	4.1
须知	xūzhī	n	notice	4.2
选修	xuǎnxiū	v	to take as an elective course	2.1
学分	xuéfēn	n	course credit	2.1

Y

Characters	Pinyin	Word Category	Definition	Lesson
牙膏	yágāo	n	toothpaste	4.2
盐	yán	n	salt	6.1
延误	yánwù	v	to delay	7.2
演奏	yǎnzòu	n, v	musical performance; to give musical performance	5.2
洋	yáng	adj	foreign	4.1
样子	yàngzi	n	appearance	4.1
邀请	yāoqǐng	v, n	to invite; invitation	2.2
依	yī	prep	according to	5.1
医疗	yīliáo	n	medical treatment	7.1
一见如故	yíjiàn rúgù	ie	friends at first sight	2.2
一向	yíxiàng	adv	consistently, up to now	4.1
以	yǐ	prep	in order to	7.2
以来	yǐlái	prep	since	7.2
以为	yǐwéi	v	to think, to believe (mistakenly)	6.1
一般	yìbān	adv	generally; ordinary	1.1
意外	yìwài	n, adj	accident; unexpected	7.1
因此	yīncǐ	conj	therefore; consequently	7.1
隐私	yǐnsī	n	privacy	3.1
饮食	yǐnshí	n	cuisine	4.1
饮食文化	yǐnshí wénhuà	n	cuisine culture	4.1
赢	yíng	v	to win	5.1
优惠	yōuhuì	adj	preferential, favorable	4.1
优惠券	yōuhuìquàn	n	coupon	4.1
游	yóu	v	to travel	1.1
油	yóu	n	oil	6.1
游记	yóujì	n	travel journal	8.2

Characters	Pinyin	Word Category	Definition	Lesson
游客	yóukè	n	tourist	8.2
由于	yóuyú	cj	can't be used	2.2
用不了	yòngbuliǎo	v	because, due to	4.2
于是	yúshì	cj	so; hence; as a result	6.2
与	yǔ	cj	and	2.2
与其……倒不如	yǔqí……dàobùrú	cj	rather than . . . it would be better to	5.1
雨伞	yǔsǎn	n	umbrella	1.1
雨衣	yǔyī	n	raincoat	1.2
预报	yùbào	n	forecast; to forecast	1.2
遇到	yùdao	rv	to come across; to encounter	7.2
原价	yuánjià	n	original price	4.1
原来	yuánlái	adv, adj	all along, turns out; original	1.2
园林	yuánlín	n	garden	8.2
原因	yuányīn	n	reason	5.2
远离	yuǎnlí	v	to be away from	7.2
乐队	yuèduì	n	band	5.2
匀	yún	adj	even	6.1
云南	Yúnnán	n	Yunnan (province)	1.2
运气	yùnqi	n	fortune, luck	5.1

Z

Characters	Pinyin	Word Category	Definition	Lesson
灾害	zāihài	n	disaster	7.2
在内	zàinèi	prep	to be included, including	3.2
再说	zàishuō	cj	what's more, besides	3.1
脏	zāng	adj	dirty	3.2
增	zēng	v	to increase, to add	7.2
增加	zēngjiā	v	to increase	7.2
招募	zhāomù	v	to recruit	2.2
着急	zháojí	adj	hurried; worried; feel anxious	7.1
者	zhě	n	person (who does something), one who (is)...	2.2
诊所	zhěnsuǒ	n	clinic	7.1
支持	zhīchí	v	to support	5.2
之后	zhīhòu	prep	after, later	3.2
之内	zhīnèi	prep	within	3.2
知识	zhīshi	n	knowledge	2.1

Characters	Pinyin	Word Category	Definition	Lesson
执照	zhízhào	n	license	7.1
质量	zhìliàng	n	quality	4.1
志愿	zhìyuàn	v, n	to volunteer; aspiration, wish	2.2
志愿者	zhìyuànzhě	n	volunteer	2.2
中国通	Zhōngguótōng	n	a China expert, an old China hand	2.1
中间	zhōngjiān	n	middle, center	8.1
种	zhǒng	mw	(used for style, kind, type, etc.)	5.2
种类	zhǒnglèi	n	type	6.2
重	zhòng	n, adj	weight; heavy	8.1
猪肉	zhūròu	n	pork	6.2
主修	zhǔxiū	v	to major in	2.1
主意	zhǔyi	n	idea	2.1
撞	zhuàng	v	to collide, to run into	7.1
着想	zhuóxiǎng	v	to consider	6.2
资料	zīliào	n	data, material, information	2.1
自然	zìrán	adj, n, adv	natural; nature; naturally	7.2
自然灾害	zìrán zāihài	n	natural disaster	7.2
走道	zǒudào	n	aisle	8.1
租	zū	v	to rent	3.1
最后	zuìhòu	adj, adv	final, last; finally, lastly	5.1
左右	zuǒyòu	adv	about, approximately	1.1
做法	zuòfǎ	n	method, way of doing/making something	6.1
座位	zuòwèi	n	seat	8.1

Vocabulary Index (English-Chinese)

The measure words index is arranged according to the lesson. The Chinese-English index is alphabetized according to English. Required Vocabulary is shown in purple.

Definition	Characters	Pinyin	Word Category	Lesson
Measure Words				
(used for repetitive times and occurrences)	遍	biàn	mw	1.1
(used as a unit of measurement of temperature)	度	dù	mw	1.1
(used to indicate a trip or trips made)	趟	tàng	mw	2.1
a section; a part	段	duàn	mw	2.1
(used for people or ranking)	名	míng	mw	2.2
(used to indicate a series or sets of things)	套	tào	mw	3.1
(used for an issue or term)	期	qī	mw	3.2
(used for appliances, instruments, etc.)	台	tái	mw	4.2
(used for recreational or sports activities)	场	chǎng	mw	5.1
(used for style, kind, type, etc.)	种	zhǒng	mw	5.1
(used for a course of food)	道	dào	mw	5.2
(used for vehicles)	辆	liàng	mw	6.1
(used for non-recreational events)	场	cháng	mw	7.1
a case or a batch	起	qǐ	mw	7.2
(used for a trip by bus, plane, etc.)	班	bān	mw	7.2
kilogram	公斤	gōngjīn	mw	7.2
pound	磅	bàng	mw	8.1
			mw	8.1

Definition	Characters	Pinyin	Word Category	Lesson
A				
an expert of China, an old China hand	中国通	Zhōngguótōng	n	2.1
a little	少许	shǎoxǔ	adj	6.1
a sea of people, huge crowds of people	人山人海	rénshān rénhǎi	ie	8.2
about, approximately	左右	zuǒyòu	adv	1.1
accident	事故	shìgù	n	7.1
accident; unexpected	意外	yìwài	n, adj	7.1
according to	依	yī	prep	5.1
to acquire; to learn from experience	体会	tǐhuì	v	8.2
actually; truly (intensifier before a negative)	并	bìng	adv	7.1
advantage, benefit	好处	hǎochu	n	3.1
advertisement	广告	guǎnggào	n	3.2
to be afraid, to fear	恐怕	kǒngpà	v	3.1
after, later	之后	zhīhòu	prep	3.2
aim; destination	目的	mùdì	n	8.1
air-conditioner	空调	kōngtiáo	n	3.2
airline, airline company	航空公司	hángkōng gōngsī	n	8.1
aisle	走道	zǒudào	n	8.1
all	所有	suǒyǒu	adj	4.2
all along, turns out; original	原来	yuánlái	adv, adj	1.2
all over	遍	biàn	adv	1.1
almost, nearly	几乎	jīhū	adv	6.2
ambulance	救护车	jiùhùchē	n	7.1
and	与	yǔ	cj	2.2
and, besides, moreover	并且	bìngqiě	cj	4.1
another day, some other day	改天	gǎitiān	n	1.2
anxious, worry	急	jí	adj	3.2
apartment	公寓	gōngyù	n	3.1
appearance	样子	yàngzi	n	4.1
appetite	胃口	wèikǒu	n	6.2
to apply	申请	shēnqǐng	v	2.1
to appreciate, to admire	欣赏	xīnshǎng	v	5.2
appropriate amount	适量	shìliàng	adj	6.1
as a matter of fact, actually	其实	qíshí	adv	4.2
to ask someone to go with	叫上	jiàoshang	v	1.2
audience	观众	guānzhòng	n	5.2

Definition	Characters	Pinyin	Word Category	Lesson
audition, interview; to have an interview or audition	面试	miànshì	n, v	1.1
average; on the average	平均	píngjūn	adj, adv	1.1
aviation	航空	hángkōng	v	8.1
to avoid worry and save effort	省心省力	shěngxīn shěnglì	vo	3.1
to be away from	远离	yuǎnlí	v	7.2

B

Definition	Characters	Pinyin	Word Category	Lesson
ball-team member	球员	qiúyuán	n	5.1
band	乐队	yuèduì	n	5.2
basketball	篮球	lánqiú	n	5.1
basketball star	篮球明星	lánqiú míngxīng	n	5.1
to be fascinated by	迷上	míshàng	rv	1.1
to be good at	拿手	náshǒu	adj	6.2
to be in charge of; conscientious	负责	fùzé	v, adj	2.2
be out of luck, unlucky	倒霉	dǎoméi	adj	7.1
be popular	受欢迎	shòu huānyíng	adj	2.2
to be told; to hear of	听说	tīngshuō	v	1.2
because, due to	由于	yóuyú	cj	2.2
to become due; to expire	到期	dàoqī	vo	3.2
to become enchanted with	迷	mí	v	1.1
to become, to turn into	变成	biànchéng	rv	2.1
beef	牛肉	niúròu	n	6.2
below zero	零下	língxià	n	1.1
bill, cost, fee	费	fèi	n	3.1
to blame	怪	guài	v	7.1
blog	博客	bókè	n	4.1
to blow	刮	guā	v	1.2
to blow	吹	chuī	v	5.1
to blow a whistle	吹哨	chuīshào	vo	5.1
to board; to climb	登	dēng	v	8.1
boarding pass	登机牌	dēngjīpái	n	8.1
boat, ship	船	chuán	n	8.1
to book	订	dìng	v	8.1
books	书本	shūběn	n	2.1
both . . . and . . .	既…又…	jì…yòu…	prep	4.1

Definition	Characters	Pinyin	Word Category	Lesson
box, chest	箱	xiāng	n	3.2
brand	牌子	páizi	n	4.2
Brazil	巴西	Bāxī	n	2.2
broken	坏	huài	adj	4.2
to bump into; to hit	碰	pèng	v	2.2
to burn, to scald; very hot	烫	tàng	v, adj	8.2
but; however	不过	búguò	cj	2.1
by the way; that's right	对了	duìle	interj	1.1
by the window	靠窗户	kào chuānghu	vo	8.1

C

camera	相机	xiàngjī	n	4.1
can't be used	用不了	yòngbuliǎo	v	4.2
captain	队长	duìzhǎng	n	5.1
card	牌	pái	n	8.1
careful, attentive	细心	xìxīn	adj	3.1
careless	粗心	cūxīn	adj	3.1
to catch up with; to be in time for, to be able to make something	赶上	gǎnshang	rv	8.1
Celsius (°C), °C = (°F - 32) / 1.8	摄氏	shèshì	n	1.1
champion	冠军	guànjūn	n	5.1
change; to change	改变	gǎibiàn	n, v	8.2
character	性格	xìnggé	n	2.2
to check; to investigate	查	chá	v	2.1
chicken meat	鸡肉	jīròu	n	6.1
class, shift	班	bān	n	7.2
clear	清楚	qīngchu	adj	4.2
climate	气候	qìhòu	n	1.2
to climb	爬	pá	v	1.2
clinic	诊所	zhénsuǒ	n	7.1
coach	教练	jiàoliàn	n	5.1
to collide, to run into	撞	zhuàng	v	7.1
combination, fusion	结合	jiéhé	n	5.2
to come across; to encounter	遇到	yùdao	rv	7.2
come from	来自	láizì	v	5.2
complaint	投诉	tóusù	n	4.1

Definition	Characters	Pinyin	Word Category	Lesson
to consider	着想	zhuóxiǎng	v	6.2
to consign or check for shipment	托运	tuōyùn	v	8.1
consistently, up to now	一向	yíxiàng	adv	4.1
to continue	继续	jìxù	v	1.1
contract	合同	hétong	n	3.1
conveniently; in passing	顺便	shùnbiàn	adv	2.1
cooked	熟	shú	adj	6.1
cooking	烹饪	pēngrèn	n	6.2
cooking wine	料酒	liàojiǔ	n	6.1
to coordinate, to cooperate	配合	pèihé	v	5.1
cost, expenses, charges	费用	fèiyong	n	3.1
coupon	优惠券	yōuhuìquàn	n	4.1
course credit	学分	xuéfēn	n	2.1
to cover, to interview	采访	cǎifǎng	v	5.2
to crouch	蹲下	dūnxia	rv	7.2
cuisine	饮食	yǐnshí	n	4.1
cuisine culture	饮食文化	yǐnshí wénhuà	n	4.1
custom	风俗	fēngsú	n	8.2
customer	顾客	gùkè	n	4.2
to cut	切	qiē	v	6.1

D

Definition	Characters	Pinyin	Word Category	Lesson
daily necessities	日用品	rìyòngpǐn	n	4.2
damage; to damage	损坏	sǔnhuài	n, v	4.2
dance	舞蹈	wǔdǎo	n	1.1
dance troupe	舞蹈团	wǔdǎotuán	n	1.1
dangerous	危险	wēixiǎn	adj	7.1
data, material, information	资料	zīliào	n	2.1
daytime	白天	báitiān	n	1.2
dear; darling	亲爱的	qīn'àide	adj, n	1.1
to decide; decision	决定	juédìng	v, n	2.2
deep; profound	深	shēn	adj	8.2
degree	度	dù	n	1.1
to delay	延误	yánwù	v	7.2
delicious food	美食	měishì	n	4.1
to deliver goods	送货	sònghuò	vo	4.1

Definition	Characters	Pinyin	Word Category	Lesson
to depart, to set out	出发	chūfā	v	1.2
department store	百货公司	bǎihuò gōngsī	n	4.2
destination	目的地	mùdìdì	n	8.1
to develop; development	发展	fāzhǎn	v, n	2.2
diary	日记	rìjì	n	2.2
to dice	切丁	qiēdīng	v	6.1
to dice (in cooking)	丁	dīng	v	6.1
digital camera	数码相机	shùmǎ xiàngjī	n	4.1
dirty	脏	zāng	adj	3.2
disadvantage	坏处	huàichu	n	3.1
disaster	灾害	zāihài	n	7.2
to discount	打折	dǎzhé	v	4.1
to discuss, to judge	评	píng	v	5.2
to discuss; discussion	讨论	tǎolùn	v, n	2.1
dish; snack; refreshments	小吃	xiǎochī	n	8.2
disorderly, messy	乱	luàn	adj	3.1
distinguishing feature or quality	特色	tèsè	n	6.2
dream	梦想	mèngxiǎng	n	5.2
dream; to dream	梦	mèng	n, v	5.2
to drive	驾驶	jiàshǐ	v	7.1
driver	司机	sījī	n	7.1
driver's license	驾驶执照	jiàshǐ zhízhào	n	7.1
to drop to; to fall to	下降到	xiàjiàngdào	v	1.2
dry, arid	干燥	gānzào	adj	1.2

E

Definition	Characters	Pinyin	Word Category	Lesson
each, every	各	gè	adj	1.1
earth	地球	dìqiú	n	2.2
earthquake	地震	dìzhèn	n	7.2
to eat up	吃掉	chīdiào	rv	5.1
electrical appliance	电器	diànqì	n	3.2
electricity	电	diàn	n	3.1
emergency room	急诊室	jízhěnshì	n	7.2
to end, to finish	结束	jiéshù	v	1.2
enough	够	gòu	adv	6.2
entrance ticket, admission ticket	门票	ménpiào	n	8.2

Definition	Characters	Pinyin	Word Category	Lesson
even	匀	yún	adj	6.1
ever since; from . . . on	从……起	cóng……qǐ	cj	8.2
to examine, to check; examination	检查	jiǎnchá	v, n	7.1
to exceed	超过	chāoguò	rv	2.2
to exceed	超	chāo	v	8.1
to exchange	换	huàn	v	4.2
expert	通	tōng	n	2.1
to expire	过期	guòqī	vo	6.2

F

Definition	Characters	Pinyin	Word Category	Lesson
Fahrenheit (°F), °F = °C x 1.8 + 32	华氏	huáshì	n	1.1
fair	公平	gōngpíng	adj	5.1
family routine	家常	jiācháng	adj	6.1
family; household	家庭	jiātíng	n	3.2
famous brand	名牌	míngpái	n	4.1
favorable impression	好感	hǎogǎn	n	8.2
field	场	chǎng	n	5.1
fierce	厉害	lìhai	adj	5.1
to fill out the form	填表格	tián biǎogé	vo	2.1
final, last; finally, lastly	最后	zuìhòu	adj, adv	5.1
to find, to discover	发现	fāxiàn	v	3.2
fire	火	huǒ	n	6.1
firsthand, personally	亲自	qīnzì	adv	8.2
flavorful, delicious; delicacy	美味	měiwèi	adj, n	6.2
flood, accumulated water; to flood	积水	jīshuǐ	n, v	7.2
Flying Fish	飞鱼	Fēiyú	n	5.1
folk instrumental music	民乐	mínyuè	n	5.2
for the purpose of; for the sake of	为了	wèile	prep	2.1
forecast; to forecast	预报	yùbào	n	1.2
foreign	洋	yáng	adj	4.1
forgetful, always forgetful	丢三落四	diūsān làsì	ie	7.1
form, shape, format	形式	xíngshì	n	5.2
fortune, luck	运气	yùnqi	n	5.1
to foul, to break the rules	犯规	fànguī	vo	5.1
free of charge, free, gratis	免费	miǎnfèi	vo	4.1
frequently encountered; commonly seen	常见	chángjiàn	adj	7.2

Definition	Characters	Pinyin	Word Category	Lesson
fresh	新鲜	xīnxiān	adj	6.2
friends at first sight	一见如故	yíjiàn rúgù	ie	2.2
full; entirely	满	mǎn	adj, adv	3.2
furniture	家具	jiājù	n	3.2

G

to gain, to achieve	获得	huòdé	v	5.2
garden	园林	yuánlín	n	8.2
garlic	蒜	suàn	n	6.2
generally; ordinary	一般	yìbān	adv	1.1
to get	得	dé	v	5.2
to get along with	相处	xiāngchǔ	v	3.1
giant panda	大熊猫	dàxióngmāo	n	4.1
to give up, to let go	放弃	fàngqì	v	5.2
to go out	外出	wàichū	v	7.2
to go through	通行	tōngxíng	v	7.1
goods	货	huò	n	4.1
goods	物品	wùpǐn	n	7.2
gram	克	kè	n	6.1
green onion, scallion	葱	cōng	n	6.1
group	团	tuán	n	1.1
guarantee period, warranty period	保修期	bǎoxiū qī	n	4.1
guarantee, warranty; to guarantee. to warrant	保证	bǎozhèng	n, v	4.2

H

to handle	办	bàn	v	8.1
heater	电暖器	diànnuǎnqì	n	4.2
height	个子	gèzi	n	2.2
high	高	gāo	adj	1.2
high heat	大火	dàhuǒ	n	6.1
to hike; to climb a mountain	爬山	páshān	vo	1.2
hill; mountain	山	shān	n	1.2
hobby, interest	爱好	àihào	n	2.2
to hold	举办	jǔbàn	v	2.2
home cooking	家常菜	jiāchángcài	n	6.1
hot pepper	辣椒	làjiāo	n	6.1

Definition	Characters	Pinyin	Word Category	Lesson
household chores, household duties	家务	jiāwù	n	3.1
household electrical appliance	家用电器	jiāyòng diànqì	n	3.2
however, but	却	què	cj	8.1
humid, muggy	闷热	mēnrè	adj	1.2
humid; damp	潮湿	cháoshī	adj	1.2
hurried; worried; feel anxious	着急	zháojí	adj	7.1

I

Definition	Characters	Pinyin	Word Category	Lesson
ice; to be freezing	冰	bīng	n, v	3.2
idea	主意	zhǔyi	n	2.1
ideal	理想	lǐxiǎng	adj, n	3.1
identity card	身份证	shēnfènzhèng	n	7.1
image, picture	图片	túpiàn	n	7.2
impatient, short-tempered	心急	xīnjí	adj	8.2
impression; to feel	感受	gǎnshòu	n, v	8.2
in addition	此外	cǐwài	cj	7.2
in addition; other	另外	lìngwài	adv, adj	5.1
in order to	以	yǐ	prep	7.2
in ordinary, normal times	平时	píngshí	adv	3.1
in reality; as a matter of fact	实际上	shíjìshang	adv	8.2
to include	包括	bāokuò	v	3.2
to include, to contain	包	bāo	v	3.1
to be included, including	在内	zàinèi	prep	3.2
to increase	增加	zēngjiā	v	7.2
to increase, to add	增	zēng	v	7.2
indeed; as expected; sure enough	果然	guǒrán	adv	6.2
to be inferior to, not as good as	不如	bùrú	v	4.1
(injury/illness) not serious; light	轻	qīng	adj	7.1
inn, hotel	旅馆	lǚguǎn	n	8.2
inside and outside	内外	nèiwài	n	3.1
to invite; invitation	邀请	yāoqǐng	v, n	2.2
itinerary	行程	xíngchéng	n	8.2

J

Definition	Characters	Pinyin	Word Category	Lesson
to join; to add	加入	jiārù	v	2.2
to join; to enter	入	rù	v	2.2

Definition	Characters	Pinyin	Word Category	Lesson
journalist, reporter	记者	jìzhě	n	5.2
judge, jury	评委	píngwěi	n	5.2
just now; a moment ago	刚才	gāngcái	n	8.1

K

Definition	Characters	Pinyin	Word Category	Lesson
kind	类	lèi	n	6.2
knowledge	知识	zhīshi	n	2.1
Kung Pao Chicken (spicy fried diced chicken)	宫保鸡丁	Gōngbǎojīdīng	n	6.1
Kunming (city)	昆明	Kūnmíng	n	1.2

L

Definition	Characters	Pinyin	Word Category	Lesson
landlord	房东	fángdōng	n	3.2
large-scale	大型	dàxíng	adj	7.2
to leave . . . empty; empty; spare time	空	kōng, kòng	v, adj, n	3.2
to be left; surplus	剩	shèng	v, adj	3.1
license	执照	zhízhào	n	7.1
to be like	如	rú	adj	1.2
like spring all year-round	四季如春	sìjì rúchūn	ie	1.2
like, love	喜爱	xǐài	n	5.2
London	伦敦	Lúndūn	n	1.1
long time	久	jiǔ	adj	1.2
long time no see	好久不见	hǎojiǔ bújiàn	ie	1.2
to lose	输	shū	v	5.1
to lose	丢	diū	v	7.1
low	低	dī	adj	1.2
lucky; good luck	幸运	xìngyùn	adj, n	3.2
luggage	行李	xíngli	n	8.1

M

Definition	Characters	Pinyin	Word Category	Lesson
to major in	主修	zhǔxiū	v	2.1
to make, to cause	令	lìng	v	5.2
Mapo Tofu	麻婆豆腐	Mápódòufu	n	6.2
market	商场	shāngchǎng	n	4.2
material, ingredients	材料	cáiliào	n	6.1
maybe, perhaps	说不定	shuōbudìng	adv	1.1
medical treatment	医疗	yīliáo	n	7.1

Definition	Characters	Pinyin	Word Category	Lesson
to meet unexpectedly, to run into	碰见	pèngjian	rv	2.2
member	成员	chéngyuán	n	2.2
merchandise, goods, commodity	商品	shāngpǐn	n	4.2
meter	米	mǐ	n	2.2
method; means	办法	bànfǎ	n	2.1
method, way of doing/making something	做法	zuòfǎ	n	6.1
middle, center	中间	zhōngjiān	n	8.1
to minor in; minor	辅修	fǔxiū	v, n	2.1
to be missing, to leave behind, to forget to bring	落	là	v	7.1
to mix	拌	bàn	v	6.1
to mix evenly	拌匀	bànyún	v	6.1
Mountain Lion	山猫	Shānmāo	n	5.1
to move	搬	bān	v	3.2
to move house	搬家	bānjiā	vo	3.2
musical performance; to give a musical performance	演奏	yǎnzòu	n, v	5.2
must	必须	bìxū	av	3.2

N

Definition	Characters	Pinyin	Word Category	Lesson
natural disaster	自然灾害	zìrán zāihài	n	7.2
natural; nature; naturally	自然	zìrán	adj, n, adv	7.2
near; to depend	靠	kào	adj, v	8.1
nearby	附近	fùjìn	adv	3.2
necessary; indispensable	必需	bìxū	adj	2.1
news	消息	xiāoxi	n	2.1
newspaper	报纸	bàozhǐ	n	3.2
no matter what . . . all; regardless of . . . all	无论……都	wúlùn……dōu	cj	6.1
no matter . . . all, regardless of . . . all	不管……都	bùguǎn……dōu	prep	4.2
not necessarily	不见得	bújiàndé	adv	2.1
notice	须知	xūzhī	n	4.2
notification	通知	tōngzhī	n	3.2
novel, fiction	小说	xiǎoshuō	n	2.1
numeral; digital	数码	shùmǎ	n, adj	4.1

Definition	Characters	Pinyin	Word Category	Lesson
O				
to obtain a visa, to apply for a visa	办签证	bàn qiānzhèng	vo	8.1
to occur; to appear	出现	chūxiàn	v	7.2
oil	油	yóu	n	6.1
old	旧	jiù	adj	3.2
only, merely, nothing more than	不过……而已	búguò……éryǐ	cj	5.1
optimistic	开朗	kāilǎng	adj	2.2
organization; agency	社	shè	n	2.2
original price	原价	yuánjià	n	4.1
overweight	超重	chāozhòng	adj, n	8.1
P				
packaging	包装	bāozhuāng	n	4.2
Paris	巴黎	Bālí	n	1.1
part	部分	bùfen	n	4.2
partner, companion	伙伴	huǒbàn	n	5.2
passenger	乘客	chéng kè	n	7.1
to pay money	付款	fù kuǎn	vo	4.2
to pay more or close attention to	关注	guānzhù	v	7.2
pedicab	三轮车	sānlúnchē	n	7.1
perfect	完美	wánměi	adj	5.2
period of time	期	qī	n	3.2
person (who does something), one who (is)...	者	zhě	n	2.2
personnel, staff	人员	rényuán	n	8.1
place, site, locale	地点	dìdiǎn	n	3.1
pleasantly cool	凉快	liángkuai	adj	1.1
policeman	警察	jǐngchá	n	7.1
policy, conditions	条件	tiáojiàn	n	4.2
pork	猪肉	zhūròu	n	6.2
postcard	明信片	míngxìnpiàn	n	1.1
powerful	强	qiáng	adj	5.1
preferential, favorable	优惠	yōuhuì	adj	4.1
price	价格	jiàgé	n	4.1
privacy	隐私	yǐnsī	n	3.1
product	产品	chǎnpǐn	n	4.1

Definition	Characters	Pinyin	Word Category	Lesson
to prohibit, to forbid	禁止	jìnzhǐ	v	7.1
project; item	项目	xiàngmù	n	2.2
protection; to protect	保护	bǎohù	n, v	2.2

Q

quality	质量	zhìliàng	n	4.1
quantity	量	liàng	n	6.1

R

raincoat	雨衣	yǔyī	n	1.2
rainstorm	暴雨	bàoyǔ	n	7.2
rare; hard to come by	难得	nándé	adj	6.2
rather than . . . it would be better to	与其……倒不如	yǔqí……dàobùrú	cj	5.1
ratio	比	bǐ	n	5.1
real, authentic	地道	dìdao	adj	2.1
to realize, to achieve	实现	shíxiàn	v	5.2
really, definitely, indeed	确实	quèshí	adv	3.1
reason	原因	yuányīn	n	5.2
receipt	收据	shōujù	n	4.2
to receive; to bear	受	shòu	v	2.2
recipe, cookbook	食谱	shípǔ	n	6.1
to recover; to restore to health	康复	kāngfù	v, n	7.2
to recruit	招募	zhāomù	v	2.2
to reduce	减少	jiǎnshǎo	v	7.2
to reduce the price, to be discounted	减价	jiǎnjià	vo	6.2
referee	裁判	cáipàn	n	5.1
refrigerator	冰箱	bīngxiāng	n	3.2
regarding; about	关于	guānyú	prep	7.2
to remind, to warn	提醒	tíxǐng	v	4.1
rent	房租	fángzū	n	3.1
to rent	租	zū	v	3.1
to rent together	合租	hézū	v	3.1
to rent, to let	出租	chūzū	v	3.2
to repair	修	xiū	v	4.1
report; to report	报告	bàogào	n, v	2.1
to result in; to lead to; to cause	导致	dǎozhì	v	7.2

Definition	Characters	Pinyin	Word Category	Lesson
result; grades	成绩	chéngjì	n	2.1
to return	退	tuì	v	4.2
to return merchandise/goods	退货	tuìhuò	vo	4.2
to rise, to go up	上升	shàngshēng	v	1.2
road	马路	mǎlù	n	3.2
route, itinerary	路线	lùxiàn	n	8.2
rule	规定	guīdìng	n	8.1
to rush	闯	chuǎng	v	7.1

S

Definition	Characters	Pinyin	Word Category	Lesson
saliva, drool, dribble	口水	kǒushuǐ	n	6.2
salt	盐	yán	n	6.1
to sample	试吃	shìchī	v	6.2
sandstorm	沙尘暴	shāchénbào	n	7.2
satisfied	满意	mǎnyì	adj	3.2
to save	省	shěng	v	3.1
savory, appetizing	香	xiāng	adj	6.2
scenery	风景	fēngjǐng	n	1.2
scheduled flight	航班	hángbān	n	7.2
scholarship	奖学金	jiǎngxuéjīn	n	2.1
school magazine	校刊	xiàokān	n	5.2
to scoop out, to fill	盛	chéng	v	6.1
score	比分	bǐfēn	n	5.1
seafood	海鲜	hǎixiān	n	6.2
season	季节	jìjié	n	1.1
season	季	jì	n	1.2
seasoning	调味料	tiáowèiliào	n	6.2
seat	座位	zuòwèi	n	8.1
seeing is believing	百闻不如一见	bǎiwén bùrú yíjiàn	ie	8.2
to sell	售	shòu	v	4.2
to set out on a journey	上路	shànglù	vo	8.2
Shanghai	上海	Shànghǎi	n	8.2
to share	分享	fēnxiǎng	v	4.1
shelled peanut	花生米	huāshēngmǐ	n	6.1
shopping; to go shopping	购物	gòuwù	n, vo	4.1
to be short of, to be missing	差	chà	v	6.2

Definition	Characters	Pinyin	Word Category	Lesson
to show	出示	chūshì	v	4.2
to sign	签	qiān	v	3.1
to sign a contract	签合同	qiān hétong	vo	3.1
to sign up	报名	bàomíng	v	8.2
since	以来	yǐlái	prep	7.2
sir (respectful formal address for a male elder)	师傅	shīfu	n	7.1
small steamed meat-filled buns with soup	小笼包	Xiǎolóngbāo	n	8.2
smooth, without a hitch	顺利	shùnlì	adj	8.1
so; hence; as a result	于是	yúshì	cj	6.2
so; really; honestly	实在	shízai	adv	6.1
to be sorry, to be apologetic	抱歉	bàoqiàn	v	4.2
soy sauce	酱油	jiàngyóu	n	6.1
specialty dish, a chef's best dish	拿手菜	náshǒucài	ie	6.2
spirit	精神	jīngshén	n	5.1
spoon	匙	chí	n	6.1
sports competition season	赛季	sàijì	n	5.1
star	明星	míngxīng	n	5.1
starch	淀粉	diànfěn	n	6.1
to stay in a place, to remain	留	liú	v	1.1
to stir-fry until the food is cooked	炒熟	chǎo shú	v	6.1
to stir-fry, to sauté	炒	chǎo	v	6.1
strength	实力	shílì	n	5.1
strength, power	力	lì	n	3.1
stringed plucked instrument similar to the zither	古筝	gǔzhēng	n	5.2
to study abroad	留学	liúxué	v	2.1
style, type	款	kuǎn	n	4.1
subway	地铁	dìtiě	n	8.1
suddenly	突然	tūrán	adv	7.1
sugar	糖	táng	n	6.1
sunny day	晴天	qíngtiān	n	1.2
supermarket	超市	chāoshì	n	6.2
to support	支持	zhīchí	v	5.2
surgical mask	口罩	kǒuzhào	n	7.2
Suzhou	苏州	Sūzhōu	n	8.2

Definition	Characters	Pinyin	Word Category	Lesson
T				
to take a photograph; photography	摄影	shèyǐng	vo, n	4.1
take advantage of; to avail oneself of	趁	chèn	prep	8.2
to take as an elective course	选修	xuǎnxiū	v	2.1
to take off	起飞	qǐfēi	v	8.1
talent and skill	才艺	cáiyì	n	5.2
to taste	尝	cháng	v	6.2
tax	税	shuì	n	4.1
team	队	duì	n	5.1
team spirit	团队精神	tuánduì jīngshén	n	5.1
team, group	团队	tuánduì	n	5.1
temperature	气温	qìwēn	n	1.1
temperature	温度	wēndù	n	1.2
to thank, to be grateful	感谢	gǎnxiè	v	5.2
therefore; consequently	因此	yīncǐ	conj	7.1
to think, to believe (mistakenly)	以为	yǐwéi	v	6.1
to think/believe that	认为	rènwéi	v	4.2
thunder and lighting	雷电	léidiàn	n	7.2
ticket	券	quàn	n	4.1
toothpaste	牙膏	yágāo	n	4.2
totally, completely; complete	完全	wánquán	adv, adj	7.1
to tour guide	导游	dǎoyóu	n	8.2
to tour; tourism	旅游	lǚyóu	v, n	1.1
tourist	游客	yóukè	n	8.2
towel	毛巾	máojīn	n	4.2
traffic	交通	jiāotōng	n	3.1
traffic accident	车祸	chēhuò	n	7.1
to travel	游	yóu	v	1.1
to travel by	乘	chéng	v	7.1
travel journal	游记	yóujì	n	8.2
traveling mates	驴友	lǚyǒu	n	1.2
type	种类	zhǒnglèi	n	6.2
U				
umbrella	雨伞	yǔsǎn	n	1.1

Definition	Characters	Pinyin	Word Category	Lesson
unforgettable, memorable	难忘	nánwàng	adj	5.2
unfortunate; unfortunately	可惜	kěxī	adj, adv	3.2
unless, only if... or else, otherwise	除非……要不然	chúfēi……yàoburán	cj	8.1
(used to introduce the object before a verb)	将	jiāng	prep	6.1

V

Definition	Characters	Pinyin	Word Category	Lesson
vegetables	蔬菜	shūcài	n	6.2
versus	对	duì	v	5.1
very, fully, utterly	十分	shífēn	adv	5.2
very, rather, quite	挺	tǐng	adv	2.1
violation ticket	罚单	fádān	n	7.1
volunteer	志愿者	zhìyuànzhě	n	2.2
to volunteer; aspiration, wish	志愿	zhìyuàn	v, n	2.2

W

Definition	Characters	Pinyin	Word Category	Lesson
warm	暖和	nuǎnhuo	adj	1.1
warm in the winters and cool in the summers	冬暖夏凉	dōngnuǎn xiàliáng	ie	1.2
to wash	洗	xǐ	v	3.2
washing machine	洗衣机	xǐyījī	n	3.2
water and electricity bills	水电费	shuǐdiànfèi	n	3.1
weather forecast	天气预报	tiānqì yùbào	n	1.2
website	网站	wǎngzhàn	n	4.1
weight; heavy	重	zhòng	n, adj	8.1
what's more, besides	再说	zàishuō	cj	3.1
when	当	dāng	cj	2.2
whistle	哨	shào	n	5.1
will, about to	将	jiāng	adv	8.1
to win	赢	yíng	v	5.1
wind	风	fēng	n	1.2
window	窗户	chuānghu	n	8.1
to be windy	刮风	guāfēng	v	1.2
winter	冬季	dōngjì	n	1.1
within	之内	zhīnèi	prep	3.2
wok	锅	guō	n	6.1
worried; worry, trouble	烦恼	fánnǎo	adj, n	2.2
to be worth the price	划算	huásuàn	adj	4.1

Definition	Characters	Pinyin	Word Category	Lesson
wound	伤	shāng	n	7.1
to be wounded, to be injured	受伤	shòushāng	vo	7.1

Y

Definition	Characters	Pinyin	Word Category	Lesson
Yunnan (province)	云南	Yúnnán	n	1.2